THE WORLD THEATRE OF WAGNER

CHARLES OSBORNE

THE WORLD THEATRE OF WAGNER

A CELEBRATION OF 150 YEARS OF WAGNER PRODUCTIONS

PREFACE BY
SIR COLIN DAVIS

MACMILLAN PUBLISHING CO., INC.
NEW YORK

Macmillan Publishing Co., Inc.
866 Third Avenue, New York, N.Y. 10022
Collier Macmillan Canada, Inc.

Designed and produced for Macmillan Publishing Co. Inc.
by Bellew & Higton Publishers Ltd,
17–21 Conway Street, London W1P 6JD

Library of Congress Cataloging in Publication Data

Osborne, Charles, 1927–
The world theatre of Wagner.

Includes index.
1. Wagner, Richard, 1813–1883. Operas.
2. Opera -- Production and direction. I. Title.
MT100.W208 782.1'092'4 82-130
AACR2

ISBN 0 02 594050 3

First American Edition 1982

10 9 8 7 6 5 4 3 2 1

Printed in Hong Kong

CONTENTS

	PREFACE BY SIR COLIN DAVIS: WAGNER ON STAGE 6
I	THE EARLY OPERAS: DIE HOCHZEIT DIE FEEN DAS LIEBESVERBOT 11
II	RIENZI 17
III	DER FLIEGENDE HOLLÄNDER 27
IV	TANNHÄUSER 43
V	LOHENGRIN 59
VI	TRISTAN UND ISOLDE 75
VII	DIE MEISTERSINGER VON NÜRNBERG 91
VIII	DER RING DES NIBELUNGEN 111
IX	PARSIFAL 170
X	BIOGRAPHICAL DICTIONARY 193
	INDEX 221
	ACKNOWLEDGEMENTS 224

Sir Colin Davis with the orchestra of the Royal Opera House, Covent Garden.

WAGNER ON STAGE

SIR COLIN DAVIS, who became Music Director of the Royal Opera House, Covent Garden, in 1971, has conducted most of Wagner's mature works and been closely involved in major new productions such as the 1976–7 *Ring* and *Tristan und Isolde* in 1978. He was the first British conductor to take part in the Bayreuth Festival (*Tannhäuser*, 1977 – a production which was also filmed, in 1978). Gill Rowley, editor of *The World Theatre of Wagner*, spoke to him in early 1982, while he was preparing a revival of *Die Meistersinger*.

•

WAGNER was a composer with whom I could identify even as a child, whether because I liked the noises, or because the stories were about gods and dragons, I am uncertain; probably both.

When I came to prepare *The Ring* for Covent Garden, I began with the words and afterwards the music. I spent years learning the scores before I came to do the first opera. The next step, once we knew that Götz Friedrich had agreed to produce the work, was to decide what *The Ring* was about. We spent many hours arguing the production, trying to answer the questions it poses. Unlike *Meistersinger*, which is a bourgeois comedy, *The Ring* is an opera of ideas, and these can fit into any framework it is possible to invent. We all did a lot of reading, talking and discovering; for example, we learned what frightful creatures the Valkyries were – they drank blood, they were necrophiles, more in tune with an ancient barbaric world than with the nineteenth-century theatrical tradition. But the key to it all was the set: we wanted a general-purpose set for all four operas, such as one might use for a medieval miracle play – an area in which to present a fable. Friedrich came up with the idea of the hydraulically manoeuvred slab, which could turn at any angle, change itself into a flight of steps, a mountain, or whatever, and Josef Svoboda, a very clever man, worked out the practicalities with the technical department. 'This is my space,' as Shakespeare's Antony says – and as Friedrich might have said of this wonderful toy.

Once the set was devised we knew it could not be a realistic production. *The Ring* is a tale of fraud, corruption – it need be rooted in no particular era; it is not a vehicle for the naturalistic magic of forests, mountains and weather, and it takes place over many years. It's a sort of odyssey – Wotan's journey.

For *Rheingold* we had in many ways an ideal situation. We all discussed it together, deciding that it is above all a morality play – like Brecht's *Mahagonny*. But what were the people supposed to look like? They're not real people in *Rheingold*, they're symbols, so they should wear 'the face [they] had before the world was made', as Yeats has it. We didn't see the Nibelungs as the proletariat fighting the capitalists; there is no need to: the notions of the downtrodden rising against the rulers or the sexuality inherent in the relationship of father and daughter are by no means ideas that were born in the nineteenth century ... they can all be found in Homer, Euripides – they can be traced through a temporal line. But perhaps the production benefited from the Marxist/dreamer combination [Friedrich/Davis] that some saw it as.

Walküre was very different from *Rheingold*. It all hinges

on emotions, and has more to do with Ibsen, or Strindberg – *The Dance of Death* – than the frictions between gods and men. In all the operas one is faced with the problem of Wagner's detailed directions for staging: eight women careering around the stage on horseback, for example, is not a practical idea [*Walküre*]. It leads one to discard Wagner's own instructions.

Tannhäuser, on the other hand, is not at all an impractical piece, apart from that opening ballet sequence – the scene on the Venusberg; he was trying to put a poetic idea on stage here and it is difficult to make it work. The rest of *Tannhäuser* is simply a question of conflict among the people, a drama

Sir Colin Davis rehearsing DIE MEISTERSINGER: (opposite) with principals (left to right) Hans Sotin (Sachs), Reiner Goldberg (Walther), Phyllis Cannan (Magdalene) and Lucia Popp (Eva); (below) with Hans Sotin, Christopher McManus at the piano and Reiner Goldberg; (right) assistant producer Jeremy Sutcliffe rehearses Robert Tear (David).

without the supernatural or natural problems of *Lohengrin*, *Parsifal* and *The Ring*. *Meistersinger* is closer to Mozart than any other Wagner opera. Of course he was looking back to earlier themes with the song contest and the Sachs/Eva relationship mirroring that of Wotan and Brünnhilde. It couldn't take the kind of treatment we gave *The Ring*, though it needs a naturalistic set for the people in a church, people in a town square – to reflect its story about a famous little republic. Some people regard it as Wagner's greatest work; he is happy to present to us people with whom we can identify easily, who live and have their being in a real world.

For a conductor, the main problem with Wagner's operas is practical: it is a matter of learning to pace oneself – to sustain oneself through the long hours of preparation and performance. There are great difficulties; the orchestra must know where they are, and be well rehearsed in them – the Rhine Journey, and the Funeral March in *Götterdämmerung*, for example. But despite what Wagner himself said about breaking away, in his music-dramas, from past operatic convention, the music does break up quite conveniently into scenes that one can take out and work on separately before presenting the piece as a whole.

The strangest thing for me about Wagner is that he seems to have become a musician in order to set all his words to music. He learned to be a composer after he was a writer – a compulsive writer who poured out words throughout his childhood, long letters to his mother which she probably never understood, poems ... he was his own librettist and a law unto himself in all that he did. Even he couldn't make all his productions work; no wonder it is so difficult for others to try to do so.

COLIN DAVIS

Above: orchestral rehearsal at the Royal Opera House, Covent Garden.
Opposite: scene from DIE FEEN: artist unknown.

I

THE EARLY OPERAS:
DIE HOCHZEIT
DIE FEEN
DAS LIEBESVERBOT

None of Wagner's early operas, those written before *Rienzi*, has remained in the repertory of performed works, and the very earliest of them, *Die Hochzeit*, is a mere fragment which is hardly worth staging.

Die Hochzeit (The Wedding) was planned by the young composer in his nineteenth year. Throughout his life, he was to compose only to libretti which he himself had written, and the ideas which came to him for operas came first as literary or dramatic ideas. It was not until he had completed a libretto that Wagner began consciously to think about the music of the opera on which he was working. In the summer of 1832 he began to sketch out the dramatic poem, *Die Hochzeit*, which he had completed by the end of the year. Its overwrought romantic narrative derived from an 1826 play, *Cardenio und Celinde* by Karl Immermann, and also from *Ritterzeit und Ritterwesen*, a treatise on chivalry by J. G. Büsching: Wagner had initially intended to use the material in a short story, but changed his mind and decided it would be more suitable for the basis of an opera. In his autobiography, *Mein Leben*, he summarized the plot:

Two great houses had lived in enmity, and had at last decided to end the family feud. The aged head of one of these houses invited the son of his former enemy to the wedding of his daughter with one of his faithful partisans. The wedding feast is thus used as an opportunity for reconciling the two families. Whilst the guests are full of the suspicion and fear of treachery, their young leader falls violently in love with the bride of his newly found ally. His tragic glance deeply affects her; the festive escort accompanies her to the bridal chamber, where she is to await her beloved; leaning against her tower-window she sees the same passionate eyes fixed on her, and realizes that she is face to face with a tragedy.

When he penetrates into her chamber, and embraces her with frantic passion, she pushes him backwards towards the balcony, and throws him over the parapet into the abyss, whence his mutilated remains are dragged by his companions. They at once arm themselves against the presumed treachery, and call for vengeance; tumult and confusion fill the courtyard: the interrupted wedding feast threatens to end in a night of slaughter. The venerable head of the house at last succeeds in averting the catastrophe. Messengers are sent to bear the tidings of the mysterious calamity to the relatives of the victim: the corpse itself shall be the medium of reconciliation, for, in the presence of the different generations of the suspected family, Providence itself shall decide which of its members has been guilty of treason. During the preparations for the obsequies the bride shows signs of approaching madness; she flies from her bridegroom, refuses to be united to him, and locks herself up in her tower-chamber. Only when, at night, the gloomy though gorgeous ceremony commences, does she appear at the head of her women to be present at the burial service, the gruesome solemnity of which is interrupted by the news of the approach of hostile forces and then by the armed attack of the kinsmen of the murdered man. When the avengers of the presumed treachery penetrate into the chapel and call upon the murderer to declare himself, the horrified lord of the manor points towards his daughter who, turning away from her bridegroom, falls lifeless by the coffin of her victim.

Above: stage designs by the Viennese artists Anton Brioschi and Hermann Burghart for the first production of Die Feen, Munich, 1888.

Wagner began to compose the music for *Die Hochzeit*, but had completed only an introduction, a chorus and a septet, when he abandoned the project, ostensibly because his sister Rosalie found the subject too gloomy for her taste but more likely because Wagner the composer did not share Wagner the poet's enthusiasm for the naively romantic story, with its lack of resonance, its cardboard *personae* and its situations so insignificant as to border upon the squalid. The music already composed was filed away for possible future use: within a few weeks, the would-be composer of operas was ready to make a fresh start. (The fragmentary *Hochzeit* has, in fact, been performed, at least once. It was given at the Neues Theater, Leipzig, on 13 February 1938.)

Early in 1833, Wagner began work on what was to be his first completed opera, *Die Feen* (The Fairies). He had written, in Leipzig, a libretto based on 'La donna serpente', a fable by the eighteenth-century Italian playwright Carlo Gozzi (whose plays were to provide subjects for two well-known twentieth-century operas, Prokofiev's *Love of Three Oranges* and Puccini's *Turandot*), and he completed the score of his opera during the year, in Würzburg. Excerpts from *Die Feen* were tried out at a concert in Würzburg, but the opera was never staged in Wagner's lifetime. The three-act work was finished and fully scored by the beginning of January 1834, and offered to the theatre at Leipzig. Though it was accepted,

or at least not rejected, there was never any real intention on the part of the Leipzig management to perform the work, and in due course this became clear to the young composer.

Though he had taken his basic plot from Gozzi, Wagner made numerous changes, and invented new names for his characters. Here is his synopsis:

The names of my heroes I chose from different Ossian and similar poems: my prince was called Arindal; he was loved by a fairy called Ada, who held him under her spell and kept him in fairyland, away from his realm, until his faithful friends at last found him and induced him to return, for his country was going to rack and ruin, and even its capital had fallen into the enemy's hands. The loving fairy herself sends the prince back to his country; for the oracle has decreed that she shall lay upon her lover the severest of tasks. Only by performing this task triumphantly can he make it possible for her to leave the immortal world of fairies in order to share the fate of her earthly lover, as his wife. In a moment of deepest despair about the state of his country, the fairy queen appears to him and purposely destroys his faith in her by deeds of the most cruel and inexplicable nature. Driven mad by a thousand fears, Arindal begins to imagine that all the time he has been dealing with a wicked sorceress, and tries to escape the fatal spell by pronouncing a curse upon Ada.

Wild with sorrow, the unhappy fairy sinks down, and reveals their mutual fate to the lover, now lost to her forever, and tells him that, as a punishment for having disobeyed the decree of Fate, she is doomed to be turned into stone (in Gozzi's version she becomes a serpent). Immediately afterwards it appears that all the catastrophes which the fairy had prophesied were but deceptions: victory over the enemy as well as the growing prosperity and welfare of the kingdom now follow in quick succession: Ada is taken away by the fates, and Arindal, a raving madman, remains behind alone. The terrible sufferings of his madness do not, however, satisfy the Fates: to bring about his utter ruin they appear before the repentent man and invite him to follow them to the nether world, on the pretext of enabling him to free Ada from the spell. Through the treacherous promises of the wicked fairies Arindel's madness grows into sublime exaltation; and one of his household magicians, a faithful friend, having in the meantime equipped him with magic weapons and charms, he now follows the traitresses. The latter cannot get over their astonishment when they see how Arindal overcomes one after the other of the monsters of the infernal regions: only when they arrive at the vault in which they show him the stone in human shape do they recover their hope of vanquishing the valiant prince, for, unless he can break the charm which binds Ada, he must share her fate and be doomed to remain a stone forever.

Arindel, who until then has been using the dagger and shield given him by the friendly magician, now makes use of an instrument – a lyre – which he has brought with him, and the meaning of which he had not yet understood. To the sounds of this instrument he now expresses his plaintive moans, his remorse, and his overpowering longing for his enchanted queen. The stone is moved by the magic of his love: the beloved one is released. Fairyland with all its marvels opens its portals, and the mortal learns that, owing to his former inconstancy, Ada has lost the right to become his wife on earth, but that her beloved, through his great and magic power, has earned the right to live for ever by her side in fairyland.

Clearly there are similarities between the libretto of *Die Feen* and that of Mozart's *Die Zauberflöte*; not in the details of plot but in the underlying meaning. Indeed *Die Feen*, though an immature work by the standards of Wagnerian music-drama, is an important landmark in the progression of German fairy-tale operas from Mozart and *Die Zauberflöte* to Strauss and *Die Frau ohne Schatten*, and its plot looks forward to Strauss (the spouse turned to stone) as much as it looks backward to Mozart. The juxtaposition of royal and bourgeois couples links all three operas, but Schikaneder wrote for Mozart and Hofmannsthal for Strauss with, in the one case, more wit and, in the other, more style than Wagner was able to summon up for Wagner. In his memoirs, Wagner says he wrote his own libretto for *Die Feen* because 'I was sure that nobody else could write one for me; the reason being that such a book is something quite unique and cannot be written either by a poet or by a mere man of letters.' The composer was to retain to the end of his life this arrogant belief: since it enabled him to compose a series of masterpieces he was obviously right to do so. His was not the temperament to collaborate with a 'mere man of letters'.

With *Die Feen*, his first completed opera, Wagner plunged into that world of myth and fairy-tale which he was creatively to inhabit for the remainder of his life. Musically, however, the opera represents a false start, for Wagner not only chose the kind of subject which the more established German composers of his day tended to favour, but also imitated their style. This is not particularly surprising when one bears in mind the composer's extreme youth: he was only twenty. But in view of the direction his mature genius was to take, and the grandiose scale of his later achievement, it is perhaps a trifle odd to find so few traces of originality or individuality in his first opera.

Examining *Die Feen* now with the benefit of hindsight, it is not difficult to discern adumbrations of musical and dramatic themes which were to be more fully worked out in the operas of Wagner's maturity. At the time of its composition, however, there was nothing in *Die Feen* to indicate to Wagner's fellow musicians and colleagues that this was the work of a powerful and original talent. Much of the orchestral writing is pastiche Mendelssohn, while certain effects are borrowed from Weber and, in particular, Marschner, whose three operas, *Der Vampyr*, *Der Templer und die Judin* and *Hans Heiling*, clearly had deeply impressed the young Wagner.

The first performance of *Die Feen* took place at the Nationaltheater, Munich, in 1888, five years after the death of Wagner. Ironically, the opera was received with such enthusiasm that it was taken into the repertory in Munich, and within three years had been performed fifty times. However, after 1896 performances ceased entirely until a revival in 1910. *Die Feen* did not arouse a great deal of interest beyond Munich, and it was not until 1967 that it reached Bayreuth: two semi-professional performances were given that year in the Stadthalle. It has never been performed at the Wagner Festival Theatre at Bayreuth, nor will it be until there is a deliberate change of policy on the part of the Wagner family. The Bayreuth Festival does not acknowledge any work by Wagner earlier than *Der fliegende Holländer*.

Productions of *Die Feen* have been so few and far between that they can hardly be said to have contributed to the history of Wagnerian production-style. The opera was staged in Prague in 1893, in Zurich in 1914, and in Stuttgart in 1932. Its British premiere had to wait until 1969 when an enterprising amateur group, the Midland Music Makers Grand Opera Society, gave four performances of *Die Feen* in the Great Hall of the University of Aston. The first London performance, also amateur (though with some professional stiffening), was given at the Fulham Town Hall on 3 May 1973. The opera still awaits its first American stage performance. It was given in a concert version by the New York City Opera on 24 February 1982 at the New York State Theatre. The conductor was Antonio de Almeida and the leading roles were sung by Penelope Daner and John Alexander.

It was while he still had hopes that *Die Feen* would be staged by the Leipzig Opera that Wagner began to turn his thoughts towards the composition of an opera in the Italian manner. Perhaps Bellini's Romeo and Juliet opera, *I Capuleti ed i Montecchi*, a performance of which he had seen in Leipzig in 1834, had set Wagner thinking of Shakespeare, for the play which he took as the starting point for his libretto was Shakespeare's *Measure for Measure*, to which he gave the title *Das Liebesverbot* (The Ban on Love). In his very free adaptation of the Shakespeare original, Wagner transferred its action from Vienna to Sicily, and in the process turned the play into a contrast between the puritan Teutonic spirit and the sensual warmth of the South, the composer's sympathies being decidedly with the simple, childlike Mediterraneans. Shakespeare's ironies and ambiguities were flattened out into broad farce.

Musically, *Das Liebesverbot* is shamelessly eclectic: even more so than *Die Feen*. The Marschner influence, though much less strong, is still apparent, but it is the music of Rossini, Donizetti and Bellini (composers whose operas he had been conducting) of which Wagner's fussily uninventive score is more reminiscent. Listening to it today, one is struck by the composer's first use of the theme known as the 'Dresden Amen', which was to reappear later in *Tannhäuser* and, in a different form, in *Parsifal*. (In *Das Liebesverbot* it is sung by an off-stage chorus of nuns to the words 'Salve regina coeli'.)

Wagner's flirtation with Italian models resulted in an even less satisfactory work than *Die Feen*, his earlier attempt to imitate Weber and Marschner. Yet *Das Liebesverbot* is in many respects a more interesting opera than *Die Feen*. Its libretto, though a travesty of Shakespeare's play, propagating ideas of dubious aesthetic and moral value, is really much better planned and shaped than many of the libretti of his mature operas: for these, Wagner did not have the advantage of a play already in existence whose structure he could utilize. The slipshod dramatic form and frequently mediocre versification of the mature operas must, of course, be accepted since they helped musical masterpieces into existence. But *Das Liebesverbot* leads one to wonder whether Wagnerian masterpieces of an even higher quality, operas whose texts would have been the equal of their music, might have been composed had Wagner not deluded himself into the belief that he possessed literary talent of a high order. In later life he was to describe *Das Liebesverbot* as 'atrocious, abominable, nauseating': it is none of these things, though it contains few traces of Wagner's later genius.

The impresario of the Magdeburg opera company agreed to give *Das Liebesverbot* two performances at the end of the

Above: cover illustration by Franz Stassen for a libretto of DAS LIEBESVERBOT.

season, and in due course the opera was put into rehearsal. On the orders of the police, the title was changed to *Die Novize von Palermo*: banning love was banned! Because of the expense involved in mounting the work, Wagner agreed to an arrangement whereby the management would take the entire proceeds of the first performance, the second performance constituting the composer's benefit. The company found themselves having to learn the opera in ten days, and circumstances were not improved by the fact that Wagner himself acted as both conductor and stage director. At the first performance, on 29 March 1836, the tenor forgot much of his part, and resorted to snatches of *Fra Diavolo* and *Zampa*, operas by Auber and Hérold in which he felt more at home. On the second night, the composer's benefit, Wagner peered through the curtain just before the performance was to begin to find an audience of three, all of whom, ironically, were Jews: a Madame Gottschalk who had befriended him, her husband, and 'a Polish Jew in full dress'. Suddenly there was a commotion backstage. The husband of the prima donna, Karoline Pollent, had attacked the handsome young second tenor whom he suspected of being his wife's lover. The entire company immediately joined in the quarrel, and the second performance of *Das Liebesverbot* failed to take place.

That was the end of Wagner's second opera (his first to be performed) until the twentieth century, when it was revived in Munich in 1923, Berlin in 1933, Leipzig in 1938 and Dortmund in 1957. In recent years there have been further productions; London University's opera society gave the British premiere of *Das Liebesverbot* on 15 February 1965, and the opera reached Bayreuth, though not, of course, the Festival Theatre, when it was staged in the Stadthalle on 18 August 1972 by students at an international youth festival. It has yet to be produced in the USA, though excerpts were performed by students of the Metropolitan Opera Studio in 1965. None of these twentieth-century stagings can be said to have contributed to a Wagner style of production, any more than *Das Liebesverbot* can claim properly to belong to the Wagner canon. Wagner's individual voice began to emerge clearly with his next opera, *Rienzi*.

Opposite: Rienzi, final scene of Act IV. Woodcut of the Dresden premiere, 1842, published in the Leipzig *Illustrirte Zeitung*, 12 August 1843.

II
RIENZI

Above: the tenor Joseph Tichatschek as Rienzi in the first performance of the opera, Dresden, 1842. Opposite: (above) Act II of RIENZI as seen as Her Majesty's Theatre, London, in 1879; (below) RIENZI design by Johann Kantsky, Berlin, 1895.

Having tried German opera *à la* Marschner and Italian opera *à la* Bellini, Wagner next toyed with the idea of making his mark with French grand opera *à la* Meyerbeer. He began to plan an opera to be based on a recently published novel, *Rienzi*, by the English novelist and dramatist Edward Bulwer-Lytton, which he had been reading in a German translation. In order to escape creditors, in 1839 Wagner and his wife Minna fled from Riga, where he had held a post as conductor, and managed to get to London on a small sailing vessel. In London, Wagner attempted to contact the author of *Rienzi*, whom he knew to be a Member of Parliament, by enquiring for him at the Palace of Westminster. Bulwer-Lytton, however, was out of town. By now the composer had written his own libretto, based partly on Bulwer-Lytton and partly on a play by Mary Russell Mitford, and had even begun to compose the music. He was, in fact, completing the orchestration of the second of *Rienzi*'s five acts.

After a fruitless week in London, the Wagners made their way to Paris where the rest of *Rienzi* was composed during the following year, the final act being fully scored by November 1840. En route to Paris, having secured an introduction to Meyerbeer, who happened to be in Boulogne, Wagner read the celebrated composer more than half of the *Rienzi* libretto and showed him what he had written of the score. Meyerbeer complimented the young composer on his meticulous calligraphy and agreed to examine the score at leisure. He also gave Wagner introductions to men of influence in the musical world of Paris, including both the administrator and the chief conductor of the Paris Opéra. However, it was not the Paris Opéra which eventually accepted *Rienzi* for performance, but the Dresden Opera, to whose management Wagner had also been recommended by Meyerbeer. Although the opera was accepted as early as June 1841, it was not until October 1842 that *Rienzi* was produced in Dresden, by which time Wagner had composed his next opera, *Der fliegende Holländer*.

Though *Rienzi*'s structure partly derives from Mary Russell Mitford's 1828 play, Bulwer-Lytton's three-volume historical novel is the real parent of Wagner's opera. *Rienzi, the Last of the Roman Tribunes* was published in England in 1835, and appeared in German translation towards the end of 1836. The historical Cola di Rienzi was born Nicolaus Laurenti in 1313, the son of a Roman innkeeper and a washerwoman. He studied law, acquired a knowledge of history,

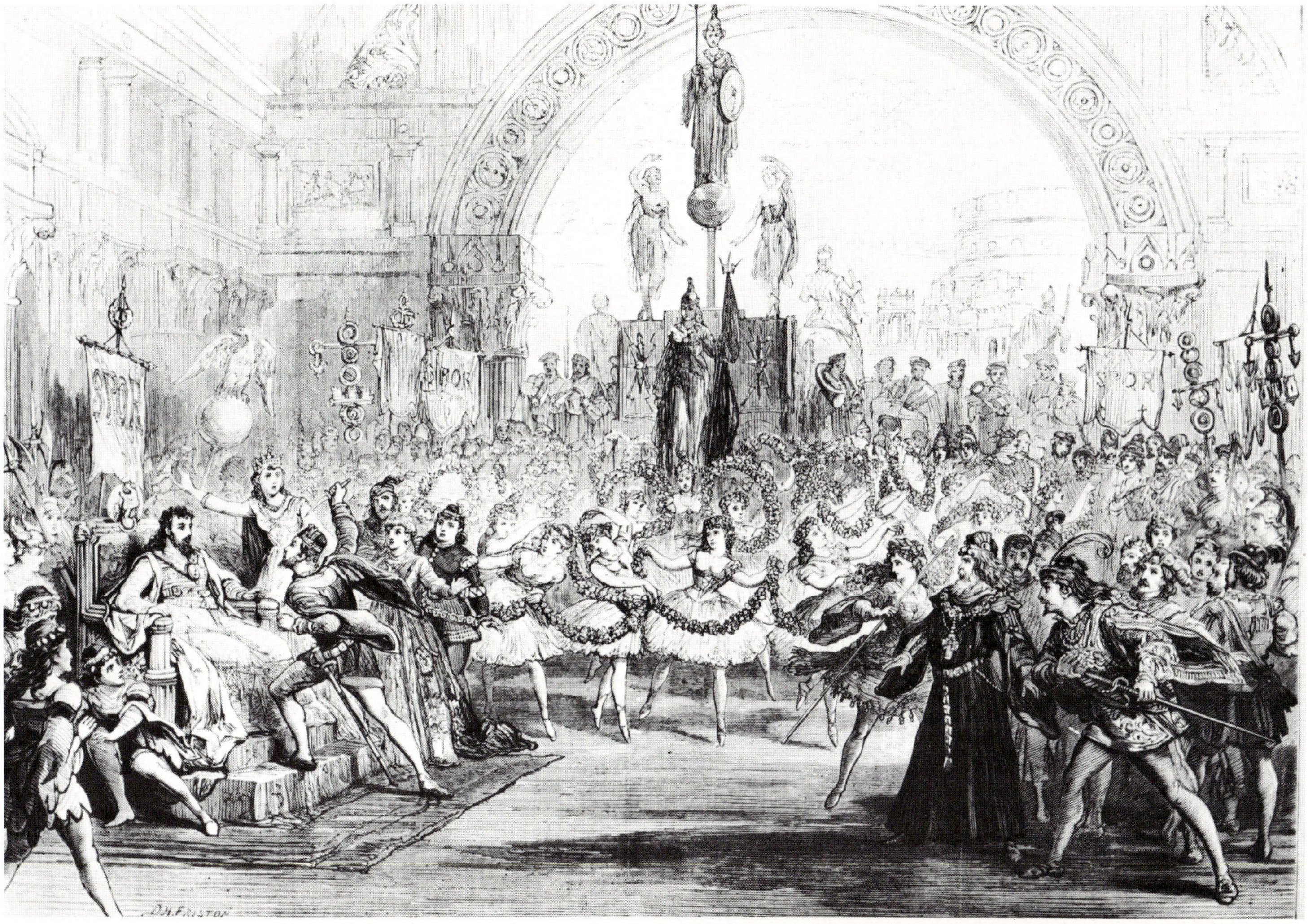

and became a friend of the poet Petrarch. In 1347, with the support of the populace, Rienzi overthrew the rule of the patricians, set himself up as tribune of the people, and summoned an Italian national parliament. Expelled by his opponents the following year, he returned in 1352 and in 1354 was appointed senator by the pope. Two months later, he was slain by his baronial opponents.

The principal characters in Wagner's opera are Rienzi; his sister, Irene; Stefano Colonna, a patrician; his son, Adriano; and Paolo Orsini, another patrician. At the beginning of the opera, Orsini and his followers attempt to abduct Irene, but are foiled by Colonna, whose son, Adriano, succeeds in freeing Irene. The populace joins in the fight between the two noble families, and order is restored only when Rienzi appears. Rienzi tells Adriano of his plan to seize power from the nobles and make Rome a free city; because of his love for Irene, Adriano agrees to support Rienzi. In Act II, the nobles having been defeated, Orsini attempts to kill Rienzi during the triumphal celebrations. Orsini and Colonna are condemned to death, but Rienzi yields to the entreaties of Adriano and Irene and spares them. In Act III the populace is moved to anger against the patricians who have again gathered an army to move against Rienzi. Colonna is killed, Adriano blames Rienzi and swears revenge, and the magnanimous Rienzi prevents the people from attacking Adriano. Adriano plots against Rienzi in Act IV, and in the final act the people themselves move in exasperation and anger against Rienzi. Firebrands are hurled into the Capitol, while Rienzi and Irene stand on the balcony in each other's arms. When Adriano attempts to enter the burning building, the tower collapses and he, Rienzi and Irene are buried in the ruins.

The libretto which Wagner fashioned for *Rienzi* reveals clearly the composer's adherence at this stage of his career to the style and content of Parisian grand opera. The historical subject, its known fact intermingled with romantic fiction, the division into the five acts of Meyerbeer and his imitators, the love of grandiose stage effects and huge ensembles – all these are characteristic of the kind of opera which was most popular in Paris at that time. Though Wagner had produced his libretto in German, he would have been willing, at the wave of a contract, to re-draft it in French, for it was his hope that *Rienzi* would be created as a French opera on the Meyerbeerian plan. That it was born as a kind of hybrid, a French grand opera in German, was due entirely to the fact that Dresden's was the only opera management to be seriously interested in Wagner's work.

Selecting from Bulwer-Lytton's novel those scenes which were of most use to him in order to display Rienzi as an idealist who fights, suffers and dies for his ideals, Wagner eliminated the character of Rienzi's wife and condensed the political leader's two periods of rule into one. 'Grand opera', he wrote, 'with all its scenic and musical splendour, its effective musical mass-passions, served me as a model; and it was my artistic ambition not just to imitate it but to surpass its previous realizations with ruthless extravagance.' This ruthless extravagance necessarily led to ruthless length, but not to any special care regarding the diction of the libretto as opposed to its shape: 'I applied no greater care with regard to diction and verse than seemed necessary in order to produce a good, not trivial, opera text.'

As early as July, three months before the premiere, Wagner began to involve himself actively in Dresden in preparations for the staging of *Rienzi*. The opera cannot have been an easy one for the recently opened Dresden Opera House to perform: it was inordinately long, its large cast and chorus were expensive to dress, and the orchestra found the music extremely difficult. Fortunately, the principal singers were first-rate. Joseph Tichatschek was cast in the title-role. The role of Adriano, Colonna's young son, which Wagner had written for a mezzo-soprano, was sung by the famous Wilhelmine Schröder-Devrient, despite the fact that she did not

Above: Ludwig Sievert's design for his RIENZI décor, Augsburg, 1954. Left: Ludwig Sievert's permanent set for this open-air production. Opposite: (left to right) Paula Brivkalne (Irene), Wolfgang Windgassen (Rienzi) and Josef Traxel (Adriano Colonna) in Wieland Wagner's production of RIENZI, Stuttgart, 1957.

care for the role and that her matronly figure was hardly seen to its best advantage in male costume.

The first performance, in Dresden on 20 October, was conducted by the theatre's music director Karl Reissiger. It began at six in the evening and did not end until shortly before midnight. On this occasion the stamina of performers and audience appears to have been greater than that of the composer:

I noticed that the first two acts had taken as long as, for instance, the whole of *Der Freischütz*. On account of its warlike calls to arms, the third act begins with an exceptional uproar, and when at its close the clock over the stage pointed to ten, which meant that the performance had already lasted a whole four hours, I became absolutely desperate. The fact that, after this act also, I was again loudly called for I regarded merely as a final courtesy on the part of the audience who no doubt wished to signify that they had had quite enough for one evening and would now leave the house in a body. As we still had two acts to go, I thought it certain that we should not be able to finish the piece, and considered apologizing for my lack of wisdom in not having previously effected the necessary curtailments ... But my astonishment at finding the audience

still there in full muster, even in the last act towards midnight, filled me with unbounded perplexity. I could no longer trust my eyes or ears, and regarded the entire evening as a nightmare. It was past midnight, however, when for the last time I had to obey the thunderous calls of the audience, side by side with my faithful singers.

There can be no doubt of the success of *Rienzi*'s premiere. At a few subsequent performances the opera was given in two parts, as *Rienzis Grösse* (Rienzi's Greatness) and *Rienzis Fall* (Rienzi's Fall), one part per evening. But audiences complained at having to pay twice for what had originally been one opera, so the management reverted to performing the work on one evening, though with substantial cuts. This shortened version of 1843 remained for many years Wagner's most popular opera.

Musically, *Rienzi* reveals Wagner still to be searching for his own individual voice. Nevertheless, the skill with which the composer, in his mid-twenties, handled the vast resources he was determined to deploy was quite remarkable. The score is set out in separate numbers, recitative alternating with melody. But Wagner's recitative, though conventional in style, is considerably more expressive than that of his model, Meyerbeer. It was not to be banished entirely in his next opera, *Der fliegende Holländer*, either, but would be considerably reduced as Wagner moved towards his not yet clearly formulated concept of endless melody. Though there is much of Meyerbeer in the music of *Rienzi*, in the processional rhythms and the great choruses, and even in the broad melody of Rienzi's prayer in Act V, it is in the prayer that one first catches something of the manner of the mature

Left: RIENZI, artist unknown. Below: a scene from the 1964 production of RIENZI at La Scala, Milan. The scenery and costumes were designed by Nicola Benois and the producer was Herbert Graf.

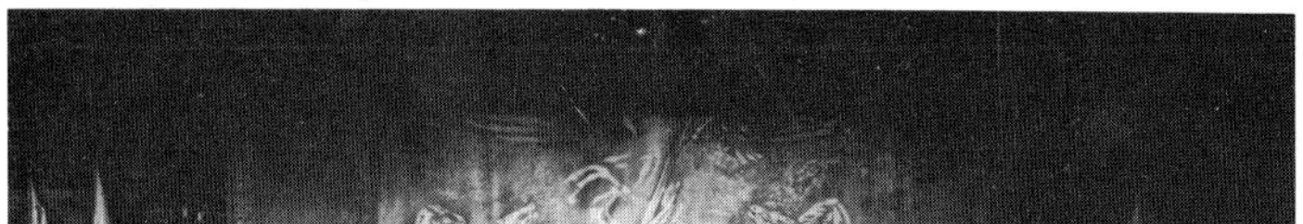

Top, left to right: Ursula Brömme (Adriano), Elisabeth Rose (Irene) and Gustav Papp (Rienzi) in a production by Heinrich Voigt, Leipzig, 1962.
Above: scene from the 1967 production of RIENZI in Munich. The opera was produced by Heinz Arnold in a courtyard of the Residenzplatz.
Right: the open-air setting of this 1967 production of RIENZI in Munich allowed a much larger performing area than would have been possible in a theatre.

Wagner. This particular tune, Janus-like, faces not only backwards, toward the pomp of grand opera, but also forward towards the sweeping lines and emotional depths of Wagnerian music-drama.

That *Rienzi* should still occasionally be performed, while *Die Feen* and *Das Liebesverbot* are almost totally neglected, is perhaps somewhat unfair, though understandable. Despite the fact that with *Rienzi* Wagner set out to compose an opera of the kind he thought Parisian audiences would appreciate, it is a transitional work, and, as such, of somewhat more interest to opera audiences of today than Wagner's two earlier false starts. In Dresden, it remained in the repertory, reaching its 100th performance in 1873 and its 200th in 1908. After Dresden, *Rienzi* was produced in Hamburg, in 1844, and in Berlin in 1847. It took longer to establish itself outside Germany, reaching Prague in 1859, Paris in 1869, Vienna in 1871, Venice in 1874, New York in 1878 and London in 1879. The opera has never been performed at Bayreuth. It cannot be said to have appealed greatly in either London or New York, having last been performed in New York in 1923, and in London not since 1879. Performances elsewhere in Great Britain in recent years have been by amateurs: the Midland Music Makers in Birmingham in 1957 and Reading University Opera in 1973. Concert performances are less infrequent. In this form a truncated *Rienzi* has been heard at St Pancras Town Hall, London, in 1966 and Carnegie Hall, New York, in 1980. There have also been concert performances in Vienna in 1950 and again in 1960, in Turin in 1963, West Berlin (1974 and 1980), Perugia (1980), and elsewhere, but always with huge cuts.

An open-air production at Augsburg in 1954 was said to be 'grandiose and impressive'. The designer, Ludwig Sievert, constructed 'an enormous fixed set, with much variety of level and locality. The brick walls at the back allowed of real flames, huge spectacular flames, for the climax.'

In 1957 Wieland Wagner, the composer's grandson who was then in mid-career at Bayreuth, staged *Rienzi* in Stuttgart. The correspondent of *Opera* described it thus:

> One had the feeling that he could not decide whether to produce it as 'grand opera' or embark on yet another of his experimental productions. So the overall impression was that of a grand spectacle onto which were tacked some of Wieland Wagner's well-known modern scenic tricks. The stabbing of Rienzi was reminiscent of the Act II riot scene of the Bayreuth *Meistersinger*. And the friends of Neu-Bayreuth this time got the shock of their lives; the appearance of the messengers of peace, all dressed in gold and white and with golden wings, can only be described as *Kitsch*. However, the little ballet angels that accompanied this scene with rather silly hopping-round movements have been removed. Wieland Wagner's adaptation, though, was very effective: it extended the opera to nine instead of the original five scenes and also reduced the work from five hours to three and a half. This clarified the plot and could have formed a most satisfying basis for the production.

An interesting innovation, and one that has been incorporated in other productions, was the casting of a tenor instead of a mezzo-soprano as Adriano. The advantage can only have been in terms of dramatic verisimilitude, for a tenor Adriano cannot sing the role entirely as written and remain completely audible.

It was in 1957, also, that a poll conducted at the Bayreuth Festival invited audiences and critics to vote on whether or not *Rienzi* should be officially admitted to the canon and performed at Bayreuth. The answer was in the negative.

Most recent productions of *Rienzi* have been in provincial theatres in Germany (Dessau, 1957; Magdeburg, 1959) or abroad (Bratislava, 1967; Graz, 1970; Trieste, 1968), though occasionally the opera has been taken up by a prestigious company such as Leipzig (1962), La Scala, Milan (1964) or Munich (1967). But the style of production for which *Rienzi* cries out is too expensive for most theatres and not to the taste of the others. The conventional representational style adopted at La Scala by the director Herbert Graf and the designer Nicola Benois was generally disliked, and the open-air Munich production by Heinz Arnold, whose designer, Johannes Dreher, used lighting and movable scenery to turn the Munich Residenz into a piece of Rome, was equally unsuccessful with critics and audiences. The Trieste 1968 production (the local premiere of the opera) presented the work stripped of all its grand opera trappings. It was staged by the Trieste director and designer Gianrico Becher who designed and built all the sets in wood. The Roman Forum scene with its arches and broken columns was splendidly impressive, and the costumes of the crowd of 400, 'a glowing fusion of red and brown in a sumptuously harmonious stage picture', was greeted with acclaim. There are, it seems, ways of staging *Rienzi* which modern audiences will find acceptable.

Opposite: cover of a composition entitled
'The Flying Dutchman Galop'
by W. Williams, based on themes from Wagner's opera.

III
DER FLIEGENDE HOLLÄNDER

In his later operas, Wagner gave himself libretti whose origins were so lost in myth and history that he was able to claim himself to be the creator of the plot, the artistic shaper of events. *Der fliegende Holländer* (The Flying Dutchman), the earliest of his mature works, is also based on a myth, but it is a myth with which other artists, novelists and playwrights had tampered, and it is through them that Wagner was drawn to the subject. When, in 1838, he first encountered the legend of the Flying Dutchman in Heinrich Heine's 'Memoirs of Herr von Schnabelewopski', Wagner realized it would make good operatic material. But he was then at work on the composition of *Rienzi*, so for the time being the Dutchman was set aside.

Wagner's escape from Riga to London was made on the *Thetis*, a small vessel of not more than 100 tons. In his autobiography the composer described the horrors of the voyage: a violent storm had arisen, and the Captain was driven to seek refuge on the Norwegian coast.

And how relieved I was to behold that far-reaching rocky coast, towards which we were being driven at such speed! A Norwegian pilot came to meet us in a small boat and, with experienced hand, assumed control of the Thetis, whereupon in a very short time I was to have one of the most marvellous and most beautiful impressions of my life. What I had taken to be a continuous line of cliffs turned out on our approach to be a series of separate rocks projecting from the sea. Having sailed past them, we perceived that we were surrounded, not only in front and at the sides, but also at our back, by these reefs, which closed in behind us so near together that they seemed to form a single chain of rocks. At the same time, the hurricane was so broken by the rocks in our rear that the further we sailed through this ever-changing labyrinth of projecting rocks, the calmer the sea became, until at last the vessel's progress was perfectly smooth and quiet as we entered one of these long sea-roads running through a giant ravine – for such the Norwegian fjords appeared to me. A feeling of indescribable content come over me when the enormous granite walls echoed the hail of the crew as they cast anchor and furled the sails. The sharp rhythm of this call clung to me like an omen of good cheer, and shaped itself presently into the theme of the seamen's song in my Flying Dutchman. The idea of this opera was, even at that time, ever present in my mind, and it now took on a definite poetic and musical colour under the influence of my recent impressions.

For almost a year, Wagner had been considering the possibility of writing an opera on the legend which he had read

about in Heine. The legend was not created by Heine, but had been widely known for many years. A Dutch sea captain swears that he will round a certain dangerous cape in rough weather, even if he should go on sailing until the day of judgement. His oath is noted in high places, and he and his ship are thereafter condemned to sail on throughout eternity. A detail in several accounts of the legend involves the phantom ship hailing other vessels, and asking them to deliver letters from the crew to their families in Holland. But the letters turn out to be addressed to people long since dead.

The story is sometimes referred to as 'the English legend', and, although it may not have originated in England, it certainly makes several appearances in English literature and drama in the early nineteenth century. An anonymous story, 'Vanderdecken's Message Home, or The Tenacity of Natural Affection', appeared in *Blackwood's Magazine* in May 1821, and five years later a three-act play called 'The Flying Dutchman, or The Phantom Ship' was produced in London at the Adelphi Theatre. In 1839, Captain Marryat's novel *The Phantom Ship*, based on the legend, was published.

Heine's 'Memoirs of Herr von Schnabelewopski' mentions the Flying Dutchman in only one chapter, when Schnabelewopski visits a theatre in Amsterdam and sees a play on the subject. The action of the play is described in detail by Heine, and includes an element lacking in earlier versions of the legend: the possibility for the Dutchman of redemption through the love of a faithful woman. It was surely this which aroused Wagner's creative interest in the Dutchman, for the concept of redemption through love was thereafter to pervade almost every opera he composed.

The precise meaning of the Flying Dutchman myth, as far as Wagner was concerned, was revealed by the composer in 'A Communication to My Friends':

The figure of the Flying Dutchman is a mythical creation of the folk: a primal trait of human nature speaks out from it with heart-enthralling force. This trait, in its most universal meaning, is the

Opposite: drawing from the Leipzig *Illustrirte Zeitung*, 7 October 1843, showing the final scene of the opera as seen at the Dresden premiere in 1843. As the Dutchman's ship founders in the harbour, Senta flings herself into the sea to prove her fidelity to the Dutchman. Below left: two drawings from the *Illustrirte Zeitung*, 7 October 1843: Michael Wächter as the Dutchman and Wilhelmine Schröder-Devrient as Senta. Below: painting (1870) by Theodor Pixis of the final scene from DER FLIEGENDE HOLLÄNDER, as seen at Drury Lane Theatre, London.

longing after rest, from amid the storms of life. In the blithe world of Greece we meet with it in the wanderings of Ulysses and his longing after home, house, hearth and wife: the attainable, and at last attained, reward of the city-loving son of ancient Hellas. The Christian, without a home on earth, embodied this trait in the figure of the Wandering Jew: for that wanderer, forever doomed to a long-since out-lived life, without an aim, without a joy, there bloomed no earthly ransom; death was the sole remaining goal of all his strivings; his only hope, the laying down of being.

If the Dutchman bears characteristics of Wagner's Jew, then that Jew is a wanderer who carries on his own shoulders the *Weltschmerz* of his race. But unlike the 'Wandering Jew' who does not share the Christian idea of salvation, the Dutchman can be redeemed. Wagner's Dutchman, then, embodies the composer's earliest use of a Wandering Jew theme, just as Kundry in *Parsifal* many years later represents his mature attitude to the subject. His Dutchman carries his own *Weltschmerz*. But unlike the Wandering Jew, he can be redeemed by the love of a faithful woman. In contemplating this touch, added to the legend by Heine, Wagner not only makes a creative leap into the world of the Goethean *Ewigweibliche* but also anticipates Ibsen in creating the new woman. The woman sought by Wagner's Dutchman is, as the composer himself pointed out, 'no longer the home-tending Penelope of Ulysses, as courted in the days of old, but the quintessence of womankind; and yet the still unmanifest, the longed-for, the dreamed-of, the infinitely womanly woman – let me out with it in one phrase: the woman of the future'.

Below: Astrid Varnay as Senta in Act II of DER FLIEGENDE HOLLÄNDER in Wolfgang Wagner's Bayreuth production, 1955.

Opposite: (above) Max Brückner's design for the last act of DER FLIEGENDE HOLLÄNDER, Bayreuth, 1901; (below) Emil Preetorius's design for Act II, Bayreuth, 1939.

Brückner

In other words, the woman sought by Wagner's Dutchman is closer to Ibsen's Rebecca West than to Ulysses' Penelope.

Of course, the Dutchman is not only the Wandering Jew. He is also, and most significantly, the artist, and not merely the artist in general but Wagner in particular: a Wagner who, at this stage of his life, was willing to accept his wife Minna as his redeemer. In his first sketch for the opera, the heroine's name is, in fact, not Senta but Minna, and much of the composer's own self-pity finds its way into the mouth of the Dutchman: '*War ich unsel'ger Spielwerk deines Spottes, als die Erolösung du mir zeigtest an?*' (Was I the unhappy plaything of your mockery when you showed me the way of redemption?)

Heine's cynical conclusion that the moral to be drawn from the play is that women should refrain from marrying Flying Dutchmen and that men can, in the last resort, expect no better from women than betrayal and destruction, is not one which Wagner would have had the proper temperament to endorse. It is, in fact, the composer's lack of humour, his ability to accept every aspect of the myth with the greatest solemnity, that enabled him to compose so hypnotically compelling an opera on the subject. Many years later, when he came to see himself as Parsifal, even not so many years later when he saw himself as Lohengrin, a certain garrulity and lack of proportion had begun to obtrude themselves upon Wagner's artistic instincts. However, in his twenties when he wrote *Der fliegende Holländer*, composing the entire score in seven weeks, he was young enough for this not to be the case. Indeed, the opera is Wagner's most concise work for the stage. Its libretto was initially planned in one long act, and it was always Wagner's intention that the opera should be played straight through, without breaks in the music. He was, he claimed, 'influenced by the consideration that I could in this way confine it to the simple dramatic developments between the principal characters, without troubling about the tiresome operatic accessories. From a practical point of view, I thought I could rely on a better prospect for the acceptance of my proposed work if it were cast in the form of a one-act opera, such as was frequently given as a curtain raiser before a ballet at the Grand Opera.'

Act II of the Dutchman, with set design by Dave Gano, New Orleans, 1979. Opposite: (above) Act II, at the Teatro Colón, Buenos Aires, 1973; (below) Act I of Wieland Wagner's Bayreuth production, 1959.

Der fliegende Holländer would have made an enormously lengthy curtain-raiser. As it happened, practical considerations dictated the three-act structure at the opera's first performance in Dresden in 1843; nevertheless, it has frequently been produced in this century in its one-act version (the first time being at Bayreuth in 1901), and it gains immeasurably from being performed as Wagner originally intended it should be. In order to stage the work in one act, certain minor cuts are necessary, so that the postlude of one act of the published score flows readily into the prelude of the next.

Wagner's involvement in humanizing the myth of the Dutchman did not end with his composition of the words and music of the opera. He left detailed and fascinating notes on how the characters should be conceived and performed. In an essay 'Remarks on Performing the opera *The Flying Dutchman*', published in 1853, ten years after the premiere, he examined the Dutchman's first scene in great detail, instructing the singer how and where to move, and on which bar to make what gesture:

> His first entry is most solemn and earnest; the measured slowness of his landing should offer a marked contrast with his vessel's weirdly rapid passage through the seas. During the deep trumpet notes (B minor) at quite the close of the introductory scene he has come off board, along a plank lowered by one of the crew to a shelf of rock on the shore; his rolling gait, proper to seafolk on first treading dry land after a long voyage, is accompanied by a wave-like figure for the violins and "tenors": with the first crotchet of the third bar he makes his second step – always with folded arms and sunken head; his third and fourth steps coincide with the notes of the eighth and tenth bars. From here on, his movements will follow the dictates of his general delivery, yet the actor must never let himself be betrayed into exaggerated stridings to and fro: a certain terrible repose in his outward demeanour, even amid the most passionate expression of inward anguish and despair, will give the characteristic stamp to this impersonation.

Opposite: the DUTCHMAN as seen in a BBC Television production, 1975, with Norman Bailey in the title-role.
Above: Act I at La Scala, Milan, as performed in 1965–6.

Top: Gwyneth Jones as Senta at Covent Garden, 1966. Above: Donald McIntyre (the Dutchman), Rita Hunter (Senta), Don Garrard (Daland) at Sadler's Wells Theatre, 1964. Opposite: in 1968, the leading roles at Sadler's Wells were performed by Norman Bailey and Elizabeth Fretwell.

The first phrases are to be sung without a trace of passion (almost in strict beat, like the whole of this recitative), as though the man were tired out; at the words, declaimed with bitter ire, "Ha, stolzer Ozean", and so on, he does not break as yet into positive passion: more in terrible scorn, he merely turns his head half-round towards the sea . . .

Wagner is especially interesting, though in more general terms, on the character of Senta. She, after all, is his own invention, non-existent in the popular myth, and barely adumbrated in Heine, and the composer is concerned to ensure that she is not weakened by what he thinks of as German sentimentality:

The role of Senta will be hard to misread; one warning alone have I to give: let not the *dreamy* side of her nature be conceived in the sense of a modern sickly sentimentality! Senta, on the contrary, is an altogether robust Northern maid, and even in her apparent sentimentality she is thoroughly naive. Only in the heart of an entirely naive girl, surrounded by the idiosyncracies of northern nature, could impressions such as those of the ballad of the Flying Dutchman and the picture of the pallid seaman call forth so wondrous strong a bent, as the impulse to redeem the doomed: with her, this takes the outward form of an active monomania such, indeed, as can be found only in quite naive natures. We have been told of Norwegian maids of such a force of feeling, that death has come upon them through a sudden rigour of the heart. Much in this wise may it go, with the seeming 'morbidness' of pallid Senta.

There are also instructions for the performers of the other roles. Erik must not be portrayed as 'a sentimental whiner: on the contrary, he is stormy, impulsive and sombre, like every man who lives alone, particularly in the northern highlands. Whoever should give a sugary rendering to his Cavatina in Act III', writes Wagner, 'would do me a sorry service, for it ought instead to breathe distress and heartache.' And he beseeches the exponent of the role of Daland, Senta's father, 'not to drag his role into the region of the positively comic: he is a rough-hewn figure from the life of everyday, a sailor who scoffs at storms and danger for the sake of gain, and with whom, for instance, the – certainly apparent – sale of his daughter to a rich man ought not to seem at all disgraceful: he thinks and deals, like a hundred thousand others, without the least suspicion that he is doing any wrong.'

Der fliegende Holländer is Wagner's first real encounter with folk myth. But he came to it fully-fledged, and the fruit of the encounter is an opera which is in no sense an

Overleaf: Harry Kupfer's production, Bayreuth, 1978. Senta (Lisbeth Balslev), dreaming, sees the arrival of the Dutchman (Simon Estes) and his ship; (opposite) Ponnelle's controversial San Francisco production (1979), entirely staged on the deck of a ship, again with Simon Estes.

apprentice-work. That he was to deal differently with myth, and with a different kind of myth, in his greatest works, *Tristan und Isolde*, *Der Ring des Nibelungen* and *Parsifal*, does not invalidate the fresher, crisper, more Italianate approach of *Der fliegende Holländer*, a work so filled with strong passions that it has simply no room for weak *longueurs*.

Although only four performances of *Der fliegende Holländer* were given in Dresden in 1843, after which the opera was not revived there until 1865, it made its way on to other German stages and eventually was staged in a number of foreign countries. In London, at the Theatre Royal, Drury Lane, in 1870, it became the first Wagner opera to be produced in Great Britain (it was performed in Italian as *L'olandese dannato*). The first American performance, also in Italian, was given in Philadelphia in 1876. It was for the production in Zurich during the winter of 1851–2 that Wagner, who conducted, revised some of the orchestration and changed the ending of the overture to the form in which it is known today. The opera reached Covent Garden, still in Italian but this time as *Il vascello fantasma*, in 1877. It was not staged at Bayreuth until 1901, since which time it has been produced there at quite frequent intervals. It is, in fact, the earliest Wagner opera in the Bayreuth repertoire.

Productions of *Der fliegende Höllander* have, over the years, followed various changes in taste and advances in stage technique, although until after World War II most stagings were basically representational. The 1901 Bayreuth production, staged by the composer's widow, Cosima, respected Wagner's wishes by presenting the opera in one continuous act, but Cosima's approach to the work was pedantic rather than creative. The next Bayreuth production, however (for which Wagner's son Siegfried was responsible), replaced the painted scenery of Cosima's time with three-dimensional stage sets. After that staging, in 1914, the opera was not seen again at Bayreuth until 1939 when it was staged by Heinz Tietjen whose production was revived each year until 1942. Tietjen usually worked with the designer Emil Preetorius, and they were still staging *Der fliegende Höllander* in various European cities in the years immediately following the war.

Writing in 1953 of his work with Preetorius at Bayreuth in the 'thirties, Tietjen said: 'We set ourselves in the face of obstinate and often actively hostile resistance, rooted in a narrow and rigid view of a misunderstood "Old tradition",

Below: Ponnelle's permanent set for his production of Der fliegende Holländer as seen at the Met in March, 1979, after its San Francisco premiere.

to create a new tradition – one, however, which did not simply throw the old tradition overboard but sought to draw it fruitfully into our efforts of renewal. Both of us, scenic designer and producer, saw light as the basic element in the visual realization of all Wagner's works, and we sought to evolve a stage setting which restricted the use of objects to essentials and gave the main role to the adaptable and highly effective visual instrument of lighting.' This clearly paved the way for the post-war 'new Bayreuth' style of the young Wagner generation, the composer's grandsons, Wieland and Wolfgang, who took over the running of the Wagner Festivals when the theatre was allowed to re-open in 1951.

The first post-war Bayreuth *Holländer* in 1955 was produced not by Wieland, who is generally thought of as the stage architect of the new Bayreuth, but by Wolfgang, who has always been regarded as administrator first and stage director second. In its uneasy attempt to bring something of Wieland's abstraction to an opera which requires to be rooted in a real place and a specified time, Wolfgang Wagner's production fell between two styles. Four years later, it was replaced with a production by Wieland Wagner which firmly grasped the nettle of the conflict of style within the opera itself, and contrived magnificently to blend the realistic and the abstract in a staging which, uncluttered and direct, presented the work in a way which no merely passive mounting of the opera could have achieved. The characters were real, the props were real. What surrounded the villagers was mystery, and what threatened their security was the suffering Christ-figure of the Dutchman.

Der fliegende Holländer is, in a way, a more difficult work to stage than *Tristan* or *Parsifal*, because it has to be made to work on two levels, the real and the mythic, whereas the later works can rise above the real and can be made to respond to a great stage director's vision of the ideal. Wagner's Dutchman needs the sea, the sky, the rocky Norwegian coast, and the cosy fishing village: those productions fail which, in responding to the deeper meaning of the drama, neglect to provide, at least in part, these more mundane elements. Jean-Pierre Ponnelle's production in 1975 for the San Francisco Opera set most of the events in the turbulent mind of a minor character, the Steersman. The roles of the Steersman and Senta's unwanted suitor Erik were merged into one, and the opera took on the surrealistic aspect of a dream. The result was stimulating but finally unsatisfactory, since it was unable to encompass the end of the opera as Wagner envisaged it. Redemption had no place in this producer's thoughts.

A BBC Television production by Brian Large, also in 1975, missed its opportunity by failing to take advantage of the medium. The entire work was filmed in and confined to the television studio, and the set designs were visually unappealing. Bayreuth, in its most recent staging in 1978, has succumbed to the schizophrenic dream, though at Bayreuth it is Senta who is the dreamer. This conception by the East German director Harry Kupfer makes more dramatic sense than Ponnelle's equally partial view of the work, though it still does not take account of every element in Wagner's libretto. *Opera*'s critic dismissed it sternly as 'a production in which a prodigious amount of technical ingenuity, visual complexity, and theatrical skill had been lavished on a not very interesting idea – a Bright Idea that better deserved to be dismissed after five minutes' hard thinking than undertaken with the full force of East German operatic didacticism.'

An English National Opera production in 1982 respected Wagner's first thoughts concerning the opera's dramatic form by reverting to the one-act version he had originally envisaged; however, musically it stayed with the composer's revised instrumentation and thus missed an opportunity to present the work as it sounded in 1843.

Below: Act III in the Australian Opera production, Sydney Opera House, 1977.

Above: scenes from the English National Opera's 1982 production of
The Flying Dutchman at the London Coliseum, designed by Stefanos Lazaridis.
Opposite: a scene from Tannhäuser, artist unknown.

IV
TANNHÄUSER

Wagner had originally planned to call his new opera *Der Venusberg* (The Mount of Venus), but was dissuaded by his publisher, who feared that the title might cause ribald comment: 'Bad enough that some of the action be located on the Mountain of Venus.' The opera's full title is *Tannhäuser und der Sängerkrieg auf Wartburg* (Tannhäuser and the Battle of the Singers on the Wartburg), which reveals that, in writing his libretto, the composer made use of elements from two myths which had not previously been connected. He first conceived the idea for the opera in the summer of 1842, and wrote his libretto the following spring, after the premiere of *Der fliegende Holländer*. During a holiday with Minna at Teplitz in July and August of 1843, he began to compose the music, starting with the Venusberg scene, which he regarded as the most difficult and with which he was not to be completely satisfied until he had revised it a good fifteen years after the opera's initial production. The first act was finished in January 1844, the second in mid-October, and the third at the end of December. By the middle of the following April the opera had been completely scored.

The stories of the singers' contest and of Tannhäuser are found in medieval German poetry and in several nineteenth-century volumes based on the old legends. Wagner probably came across both stories in a collection of Thuringian legends by Ludwig Bechstein, published in 1835, which contained not only an account of the thirteenth-century minstrel Tannhäuser but also the story of the singers' contest on the Wartburg. A possible link between the two legends was made in 1838 in a book about the Wartburg contest which suggested that Tannhäuser was an alternative name for another medieval poet, Heinrich von Oftendingen, who took part in the contest. Other sources which Wagner admitted having consulted were '*Der getreue Eckart und der Tannenhäuser*' (Faithful Eckart and Tannenhäuser), a story by Johann Ludwig Tieck, and '*Der Kampf der Sänger*' (The Battle of the Singers), a story from E.T.A. Hoffmann's collection, *Serapionsbrüder* (The Serapion Brethren). A potential source which Wagner does not mention is Heine's poem '*Der Tännhauser*', which is to be found in the same collection of writings by Heine in which the composer found the Flying Dutchman myth.

Wagner's libretto sets the action in thirteenth-century Thuringia. In the first act, inside the Venusberg, Tannhäuser lies at the feet of the goddess Venus, while nymphs, sirens and satyrs dance among the grottoes. Satiated with the delights of carnal love, Tannhäuser begins to long for his former life and his friends, and determines to forsake Venus. When the goddess tries to prevent him, he calls on the Blessed Virgin for protection, and suddenly finds himself in a valley at the foot of the Wartburg. It is spring, a young shepherd is singing, the hymns of pilgrims traversing the valley can be heard, and Tannhäuser is overjoyed to be back in the real world. He encounters a hunting party, consisting of the Landgrave, and a group of knights, all of them former associates of Tannhäuser who greet him with delight. One of them, Wolfram, reminds him that the Landgrave's niece, Elisabeth, loves him and that his return will be a great joy to her. Tannhäuser asks to be taken to her.

The second act is set in a great hall where a song contest is to be held. The Landgrave announces that the subject of the contest is to be the nature of love. His niece Elisabeth will give to the winner whatever he is bold enough to demand. The contest begins, the knights all offering songs on the mediaeval romantic ideal of courtly love. Tannhäuser, enriched by his experiences with Venus, has a different ideal of love, and expresses it in terms of passionate ardour which at first mystify, then offend and finally outrage the other knights. Goaded by what he feels to be their lack of comprehension, Tannhäuser launches into a song of praise to Venus, at which the women rush out of the hall in horror, while the men draw their swords in righteous anger. Elisabeth implores the Landgrave to pardon Tannhäuser, whose mood

Opposite: Tannhäuser in the song contest of Act II. Woodcut of the scene as performed at the opera's 1845 premiere in Dresden.
Above: the second scene of Act I, as seen at the opera's first Paris production, at the Opéra in 1861.
Left: Joseph Tichatschek (Tannhäuser) and Wilhelmine Schröder-Devrient (Venus) in the 1845 Dresden premiere.

is now one of despair and remorse, but the Landgrave tells him that the only way to obtain forgiveness is for him to journey to Rome with the pilgrims to seek salvation. As the pilgrims' hymn is heard in the distance, Tannhäuser cries 'To Rome!' and rushes out to join them.

In the third act, set in the valley of the Wartburg, Elisabeth seeks Tannhäuser in vain among the returning pilgrims. She leaves sadly, refusing Wolfram's offer to accompany her. Wolfram encounters Tannhäuser, who has been refused absolution by the Pope. 'You have as much chance of salvation,' His Holiness had said in effect, 'as this dead staff in my hand has of bursting into bloom.' Tannhäuser is dissuaded by Wolfram from attempting to return to the Venusberg. As dawn breaks, a funeral procession appears with the body of Elisabeth, across whose bier Tannhäuser falls dead. A group of young pilgrims enters bearing the Pope's staff, which has sprouted leaves: a token that Tannhäuser has achieved salvation.

Above: TANNHÄUSER, designed by Max Brückner for Bayreuth, 1891 (top, Act I; above, Act II).
Right: Act III of the 1930 Bayreuth TANNHÄUSER, designed by Kurt Söhnlein and Friedrich Kranich.

On one level a tale of sacred and profane love, Wagner's libretto for *Tannhäuser* is also a tragic love story and even a dissertation on the decline of the romantic ideal – and a cry of despair at the standards and tastes of his materialistic nineteenth century. In 'A Communication to My Friends', the composer himself spoke of this, though in characteristically verbose language:

If at last I turned impatiently away, and owed the strength of my repugnance to the independence already developed in my nature, both as artist and as man: so did that double revolt, of man and artist, inevitably take on the form of a yearning for appeasement in a higher, nobler element: an element which in its contrast to the only pleasures that the material present spreads in modern life and modern art, could but appear to me in the guise of a pure, chaste, virginal and unseizable, and unapproachable ideal of love. What, in fine, could this love yearning, the noblest thing my heart could feel – what other could it be than a longing for release from the present, for absorption into an element of endless love, a love denied to earth and reachable through the gates of death alone? And what, again, at bottom, could such a longing be, but the yearning of love; aye, of a real love seeded in the soil of fullest sentience – yet a love that could never come to fruitage on the loathsome soil of modern sentience? How absurd, then, must those critics seem to me, who, drawing all their wit from modern wantonness, insist on reading into my *Tannhäuser* a specifically Christian and impotently pietistic drift! They recognize nothing but the fable of their own incompetence, in the story of a man whom they are utterly unable to comprehend.

The two worlds contrasted in *Tannhäuser*, the piety of the Middle Ages and the rebellious free thought of post-Renaissance man, both find sympathetic expression in Wagner's music. The eroticism of the Venusberg and the chaste utter-

Opposite: TANNHÄUSER, produced and designed by Wieland Wagner, Bayreuth, 1954 (above, Act I; below, Act II).

Below: Act II at Sadler's Wells Theatre, London, in 1959. Standing right of centre is Ronald Dowd (Tannhäuser).

ance of Elisabeth are equally convincing, and it is at those moments when one is in conflict with the other, or at moments of transition from one to the other, that Wagner's creative genius shines forth most excitingly. The *Leitmotif* technique of the later operas, already adumbrated in *Der fliegende Holländer*, is used consciously and with confidence in *Tannhäuser*, especially in the knight's Act III narration of his pilgrimage to Rome, a clear forerunner of the composer's later style with its declamatory vocal line above a symphonic accompaniment of great melodic interest. Elsewhere in the opera, for instance in Wolfram's famous song to the evening star, Wagner retains the old Italian-style recitative and cavatina with simple accompaniment.

Tannhäuser was given its first performance in Dresden on 19 October 1845, with Joseph Tichatschek in the title-role, Wagner's niece Johanna Wagner as Elisabeth and Wilhelmine Schröder-Devrient as Venus. Though its initial reception was lukewarm, the opera caught on at its third performance. But four years were to pass before it was staged elsewhere, and ten years or more before it was seen on other important stages such as Berlin, Munich and Vienna. The opera was thought to be generally too slow and stately for its subject matter. It has, however, maintained a place in the repertory, though it has never excited the admiration accorded to Wagner's next opera, *Lohengrin*, nor has it achieved the popular success of his previous opera, *Der fliegende Holländer*.

Wagner revised *Tannhäuser* for its Paris production in 1861, altering the opening scene and developing and expanding the Venusberg music. Though stylistically the 1845 score is more unified, there can be no doubt that the infiltration of the more mature Wagner into a work he had conceived more than fifteen years earlier makes the opera even more interesting to modern audiences.

New York's first *Tannhäuser* was a production of the original Dresden version at the Stadt Theater, on 4 April 1859, when it became the first opera by Wagner to be staged anywhere in the Americas. This seems to have been a thoroughly German-community occasion: one critic wrote

Below: Act II at La Scala, in 1967, when the opera was produced by Frank de Quell, with sets by Peter Bisseger.

Opposite: Richard Cassilly (Tannhäuser) and Jessye Norman (Elisabeth) at Covent Garden, 1973, in Vaclav Kaslik's ill-fated production.

that 'objections were made ... to the thoroughly German atmosphere pervading the whole affair. Boys went through the aisles with beer in stone mugs for the thirsty, and huge chunks of *Schweizerkäs* for the hungry.' The opera was not staged in London until 1875 when it reached Covent Garden in a performance of which the critic Herman Klein wrote 'the less said the better: it satisfied curiosity without affording a true idea of the opera.'

By the time *Tannhäuser* came to be produced at Bayreuth, in 1891, it had become one of Wagner's most popular operas. The composer having died eight years earlier without really having produced a definitive performing edition of the work, his widow Cosima had to decide whether to stage the Dresden or Paris version or one of the other versions prepared either by Wagner himself (for the first Vienna production) or by someone else. That she was fully conscious of the difficulties involved is revealed in a letter Cosima Wagner later wrote to a Berlin publisher:

Below: Grace Bumbry, Bayreuth's 'Black Venus', in Wieland Wagner's production (1961).

> If we were to make an operatic production (even in the best sense of the word), it was inevitable that the musical riches of the first scene would make not only the following scene but also the second and third acts appear pale and flat... Whereas, if we could succeed in bringing to realization the characters with their tragic destiny and the life of the Middle Ages, the musical riches I spoke of would be seen as part of Venus's magic wiles and the simpler means would appear as the natural expression of the other way of life. The warmth in the welcoming of Tannhäuser (in Act One), the utmost simplicity and clarity in the enunciation of the words, the avoidance in positioning, expression, tempo etc. of everything that could remind one of a septet – this was our one endeavour.

When Cosima's production of *Tannhäuser* was staged in Bayreuth in 1891, it was clear to many that her emphasis upon the dramatic qualities of the work had given the opera a new and enhanced stature. The young Richard Strauss wrote that 'the opera *Tannhäuser* has been resurrected as a drama'. The Bayreuth style was in the process of being formulated, a style with its basis in what seems today the simple commonsense of a complete fusion of the stage action with the music. Daniela, Cosima's daughter (by von Bülow) who assisted her mother in the running of the Festival Theatre, wrote that in Bayreuth productions there was 'no theme, no melodic phrase which has not to be given visual expression through gesture, movement, positioning and mime.'

Already one senses the danger that intelligent staging might degenerate into over-fussy, stylized movement, with little or no opportunity on the part of individual performers to use their own imaginations, their own temperaments, to inform their interpretations. It was not long before Cosima's productions were being criticized for their mechanical precision. Her 1891 *Tannhäuser* was revived the following year and again in 1894, after which it was not seen at Bayreuth until 1904. In 1908 Cosima relinquished active direction of the Festival performances to her (and Wagner's) son Siegfried, then in his late thirties. He was to be in charge of Bayreuth for twenty-two years, but it was not until his final year, 1930, the year in which both he and his mother died, that Siegfried allowed *Tannhäuser* to be staged again, though he had intended to stage the opera in 1927.

Siegfried Wagner's 1930 *Tannhäuser*, conducted by Toscanini, substituted a three-dimensional, somewhat lavish realism for his mother's essentially nineteenth-century flat-painted romanticism, realistic though that had been thought in its day, and the new scenery was the joint creation of Siegfried Wagner and his designer Kurt Söhnlein. The production was revived in 1931, after which *Tannhäuser* disappeared from Bayreuth throughout the entire Nazi period, when Siegfried Wagner's widow Winifred assumed control. It was not to reappear at Bayreuth until the post-war administration of Winifred's sons, Wieland and Wolfgang Wagner, which restored artistic and political respectability to the Festival.

The 1891 staging of Cosima Wagner, especially of the opening scene in the Venusberg, had deeply impressed the young Richard Strauss (who was to conduct its 1894 revival). 'In that performance', Strauss wrote, 'there was complete agreement between the living gesture, embodied in a dance of formal Greek beauty, and its moving expression in the language of the modern orchestra, an agreement which constituted a stylistic achievement of the first order. The spectator was justified in saying of this first scene of *Tannhäuser* in the Bayreuth performance: this is *the* Venusberg and I have seen a true picture of Hellenic *joie de vivre*.' All the means of expression used by Wagner – sculpture, painting, poetry and music – were, Strauss thought, equally matched.

It is doubtful if any spectator at Wieland Wagner's Bayreuth *Tannhäuser* in 1954 would have felt justified in reacting with such certainty to what he was being shown on the stage. The elderly and conservative found Wieland's abstract décors difficult to come to terms with, but even so young and open-minded a critic as Andrew Porter, writing in *Opera*, had serious reservations:

Wieland Wagner's new production of *Tannhäuser* at Bayreuth this summer is peculiarly disturbing. Formerly one has been able to justify his innovations by claiming that – quite apart from their striking visual impact and the resultant dramatic power – they have enabled the listener to concentrate on the music and the dramatic action undistracted by the absurdities inherent (though not always apparent) in the traditional methods of Wagnerian staging ... But in *Tannhäuser* Wieland Wagner has introduced absurdities of his own, worse than any of the old ones. The basic fault – and it is perhaps the most serious one that an opera producer can commit – seems to be that he has placed visual spectacle before the music: he has imposed his own designs on the music, and the designs do not fit.

Below: (left) Act II in Vienna, 1963, with the distinguished Dutch soprano Gré Brouwenstijn as Elisabeth. Below: Elizabeth Connell as Venus in a 1973 Australian Opera production by Bernd Benthaak, designed by Ralph Koltai. Overleaf: the opening scene in Götz Friedrich's politically-slanted Bayreuth production, designed by Jürgen Rose and first staged in 1972; (inset) Act II.

The Venusberg, in that production, was set 'within a sort of gigantic shell, the main figures on the stage being anonymous male and female forms which danced a grave *pas de deux* while Venus and Tannhäuser reclined far away in the background', according to Geoffrey Skelton in *Wagner at Bayreuth*.

When *Tannhäuser* was next produced at Bayreuth, in 1961, again by Wieland Wagner, the Venusberg was a dark cavern dominated by the black Venus of the American mezzo-soprano Grace Bumbry, and Wieland now saw the opera as being about a man torn between two goddesses: Elisabeth, a Virgin Mary-goddess, and Venus, a sensual, Jocastan earth-mother-goddess. It was now the characters who became abstractions, while the settings moved away from pure abstraction to flirt with a variety of styles.

Productions of *Tannhäuser* in recent years have tended to

Above: the Bacchanale from Harry Kupfer's production in Dresden, 1978.

reveal the Wieland Wagner influence, whether it be that of the 1954 or the 1961 Wieland. Characteristically, Herbert von Karajan in his Vienna production of 1963 went his own way, tempering a modern realism with imaginative and impressionistic lighting, though Karajan's final scene was described by a Viennese critic as early Cecil B. de Mille.

Bayreuth in 1972 moved away from the Wieland Wagner approach with a new production by Götz Friedrich, the pupil and assistant of the famous (though not as a Wagnerian) Komische Oper director Walter Felsenstein. A believer in producers and their ideas, rather than composers and their operas, Friedrich narrowed the conflict in *Tannhäuser* to a fight between what he would no doubt describe as the revolutionary working-class and the reactionary forces of repression. The young pilgrims were no longer young pilgrims but rebellious youths, and were dressed as such. The Landgrave's retinue wore costumes which resembled in part the Nazi SS and in part the Don Cossacks. Elisabeth and Venus were portrayed by the same singer. It was necessary to refer to the programme book to discern most of the ideas which the producer claimed to have built into his production.

When the Royal Opera House, Covent Garden, presented a new production of *Tannhäuser* in 1973, the rehearsal period was marred by fierce and bitter disagreements between the conductor, Colin Davis, and a production team headed by Vaclav Kaslik. The producer and his designers were, in the end, dismissed, and the early performances of the new production were held together, dramatically as well as musically, by Colin Davis. The Editor of *Opera* wrote:

> Even by the third performance there had been changes: the crystal ball, with which Venus played, and which obviously was to be shattered as the Venusberg collapsed, had been quietly put into cold storage; the Landgrave no longer blew his own hunting horn; and there was a general tightening up of the whole action. But nothing could disguise the fact that the permanent set severely restricts the chorus's movements; that the wigs designed for the Hall of Song scene are the most unflattering that even Covent Garden's long-suffering choristers (especially the ladies) have ever been asked to wear; and that Mr Svoboda's 'cut-outs' in the Venusberg have an hypnotic effect, at least on this listener – whose eyes were constantly drawn back to the one that looked like a flying dolphin – but as this successfully drew his attention away from the embarrassing cavortings in the Venusberg, maybe it was a good thing after all!

Traditional cliché had, in this instance, been replaced by modern cliché. A more sensible approach to *Tannhäuser* was found by the Metropolitan Opera, New York, when it engaged the Viennese director Otto Schenk to stage its new production in 1977. Patrick J. Smith described it in *Opera*:

> Otto Schenk's staging rarely called attention to itself, yet it was always imaginatively responsive to Wagner's demands, and, at the end, very moving. In this he was immeasurably aided by Günther Schneider-Siemssen's sets. These were both evocative and apt: the transformation from the Venusberg to the valley of the Wartburg effortlessly rendered, and the soft, earthy pastorale of early spring in Thuringia giving way to the austere and solid nobility of the Hall of Song, from which we returned to the twilit, late autumn outside. Schneider-Siemssen is a superior visual poet, here working in a realistic frame, and his greatest asset lies in devising sets beautiful to look at, which are also stage-wise, such as the winding dirt path from high up-stage into the valley, so that the procession of pilgrims became more than a parade across the stage.

Tannhäuser, like *Der fliegende Holländer*, but perhaps unlike Wagner's next opera, *Lohengrin*, is a work which can respond to a number of different styles of staging. What it should not be asked to do is lie down under a blanket of producers' ideas which derive from anywhere but the musical and dramatic text of the work itself.

Below: Götz Friedrich's Bayreuth production was filmed, and has been shown on television. Here, the goddess Venus (Gwyneth Jones) towers over Tannhäuser (Spas Wenkoff).

Above: scenes from Otto Schenk's traditional production of TANNHÄUSER at the Met in 1977, designed by Günther Schneider-Siemssen (top, Act I; above, Act III). Opposite: a scene from LOHENGRIN, artist unknown.

V
LOHENGRIN

Even before the premiere of *Tannhäuser*, Wagner had begun to sketch the libretto of his next opera, *Lohengrin*, during a summer visit to the famous spa resort of Marienbad (now Mariánské Lázné) in Bohemia. He had taken with him a copy of the anonymous epic *Lohengrin*, which took such a hold of him as soon as he began to read it that he found himself excitedly drafting a libretto on the subject. This detailed preliminary prose synopsis, which was not published in full until 1936 (in the Bayreuth Festival guide), differs in occasional details from the final libretto in verse. The differences, however, are not fundamental: they came about as Wagner the practical stage-director prepared for public performance the work of Wagner the visionary poet-musician. The third Wagner, that less than completely trustworthy autobiographer, claims that, when he read his libretto to friends in Dresden, the composer Robert Schumann failed to understand the musical form implicit in it, since there appeared to be no provision for individual musical numbers: 'I then had some fun in reading different parts to him in the form of arias and cavatinas, after which he laughingly declared himself satisfied.'

Wagner's three-act libretto condenses the important elements of the old epic tale into a suitable form for opera. The action takes place in the Dukedom of Brabant in the tenth century. In Act I, Friedrich von Telramund accuses Elsa, daughter of the late Duke, of having killed her brother. The German King Heinrich calls upon Elsa to defend herself, and she recounts a dream in which a knight has appeared as her champion. The King orders a trial by combat, and the knight of her dream, in shining armour, arrives in a boat drawn by a swan. He agrees to fight for Elsa, and offers her his hand in marriage on condition that she will never ask him his name or his origin. Elsa agrees, and the knight (Lohengrin) defeats Telramund, whose life he spares.

At the beginning of Act II, Telramund and his wife, Ortrud, an adherent of the old pre-Christian religion, are brooding on the turn of events. By guile, Ortrud persuades the ingenuous Elsa to take pity on her, and begins to sow in Elsa's mind a distrust of her champion. Later, Ortrud interrupts the wedding procession of Lohengrin and Elsa, and accuses the knight of having defeated Telramund by means of witchcraft.

Act III opens in the bridal chamber. Elsa and Lohengrin sing of their love for each other, but Elsa soon begins to voice her doubts, and eventually demands to know her husband's name. Immediately, Telramund and four of his followers burst into the room to attack Lohengrin, who kills Telramund with a single blow. The final scene takes place by the river-bank. Lohengrin sorrowfully informs the King and assembled nobles that he can no longer lead them into battle or even remain with Elsa. His name, he reveals, is Lohengrin. He has been sent by the Holy Grail, the keeper of which is his father, Parsifal. The swan now arrives to take Lohengrin back, but the knight first kneels in prayer and effects the transformation of the swan into Elsa's brother, the young Duke. Elsa falls lifeless to the ground.

The music of *Lohengrin* was written between 1846 and 1848. A hasty outline sketch of the entire score was followed by detailed composition of the three acts, beginning with the third. By March 1848, the opera was complete; but by the time of its first performance, under Liszt on 28 August 1850 in Weimar, Wagner had fled to Switzerland as a political refugee from Saxony. It was not until 1861 that he himself witnessed a performance of the work. The Weimar premiere, given by a company of inadequate singers and far too small an orchestra, obviously did considerably less than justice to *Lohengrin*, which was at first considered a failure. Nevertheless, the opera was staged throughout Germany during the following decade, and was eventually hailed as the apotheosis of German romantic opera. By then, its composer had left

Opposite: woodcut showing a scene from Act I of the first production of LOHENGRIN, Weimar, 1850.
Above: an artist's impression of the scene in front of the Paris Opéra on the night of the Opéra's premiere of LOHENGRIN in 1891.

Below: (left) design by Angelo Quaglio for Act II of a production of LOHENGRIN in Munich, 1865; (right) Max Brückner's design (1894) for Act III of LOHENGRIN, still being used in Bayreuth in 1908.
Overleaf: Brückner's design for Act II of LOHENGRIN, Bayreuth, 1894.

Brückner.

German romantic opera behind him and was immersed in the creation of his new type of music-drama.

Lohengrin, in fact, stands at the crossroads. Romantic in its almost Pre-Raphaelite purity and its static, two-dimensional characterization, it also contrives to anticipate the direction Wagner was to take in his next work, *Tristan und Isolde*, by virtue of its delicate balance, though not yet complete fusion, of music and drama. The music was already being made subservient to the drama whenever Wagner felt a tension of interests. An important instance of this can be found in the composer's letter to Liszt of 2 July 1850, only a few weeks before the opera's premiere:

Give my opera as it is, without cuts. Just one cut I myself prescribe: I want you to take out the second part of Lohengrin's Narration in the big final scene of the third act. After Lohengrin's words, "Sein Ritter ich, bin Lohengrin genannt", fifty-six bars are to be omitted, down to "Wo ihr mit Gott mich alle Landen saht". I have many times performed the entire work to myself, and I am now convinced that this second section of the Narration can have only a chilling effect. The passage must also be omitted from the libretto.

The passage was dutifully removed by Liszt and has only rarely been heard since. Those who have heard a set of gramophone records of the opera conducted by Erich Leinsdorf, with the cut passage restored, will know that Wagner's artistic judgement was sound, and that *Lohengrin* is better without those fifty-six bars.

Lohengrin was Wagner's sixth opera. It will be recalled that the elements of the supernatural and of redemption through love, which were now to remain constant preoccupations throughout the composer's life, had already been present in his first completed opera, *Die Feen*, and had re-appeared in more mature form in both *Der fliegende Holländer* and *Tannhäuser*. With the exception of that magnificent hymn to national pride and artistic compromise, *Die Meistersinger von Nürnberg*, which was still some years in the future, these were to be, in one form or another, the subjects of every opera and music-drama Wagner composed. The themes were interconnected: love triumphed over evil, but spiritual love triumphed over temporal, earthly passions. The conflict between the two worlds, the worlds of the flesh and the spirit, was Wagner's basic subject.

Left: a stage rehearsal for LOHENGRIN at Covent Garden in April, 1935. Standing together in the centre are Lotte Lehmann (Elsa) and Max Hirzel (Lohengrin). On the opening night, however, Hirzel was suffering from a cold, and Lauritz Melchior sang Lohengrin at less than two hours' notice. Below: Lehmann, Hirzel and, behind them, Alexander Kipnis (Heinrich) in Act II.
Opposite: Act II of Otto Erhardt's 1949 production at Covent Garden. Sylvia Fisher (Elsa) is confronted by Edith Coates (Ortrud).

The word 'spiritual' means more to some people than to others. Like so many problems, however, this can be reduced to one of semantics. For 'spiritual' one can substitute 'unconscious' or, if psychological terms are unacceptable, 'aesthetic'. For Wagner himself the terms were interchangeable. In 'A Communication to My Friends', he wrote: 'Elsa is the unconscious, the unvolitional, into which Lohengrin's conscious, volitional being yearns to be redeemed: but that yearning is itself the unconscious, unvolitional in Lohengrin, through which he feels himself akin in being to Elsa.'

Elsewhere, Wagner sees Lohengrin as saint and redeemer. However, the most useful key to the understanding of Lohengrin's character is the suggestion that he represents Wagner the misunderstood genius, just as Vanderdecken, the Flying Dutchman, represented Wagner the betrayed idealist, and Wotan was to represent Wagner the unheeded prophet. The tension between inner and outer world, sacred and profane, eternal and temporal, is also that which existed between Wagner the artist and his audience. It is upon this fact that, to a large extent, the shaky philosophical structure of Wagner's theory of music-drama is constructed. Inevitably, Wagner was led for a time seriously to contemplate Christ as an operatic subject: Wagner as crucified Messiah. He actually sketched out a libretto, which he called 'Jesus of Nazareth'.

It is not to be thought that his identification with his heroes was necessarily a conscious act on Wagner's part. Writing to a friend in 1856, the composer says that the period in which he worked in response to his intuitions began with *Der fliegende Holländer*, and asserts that, if in *Tannhäuser* or *Lohengrin* there is any underlying poetic theme, it must be looked for in the supreme tragedy of renunciation, the abnegation of the will 'which is shown there as necessary and unavoidable, and alone capable of achieving redemption'. One does not have to read very far between these Schopenhauerian lines to realize that Wagner is talking about art as much as philosophy.

In *Lohengrin*, by asking the forbidden questions, 'Who are

Opposite: (above) Act I of LOHENGRIN at Bayreuth, 1936, directed by Tietjen and designed by Preetorius; (below) Act II at Bayreuth, 1954, in which Birgit Nilsson replaced 1953's Eleanor Steber as Elsa in a revival of Wolfgang Wagner's production.

Above: Act I in the 1967 Bayreuth production, staged and designed by Wolfgang Wagner.

you? Where do you come from?', Elsa does indeed lose her saviour Lohengrin, but with those same questions she regains her brother, who is finally more real to her than the magical knight Lohengrin simply because his only existence is in the real world. The visible world has its legitimate delights, and Wagner is not, after all, the only artistic genius. This is what, despite its author, the libretto of *Lohengrin* appears at that point to be saying. The libretto, however, is not simply a peg upon which to hang the music. Although its philosophical meaning and validity may be open to question, it works magnificently in purely dramatic terms. Upon a two-dimensional, medieval fear of the unknown world, Wagner has superimposed a drama which is modern in its psychology and unerring in its poetic instinct. Thus he retains the best not of two apparent worlds but of three: the spiritual, the psychological and the aesthetic. In a sense, they are one, or rather they are three ways of looking at the same world. It is the interplay between these three views of the world, in Wagner's music and his words, which makes *Lohengrin* a great opera.

The first English production of *Lohengrin* was in 1875, when the opera was given in Italian at Covent Garden. (This was in May. In June a rival production was staged at Drury Lane, again in Italian.) It was not heard in German in London until 1882, at Drury Lane. *Lohengrin* is now one of the most popular of Wagner operas; in many cities, it was the first Wagner work performed. In the earlier years of this century, performances tended to be built around the leading singers, for there were a number of great Wagnerian artists. Productions were relatively conventional. Latterly, the reverse has been the case. The Covent Garden revival in 1925 was dominated by Lotte Lehmann, whose Elsa, according to Ernest Newman, was 'sung and acted as it had not been perhaps for twenty years'. Otto Erhardt, an imaginative and extremely musical director of the German repertoire, was responsible for the 1935 production at Covent Garden, with Lehmann again as Elsa and, at two hours' notice due to the indisposition of another tenor, Lauritz Melchior as Lohengrin. The stage pictures were sumptuous. When *Lohengrin* returned to the Covent Garden repertory after the war, in December 1949, Otto Erhardt also returned to produce the opera, which he did in the most traditional manner possible. 'After the recent adventurings into cloud-cuckoo-land at the Royal Opera [a reference to a disastrously innovative production of Strauss's *Salome* by Peter Brook] . . . here was something like a return to the old, proud standards, opera on a grand scale, finely sung, well played, and produced by Otto Erhardt with discretion and a sense of responsibility towards the music.' (The present writer attended the premiere of a new production of *Lohengrin* in Leipzig, in the company of Otto Erhardt. The producer, Joachim Herz, made Lohengrin the villain of the piece; Elsa was directed to fling back in

Lohengrin's face the ring which he gives her in Act III. 'She should not have done that', murmured Erhardt, more in sorrow than in anger.)

If, at Covent Garden in 1949, Erhardt was upholding the old, proud standards, in Bayreuth a new generation was planning to create vastly different standards. The Bayreuth Festival Theatre opened again in the summer of 1951, and in 1953 *Lohengrin* returned to Bayreuth for the first time since 1937.

Bayreuth's first *Lohengrin* production was in 1894, and Bernard Shaw, who was present, left a valuable description:

What I feel bound to record concerning the Bayreuth *Lohengrin* ... is that its stage framework is immensely more entertaining,

Below: Act II of Wieland Wagner's production, Bayreuth, 1958, with Sandor Konya (Lohengrin) and Leonie Rysanek (Elsa).

Above costume designs by Hainer Hill for Josef Gielen's 1963 Covent Garden production of LOHENGRIN.
Opposite (above) Sandor Konya (Lohengrin) and Régine Crespin (Elsa) in the same production; (below) Hainer Hill's set for Act I.

convincing and natural than it has ever seemed before. This is mainly because the stage-management is so good, especially with regard to the chorus ... The opera suffers fearfully on ordinary occasions from the surprising power of the average chorister to destroy all stage illusion the moment he shambles on the scene with his blue jaws, his reach-me-down costume, his foolish single gesture, his embarrassed eye on the prompter, and his general air of being in an opera chorus because he is fit for nothing better ... A physically and artistically superior class of singers who regard it as an honour to sing at Bayreuth, even in the chorus, certainly help the illusion as far as the Saxon and Brabantine warriors in *Lohengrin* are concerned: but this difference in raw material is as nothing compared with the difference made by the intelligent activity of the stage manager. One example will suffice. Those who know the score of *Lohengrin* are aware that in the finale to the first act there is a section, usually omitted in performance, in which the whole movement is somewhat unexpectedly repeated in a strongly contrasted key... At Bayreuth its purpose is made clear. After the combat with Telramund and the solo for Elsa which serves musically as the exposition of the theme of the finale, the men, greatly excited and enthusiastic over the victory of the strange knight, range themselves in a sort of wheel formation, of which Lohengrin is the centre, and march round him as they take up the finale from Elsa in the principal key. When the modulation comes, the women, in white robes, break into this triumphal circle, displace the men, and march round Elsa in the same way, the striking change of key being thus accompanied by a correspondingly striking change on the stage, one of the incidents of which is a particularly remarkable kaleidoscoping of the scheme of colour produced by the dresses. Here you have a piece of stage management of the true Wagnerian kind, combining into one stroke a dramatic effect the value of which was proved by the roar of excitement which burst forth as the curtains closed in ...

The 'stage manager' of that production, Cosima Wagner, was adept at matching dramatic action to its musical equivalent in her husband's music. It is a talent which a number of directors of opera who are not themselves musicians or musically trained find it difficult to acquire, though it is clearly a *sine qua non* of opera production, especially of producing Wagner.

When Shaw attended the new Bayreuth production of *Lohengrin* by Siegfried Wagner in 1908, he missed such intelligent and imaginative effects as that of the Act I finale, though he noted in a letter to a friend: 'Wonderful stage pictures, very well composed.' The 1936 production was by Heinz Tietjen, Intendant of the Prussian State Theatres, whom Winifred Wagner appointed Artistic Director of the

Bayreuth festival during the Hitler period. Bayreuth at this time became a Nazi cultural showplace, and Tietjen, who not only produced *Lohengrin* but conducted it, did his best to turn the work into a national hymn. Perhaps the Führer, who attended a performance, saw himself as Lohengrin, rescuing Germany (Elsa) from dangerous non-Aryan threats (Telramund and Ortrud).

When the opera was re-introduced to Bayreuth in 1953, it was not in an aggressively abstract staging by Wieland Wagner but in a compromise by Wolfgang. The décor had a simple dignity, and the characters were not denied their historical time and place. The arrival of the swan with Lohengrin, which must be sublime if it is not to appear ridiculous, was staged so skilfully and indeed so beautifully that it brought tears of wonder to the eyes. Lavish historical reconstruction was not what Wolfgang Wagner sought in this *Lohengrin*, but a clear and uncluttered staging which allowed the work to present itself without encumbrance. That may sound a modest aim: would that directors often succeeded in it.

When the great Otto Klemperer conducted *Lohengrin* at Covent Garden in 1963, in a new production by Josef Gielen to replace Erhardt's staging, the Editor of *Opera* spoke for many when he wrote: 'Musically this was a triumph, visually generally a mess. That just about sums up the latest chapter in Covent Garden's sorry story of seemingly not being able to make up its mind as to what its visual approach to Wagner should be.' The opening night of that production was a deeply frustrating occasion, for the work was given a performance by Klemperer and a distinguished cast of singers which few in the audience could ever have heard surpassed. The staging, however, can only be described as tattily provincial. It was not until Elijah Moshinsky's production in 1977, designed by John Napier, and staged along what one might call Wolfgang Wagner lines, that a visually acceptable *Lohengrin* was experienced again at Covent Garden.

The old guard of Wagner producers, disconcerted by the new Bayreuth of the Wagner brothers, and by Wieland Wagner's revolutionary stagings of many of the operas, seemed to lose its confidence in the 'sixties, as one opera after the other was revealed in new colours to the world by Bayreuth. Rudolf Hartmann, an experienced and generally reliable interpreter of Strauss and Wagner, produced *Lohengrin* in Munich in 1971, with not unattractive though historically questionable sets and distressingly ugly costumes by Annelies Corrodi; he also made the mistake of ignoring

Above: Schneider-Siemssen's permanent set for Karajan's Salzburg production, Easter, 1976; (above right) Anna Tomova-Sintov (Elsa) and René Kollo (Lohengrin) in that production. Right: Siegfried Jerusalem (Lohengrin) and Teresa Zylis-Gara (Elsa) in Act II, scene 2 at the Met in 1976.

Richard Wagner's own stage directions without having successful or even interesting ideas of his own with which to replace them. Among producers of Wagner in the 'sixties and 'seventies there was only one whose genius was the equal of Wieland Wagner's, though it was genius of a very different kind. One of the most distinguished of living conductors, Herbert von Karajan, has for many years insisted on being responsible for the stage production of any opera he conducts. Karajan's *Lohengrin* at his Salzburg Easter Festival in 1976, though it was beset with casting problems, was regarded by many critics as one of the most superb, scenically and musically, that they had experienced. Karajan's account of the score was certainly both exciting and moving, and the sets of Günther Schneider-Siemssen and costumes of Georges Wakhevitch, inspired by fourteenth-century illuminated manuscripts, created a world of grave and remote beauty.

Until recent years, it was Wieland Wagner's production which impressed itself most strongly and influentially upon the opera. First seen at Bayreuth in 1958, Wieland Wagner's

Above: Timo Callio (Lohengrin) and Claire Watson (Elsa) in Rudolf Hartmann's Munich production, 1971.
Opposite: René Kollo (Lohengrin) and Anna Tomova-Sintov (Elsa) in a 1977 staging at the Royal Opera House, Covent Garden.

conception of the opera rejected the historical aspects of the piece along with most of his grandfather's ideas on the staging of his own opera. *Lohengrin* was the quintessential Wieland Wagner production, its characters mythically larger than life, its action played out in some vast theatre of the mind or of the world. Much was lost of colour and pageantry, perhaps too much, but the intensity of the producer's vision was such that these considerations paled into insignificance at performances of the opera in his production. Now, however, producers of the work are beginning to recover from the unsettling influence of Wieland Wagner. Pupils of the East German Felsenstein school predictably issue didactic stagings of little value: Karajan's remains the most recent interpretation of any validity.

Above: Lohengrin (René Kollo) and Telramund (Donald McIntyre) prepare to fight, in the 1977 Covent Garden staging. Opposite: the final scene from TRISTAN UND ISOLDE, from a painting by Wilhelm von Kaulbach, 1866.

VI
TRISTAN UND ISOLDE

Above: drawing by J. Noerr of a scene from Act I of TRISTAN UND ISOLDE.
Opposite: Isolde with the dead body of Tristan, from a painting by
Wilhelm von Kaulbach, 1866.

After *Lohengrin*, the gestation period of Wagner's music-dramas was to become longer and increasingly complex; no longer did the composer proceed in an orderly manner to concentrate upon one work at a time, attend to its staging, see it upon its way on to the world stage, and then proceed to the next. Instead, he worked on several projects simultaneously. One of these was the creation of an opera based on the old Norse myths, which he had had in mind for some years (eventually *The Ring*), but at the same time he busied himself in contributing polemical articles to newspapers, and essays to musical journals, in which he attempted to clarify his thoughts on music and drama.

By the end of 1852, when he had finished the libretti of the four operas which would in due course comprise *The Ring* tetralogy, Wagner's thoughts were diverted from the old Norse gods. While living in exile in Switzerland with Minna, his first wife, Wagner had met in Zürich a rich silk merchant, Otto Wesendonk, whose young wife Mathilde had fallen under the Wagner spell. During the next few years, as the composer continued to work slowly upon *The Ring*, his friendship with Mathilde Wesendonk became more intimate. Otto Wesendonk became the composer's patron, and installed the Wagners in a house close to his own in Zürich: it was here that Wagner finally turned aside from *The Ring* and, spurred on by his passion for Mathilde, began to compose his great romantic opera, *Tristan und Isolde*.

The personal relationship of the Wagners and the Wesendonks soon became intolerable. The two women quarrelled openly and, when Minna intercepted a note which Richard had sent to Mathilde with a sketch of the Prelude to *Tristan*, a series of unpleasant scenes ensued. Wagner's behaviour to his benefactor was hardly calculated to improve matters, for the composer began to object to Wesendonk's presence in his own drawing-room when he and Mathilde were communing artistically. They had become collaborators, for Mathilde had written five poems under the influence of Wagner's *Tristan* libretto, while he in turn had set her poems to music, incorporating motifs from *Tristan*.

The foursome broke up when Minna was sent to Dresden to intercede with the authorities for a pardon for Wagner, and Otto Wesendonk took his wife on a visit to Italy. The unhappy composer, deprived of his benefactor, his muse/mistress and his domestic helpmate all at once, gloomily made his way alone to Venice to work on *Tristan und Isolde*. After seven months he had managed to complete the second act, and returned to Switzerland to finish Act III in Lucerne. The composition of the opera had occupied him from the end of 1857 to the summer of 1859. In November of that year, he and Minna set up house in Paris, and Wagner became involved in the revision of *Tannhäuser* in preparation for its production in Paris in 1861.

The origins of the Tristan and Isolde legend are lost in antiquity: the story, as found in the German Minnesinger Gottfried von Strassburg's thirteenth-century romance, contains elements from a number of disparate sources, some Celtic, some French, though it is generally thought that the legend must have originated in Wales or Cornwall. Wagner had no doubt first come across the Tristan and Isolde story in the course of his studies of medieval literature, and he had subsequently read Gottfried von Strassburg's poem in a modern German version published in 1847. The seeds of his *Tristan* were sown well before he met Mathilde Wesendonk; his love for Mathilde merely provided a convenient excuse for turning aside from *The Ring* at the moment when, for creation's more complex reasons, the need to compose his great apotheosis of romanticism welled up within him.

In a letter to Liszt, in December 1854, Wagner wrote: 'Since never in my whole life have I tasted the real happiness

Above: Max Brückner's design for Act III of TRISTAN, Bayreuth, 1886. Left: Angelo Quadro's design for Act III, based on the composer's own directions, as seen at the Munich premiere in 1865.

of love I mean to raise a monument to that most beautiful of dreams in which, from beginning to end, this love shall really sate itself to the full for once. I have in my mind a plan for a *Tristan und Isolde*, the simplest but most full-blooded musical conception.'

As always, the composer needed the poet, and in Wagner composer and poet continued to be one. He drafted his *Tristan* libretto before allowing musical ideas to come to the surface, but the words he wrote for himself eventually to set were not only written *for* a composer, they were written *by* a composer: the musico-dramatic process had begun the moment the first words of the libretto were conceived. As

Designs for Act I (top) and II (above) by Alfred Roller, for the production staged and conducted by Gustav Mahler, Vienna, 1903.

Wagner once wrote to a friend, 'I can conceive a subject only when it comes to me in such a form that I myself cannot distinguish between the contribution of the poet and that of the musician in me; and its completion in word and tone is simply the ultimate realization of something that had originally presented itself to me only in vague outlines.'

As shaped into operatic material by Wagner, the *Tristan und Isolde* legend was set out in three acts. Act I takes place on the ship on which the Cornish knight Tristan is taking the Irish princess Isolde to Cornwall to be the bride of King Mark. When Isolde sends a message to Tristan through her confidante Brangaene, he allows his squire Kurwenal to give a gruff reply. Isolde tells Brangaene how she had cured Tristan of a wound inflicted on him in battle by her betrothed whom he had killed. Isolde had not known whom she was healing, but when she discovered Tristan's identity she could not bring herself to kill him. Now, although she cannot admit to herself that she loves him, she is bitter that he is carrying her back to Cornwall for his king. She orders Brangaene to prepare a death potion for her and Tristan, but Brangaene substitutes a potion which releases inhibition and allows repressed feelings to flow forth unhindered. As they are about to land, Tristan and Isolde drink the potion and confess their love for each other.

The second act takes place in King Mark's castle in Cornwall. In the absence of Mark, who has gone hunting, Isolde plans to meet Tristan in the castle gardens at night. Ignoring the cautions of Brangaene, Isolde sends her to a tower to keep watch, and then extinguishes the torch burning by the gate of the castle, as a signal that it is safe for Tristan to come to her. Tristan arrives, and their long and passionate night of love is interrupted only by Brangaene's warning of the approach of day. Still oblivious of all but each other, the lovers are surprised by the arrival of King Mark with Melot and others. Tristan attempts no explanation to the grief-stricken king, but merely asks Isolde if she will follow him wherever he goes. She replies that she will. As Tristan kisses her he is attacked by Melot. He allows himself to be wounded, and collapses in the arms of Kurwenal.

The last act takes place in Tristan's hereditary castle in Brittany where he has been brought by Kurwenal. Tristan lies wounded and only intermittently conscious, his thoughts continually upon Isolde. The sad tune of a shepherd's pipe indicates that no ship is to be seen approaching, but eventually the tune changes to a lively one and Kurwenal is able to announce Isolde's imminent arrival to Tristan. The wounded hero tears off his bandages as Isolde rushes in, but sinks slowly to the ground and dies in her arms. A second ship arrives, with Mark, Melot and retinue. Kurwenal angrily kills Melot and is himself mortally wounded. But Mark,

Below: Adolphe Appia's design for Act III of Tristan und Isolde at La Scala, Milan, in 1923. Opposite: (above) Act III of Wieland Wagner's abstract staging at Bayreuth, 1952: Ramón Vinay (Tristan) and Hans Hotter (Kurwenal); (below) Act I at Bayreuth, in Siegfried Wagner's production with sets by Söhnlein and Kranich which was seen at Bayreuth every summer from 1927 to 1931. Overleaf: Act I of Tristan und Isolde, produced by Karajan and designed by Günther Schneider-Siemssen, at Salzburg, Easter, 1972.

having had the entire story revealed to him by Brangaene, had come to pardon Tristan and to restore Isolde to him. Isolde sings of the fulfilment of their love in the realms of night and death, and expires by Tristan's side.

Though to assume that *Tristan und Isolde* came into existence inspired purely by its composer's affair with his benefactor's wife is to respond on too simple a level to the complex question of artistic inspiration, it is none the less clear that his new opera lay much closer to Wagner's innermost being than any he had composed in the past. 'I too', he wrote in *The Music of the Future*,

> felt driven to this "Whence and wherefore?" and for long it banned me from the magic of my art. But my time of penance taught me to overcome the question. All doubt at last was taken from me, when I gave myself up to *Tristan*. Here, in perfect trustfulness, I plunged into the inner depths of soul events, and from out this inmost centre of the world I fearlessly built up its outer form. A glance at the *volumen* of this poem will show you at once that the exhaustive detail-work which a historical poet is obliged to devote to clearing up the outward bearings of his plot, to the detriment of a lucid exposition of its inner motives, I now trusted myself to apply to these latter alone. Life and death, the whole import and existence of the outer world, here hang on nothing but the inner movements of the soul. The whole affecting action comes about for the reason only that the inmost soul demands it, and steps to light with the very shape foretokened in the inner shrine.

As that passage may suggest, *Tristan und Isolde* was written under the influence not only of Mathilde Wesendonk but also of the philosopher Arthur Schopenhauer, whose principal work, *Die Welt als Wille und Vorstellung* (The World as Will and Idea), Wagner had read in 1854. From Schopenhauer's belief that in the world there is so great a gap between the ideal and the real that suffering is a natural condition of mankind grew Wagner's theoretical interest in the renunciation of the worldly. But Wagner, the most worldly of men, could embrace this belief only by turning from the outside world to the world of feeling, by renouncing day and its falseness and turning to night and love. The juxtaposition of hated day and longed-for night, the idea of day as mundane life and night as death-in-love which permeates his libretto for *Tristan und Isolde*, is a specifically Wagnerian element, playing no part in the old Celtic myth or in Gottfried von Strassburg's thirteenth-century epic.

Curiously, Wagner's original intention had been to write *Tristan und Isolde* in the style of Italian opera, as he expected that this would make the opera more readily acceptable to theatre managements. He even began negotiations to provide such an opera, for performance not in Italy but in Rio de

Janeiro, and it was only after 1857 and his involvement with Mathilde Wesendonk that the opera began to take in his mind the form in which it was finally to emerge. When he began to compose the score all thoughts of following the style of contemporary Italian opera were forgotten. The music of *Tristan und Isolde*, coming from deep within Wagner, addressed itself to deep responses in its hearers, to the intuition, to the subconscious. Although it is music which is as susceptible to analysis as anything in the composer's earlier works, to analyse *Tristan*'s leading themes, its harmonies, its chromaticism, is more than usually irrelevant to an appreciation of the work itself.

Nevertheless, though one may be reluctant to theorize about *Tristan und Isolde*, it is in this opera that Wagner's ideas about music-drama find their most felicitous expression. In *Tannhäuser* and *Lohengrin* a division of the music into separate numbers can still be quite easily discerned: it is in *Tristan* that the drama flows smoothly through uninterrupted music which appears to grow, indeed to generate spontaneously from the seed of the opera's Prelude. The score's heavily sensuous chromaticism and the ecstatic richness of its orchestration combine to give *Tristan und Isolde* a psychological strength. In this opera, Wagner has for the first time discovered how to reach simultaneously his audience's conscious and subconscious responses.

The purely literary quality of Wagner's libretto for *Tristan*

Opposite: in the film INTERRUPTED MELODY (1955), based on the life of the Wagnerian soprano Marjorie Lawrence, Eleanor Parker played the singer. In this scene Miss Parker, whose singing voice was provided by Eileen Farrell, and Heinz Blankenburg perform the love duet from TRISTAN UND ISOLDE. Below: Tatiana Troyanos (Brangaene) and Gwyneth Jones (Isolde) at the Met in 1971. Right: the Act II love duet in Wieland Wagner's 1962 TRISTAN at Bayreuth (Birgit Nilsson and Wolfgang Windgassen).

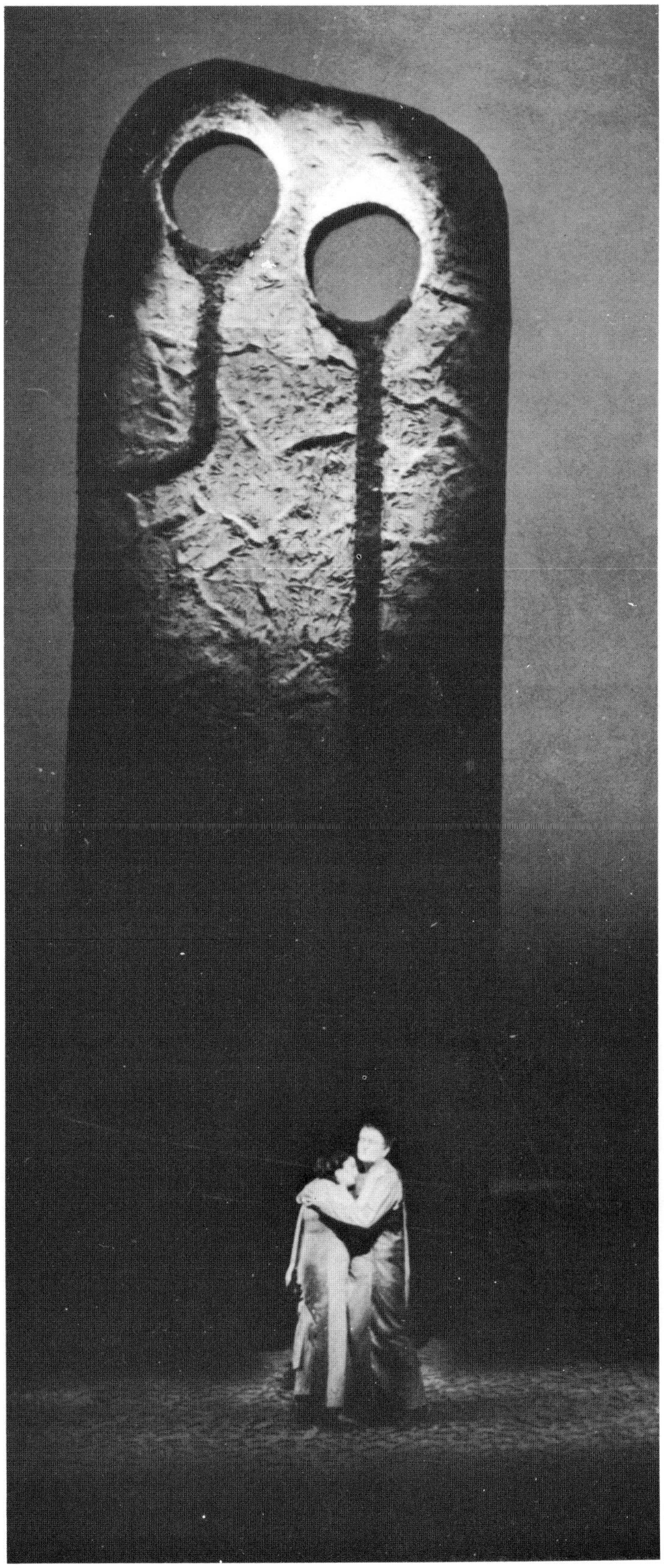

Opposite: Georg Solti at a rehearsal of TRISTAN UND ISOLDE, Covent Garden, 1972. Above: (left) Act I at Covent Garden in Peter Hall's 1971 production designed by John Bury; (right) the same production when it was revived in 1980.

und Isolde has been frequently derided, and virtually from the time of the opera's first performances. Wagner's contemporary, the Viennese music critic Eduard Hanslick (later to be satirized as Beckmesser in *Die Meistersinger*), singled out this passage:

Tristans Ehre – höchste Treu'
Tristans Elend – kühnster Trotz
Trug des Herzens, Traum der Ahnung;
Ew'ger Trauer einz'ger Trost,
Vergessens güt'ger Trank
Dich trink ich sonder Wank.

(Tristan's honour – highest loyalty
Tristan's anguish – keenest defiance
Heart's deceit, wishful dreaming;
Endless mourning the only consolation,
Oblivion's kindly draught
I drink thee unquestioningly.)

Hanslick asked: 'Are there really connoisseurs who find this sort of thing poetic, profound or even good German?' The only answer to his question may be an evasion: whether poetic and profound or merely bombastic and mediocre, this is what Wagner the composer needed from Wagner the librettist in order to create one of the most remarkable and compelling operas ever written.

When one considers the nature of the opera, and the completely new concept of music-drama which it embodies, it comes as something of a shock to realize that *Tristan und Isolde*, at its Munich premiere in 1865, was first revealed to the world in an old-fashioned, sumptuously romantic production of the kind which one would expect Wagner to have despised. But of course there was no scenic designer in the Germany of Wagner's day to match the composer's genius or even to follow the new paths he was taking.

Productions of Wagner's operas, for some years after his death, continued to adhere to the conventional visual taste of the late nineteenth century. And even Wagner himself, dissatisfied though he was with most other people's stagings of his operas, was no innovator in the field of stage design. The ideal theatre of which he dreamed, a theatre where his music-dramas could be performed as he wanted them to be, was simply a bigger and better version of the kind of opera house he already knew. When he achieved his own Wagner Festival Theatre at Bayreuth, and was able to supervise the staging of *The Ring*, it was a conventionally representational staging that he supervised.

Stage design in the nineteenth century had moved away from the elaborate machinery and architectural perspectives of the seventeenth and eighteenth centuries in the direction of what was thought at the time to be a greater realism. Modified by the tiered, amphitheatre style of most auditoria built for opera and ballet in the late eighteenth and early nineteenth centuries, this realism restricted itself to closed-in box sets for interior scenes, and panoramas, sometimes moving ones, for outdoor scenes. A number of talented stage designers worked in the theatres and opera houses, but their talents were used to provide elegant decoration rather than any integration of the scenic element into the dramatic and musical content of the work performed. The integrated visual impact, more important in opera even than in the dramatic theatre, was lost in the search for a purely academic virtuosity. The prevailing style of design veered between an exuberant romanticism and an austere neo-classicism, but the art of design continued to be thought of as subservient to the opera or drama, and was therefore rarely able to rise above the level of pastiche, even when practised by such experienced designers as Joseph Thierry in France, Carlo Ferrario (Verdi's favourite designer) in Italy, or Josef Hoffmann in Germany.

Wieland Wagner, in justification of the production style of his grandfather's operas, wrote: 'It is an insult to Wagner the composer to identify his mythological conceptions with the notorious mediocrity of nineteenth-century impotent and pseudo-naturalistic painters, who sought without making any original contribution to the process to adapt the achievements of classicism and romanticism to the taste of the *nouveau riche*.' Though not expressed in the same manner, these sentiments were clearly felt also by a twenty-year-old Swiss music student named Adolphe Appia when he first visited Bayreuth in 1882 for the premiere of *Parsifal*. Appia was to become the first modern scenic designer of real stature, not only a theorist like Gordon Craig but a practical man of the theatre like Alfred Roller. Both Appia and Roller made important contributions to Wagnerian staging.

Appia realized that, for the theatre of the future, the most far-reaching innovations would be in lighting, especially in imaginative use of the new electric light, which would enable the affinity he felt between music and light to be expressed in ways undreamed of in the gaslight era. In 1899, Appia published a book, *Die Musik und die Inszenierung* (Music and Stage Production), which contains, in an appendix, his detailed notes on how *Tristan und Isolde* should be staged. Appia begins by making the general point that, at most performances of Wagner operas, the visual setting has added nothing to one's experience of the work, and that the drama and its staging have really had little in common. He continues:

This occurs because the two are fundamentally irreconcilable: the action involved is entirely an inner, a purely spiritual one. Tristan and Isolde are in conflict with the external world, and elect to die. The attempt is aborted and they are thrown back into a life where they no longer belong. There is no need for the scenic designer to visualize this outer life, these purely external surroundings, for two reasons: firstly, because Wagner as a dramatist is not interested in them, and his concentration on the inner, or spiritual, drama of the play would in any case have prevented him from doing so. What is dramatized at the outset is a conflict in the souls of Tristan and Isolde. Later on, in the dramatic action of the play, there is no longer any conflict with the external world in which they find themselves. This will have become a vain phantom when they call upon death again. What possible relation, we ask ourselves, can stage setting have in a drama of this sort? Nevertheless, *Tristan* is a work written for the theatre, intended for the stage, and one that can be realized only in performance.

Appia then describes in detail how he would stage *Tristan und Isolde*, taking the reader through the libretto point by point, with constant reference to the score. The emphasis throughout is not on physical surroundings but on lighting. Appia concludes by summing up the ways in which his stage setting influences the production and performance:

In the first act it dramatizes in the most tangible way the conflict which eventually becomes an inner and a spiritual one in the lives of the two protagonists. The lighting plays the same negative role in Isolde's tent that it does as far as the actual setting is concerned in the second act. Outside the curtains of the tent it indicates the entire arena of conflict and prepares for the dramatic contrast which the subsequent stage pictures provide.

In the second act the greatest simplification of the stage setting is essential. However, in order to preserve its connection with the dramatic action it becomes, as indicated by the roles of the actors, a highly expressive arrangement of stage levels unified by the lighting which has the further purpose of dramatizing the action involved.

In the third act the lighting is dominant, and determines everything else in the scenic scheme. Light and shadow in the course of the drama achieve the same significance as a musical motif which, once stated and developed, has an infinite range of variation. Tristan's agony is sufficient motivation for carrying this kind of lighting to its greatest degree of expressiveness; and the audience, overwhelmed vicariously by the spiritual tragedy of the hero and heroine, would be disturbed by any form of stage setting which did not incorporate this element of design. The audience would really suffer for lack of the kind of staging I have indicated, because it needs to get through its eyes a kind of impression which, up to a given point, can equal the unexampled emotional power of the score. Light is the only medium which can continuously create this impression, and its use is motivated and justified by the score itself.

One can see that for the staging of *Tristan* the important thing is the pictorial ensemble ... A stage designer who has sufficient sensibility to accept the kind of subordination that music drama demands of him thereby proves that he is cultured enough to avoid any obvious errors of taste.

It was not until 1923 that Appia was to be given the opportunity to put into practice his ideas for staging *Tristan und Isolde*. However, at the Vienna Opera on the twentieth anniversary of Wagner's death in 1903, Alfred Roller as designer and Gustav Mahler as producer and conductor staged a *Tristan* which was, for its time, revolutionary. This famous production was praised for achieving the perfect blend of music and theatre which had always been the composer's ideal. To give appropriate visual expression to the music, Roller made use of colour and light. Each act of the opera was given its own specific, symbolic colour: an orange-red

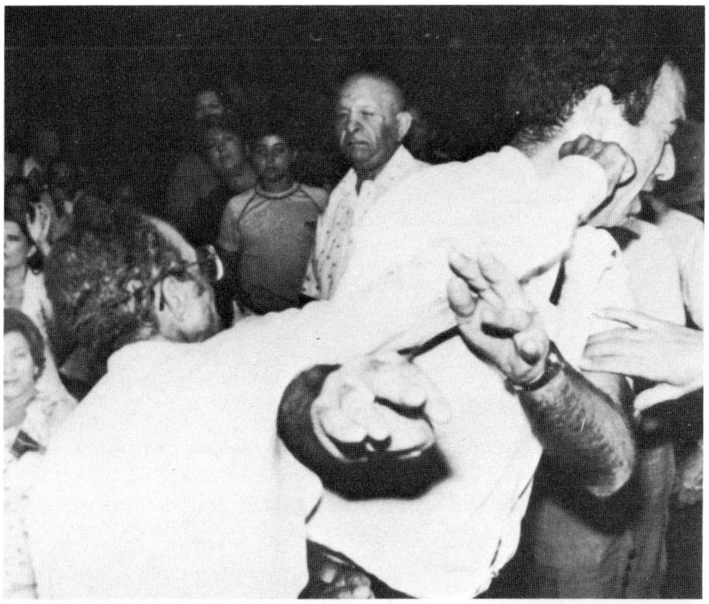

for the harsh daylight of the first act, a deep violet-blue for the ecstasy of the love scene, and in the last act a pallid grey for the world which Tristan is leaving, a greyness alleviated only by the luxuriant autumnal foliage of a lime tree which spread across the stage. The Viennese music critic Max Graf thought that the décor even seemed to take on a poetic colour of its own from the music, which in turn appeared to elaborate and deepen the dominant colour of the scene. 'The scenery', he wrote, 'actually reproduced something of the chromatic harmony of the music, subtle vibrations of light and colour producing an effect that was intrinsically musical.' The premiere was a sensation, and the '*Lichtmalerei*' (light painting) of Roller and '*Lichtmusik*' (light music) of Mahler were described and discussed at great length by critics and commentators.

In 1923 Toscanini invited Adolphe Appia to design *Tristan und Isolde* for La Scala, Milan. Announcing that his purpose was to help 'the audience see the drama through the eyes of the hero and heroine', Appia created stage-pictures from which all inessentials had been banished. The ship in Act I was, in the designer's own words, 'simple, expressive, very close, without mast, some ropes, very large helm'. The second act was apparently a triumph of darkness, with a circle of torchlight around the lovers as the only scenic element.

Though Appia's 1923 staging was met with incomprehension on the part of the Milanese public, the seeds he sowed in Milan came triumphantly to fruition thirty years later in Bayreuth, when Wieland Wagner began to stage the Wagner operas in a style clearly derived from the imaginative simplicities of Appia. 'Here for the first time in my experience', wrote Harold Rosenthal of Wieland's 1952 staging, 'was a *Tristan und Isolde* in which stage, orchestra, singers, conductor, costumes, lighting, in fact all the elements that go to make up an operatic production, were merged into a unity such as Wagner could only have dreamed of. There was no beginning or ending here; Tristan and Isolde, love and death, night and day, orchestral sound and human voice, the music and lighting were all one.'

For many years after 1952, the Adolphe Appia-Wieland Wagner concept dominated productions of the opera until, in the 1970s, other styles and methods began to urge themselves upon the work. At Covent Garden in 1971, Peter Hall and his designer John Bury interpreted Wagner's directions

Top: a scuffle among spectators at the Mann Auditorium, Tel Aviv, when the Israel Philharmonic played the Prelude to TRISTAN UND ISOLDE in October, 1981. Wagner's music is still banned in Israel. Left: Spas Wenkoff (Tristan) in Act III of a Munich staging in 1980 by Herbert Kapplmüller, which audiences greeted with boos.

literally, in a production whose Pre-Raphaelite surface representationalism was allied to a poetic symbolism which seemed to reach the heart of the work just as surely as Bayreuth's austerity had done. In the same year, August Everding produced the opera at the Metropolitan Opera House, New York, along similar lines to Peter Hall though in settings of more sumptuous beauty by Gunther Schneider-Siemssen. For his 1972 production at Salzburg, Herbert von Karajan also turned to Schneider-Siemssen, who this time designed a semi-abstract world of muted colour.

Tristan und Isolde continues to challenge producers and designers. A 1980 staging in Munich by Everding, with aggressively dominating designs by Herbert Kapplmüller which were greeted with boos, was generally regarded as an interesting series of reflections on the opera rather than a fresh interpretation of it. A new production at Bayreuth in 1981, replacing a 1976 staging by Everding designed by Svoboda, was produced and designed by Jean-Pierre Ponnelle. It was ravishing to the eye but remote from the world of the opera.

Understandably no Wagner opera has been staged in the state of Israel, where memories of the Nazi holocaust are inextricably linked to Wagner's anti-Semitism. Courageously, the Israel Philharmonic Orchestra under its permanent conductor Zubin Mehta attempted at a concert in Tel Aviv in the autumn of 1981 to play the Prelude and Liebestod from *Tristan und Isolde* as an encore at the end of a non-Wagner concert. The performance was interrupted by vociferous protesters, many of them survivors from Hitler's concentration camps. The way in which any future performances of Wagner's music are handled in Israel remains to be seen.

Above: Act I of the 1981 Bayreuth Tristan und Isolde, produced and designed by Jean-Pierre Ponnelle. Opposite: Eva and Hans Sachs: a scene from Act II of Die Meistersinger, from a painting by Theodor Pixis, 1868.

VII

DIE MEISTERSINGER VON NÜRNBERG

The idea of an opera about the old medieval guilds and the mastersingers had been in Wagner's mind for several years before he began actually to shape the libretto and compose the music. Originally, he had thought of the opera as a kind of comic complement to *Tannhäuser*, and at the time of the Paris production of *Tannhäuser* in 1861 he returned to it and to a draft scenario he had produced as early as 1845. In Venice and Vienna at the end of 1861 he worked on a new scenario, which he read to the publisher Schott in December. Most of the libretto was written in Paris, in a hotel on the Quai Voltaire. In a letter to Minna, Wagner remarked that it was amusing to concern oneself with the world of Hans Sachs and old Nuremberg, and then glance out of the window and see the Tuileries and the Louvre.

In Biebrich, near Mainz, Wagner began to work on the music of *Die Meistersinger*, but after an enthusiastic beginning he found the task difficult. Inspiration was lacking, and the score was built up slowly and fitfully. When his landlord's bulldog bit his thumb, the composer seized on the excuse to stop work on his score for several weeks. Schott had advanced funds to Wagner for the new opera, but knew him too well to continue subsidizing him until Wagner had produced a substantial part of the score. His emotional life as tangled as ever, Wagner had by now embarked upon a relationship with Cosima von Bülow, illegitimate daughter of Liszt and wife of the conductor Hans von Bülow. A further complication ensued when an envoy of the eighteen-year-old Ludwig II, King of Bavaria, brought to Wagner the curious news that King Ludwig was passionately interested in the composer and his music, and wished to constitute himself Wagner's protector.

Wagner immediately went to Munich and became the close friend of the young homosexual monarch, who was already well advanced towards the insanity in which he was to end his days. The composer's entourage, consisting of Bülow and Cosima, turned the usual Wagner emotional triangle into a rectangle. Cosima gave birth to Wagner's child, which Bülow accepted as his own, while Wagner received King Ludwig's bounty and his devotion. According to Wagner, he and Ludwig would spend hours sitting together, lost in mutual contemplation. For months on end, *Die Meistersinger* was abandoned, only to be taken up again for a time, and then again laid aside. However, by the end of October 1867, the score of the opera had been completed. Earlier that year, Cosima's second child by Wagner was born, and called Eva after the heroine of *Die Meistersinger*. The opera itself was revealed to the world in Munich on 21 June 1868. Its premiere was an absolute triumph, the only unfortunate incident occurring when Wagner, who had sat consort-like beside Ludwig in the royal box, outraged the feelings of the good citizens of Munich by stepping forward to acknowledge the applause.

The action of *Die Meistersinger* takes place in sixteenth-century Nuremberg. The goldsmith Veit Pogner offers the hand of his daughter Eva in marriage to the winner of the singing contest held by the Guild of Mastersingers. Eva, in church with her nurse Magdalene, has met a young knight, Walther von Stolzing, and they have fallen in love. Magdalene's admirer, the apprentice David, attempts to explain the rules of the Mastersingers to Walther. The knight's application for membership of the Guild is contested by the

Opposite: Mathilde Mallinger as Eva, the role she sang at the premiere of Die Meistersinger in Munich, 1868.
Above: (top) Max Brückner's design for Act II of Die Meistersinger when it was performed at Bayreuth for the first time in 1888; (above) the set for Act III, scene 2, designed by Kurt Söhnlein, and seen at Bayreuth between 1911 and 1924.

Above: Ludwig Sievert's design for Act II of a production at the Munich Staatsoper in 1943.
Opposite: (top) Emil Preetorius's set for Act II of Heinz Tietjen's Bayreuth production, first seen at Bayreuth in 1933; (below left) the closing scene of Die Meistersinger, designed by Wieland Wagner in his pre-abstract period at Bayreuth in 1943; (below right) the same scene eight years later: when Bayreuth re-opened after the war in 1951, the only traditional production was Rudolf Hartmann's Die meistersinger. The other operas were staged by Wieland Wagner in his new abstract style.

Town Clerk, Beckmesser, who hopes to win Eva for himself, but supported by David's master, the cobbler and poet Hans Sachs, who senses Walther's talent for song even though the young nobleman bypasses the traditional rules of composition laid down by the Guild.

The second act is set in a small square, in which Hans Sachs's workshop and the Pogner house face each other. Eva visits Sachs, of whom she is fond, and seeks his advice. Sachs resolves to help the young lovers, prevents them from eloping precipitately, and frustrates Beckmesser's attempts to serenade Eva by hammering noisily throughout the Town Clerk's song. The noise awakens the neighbours and a street fight ensues which is ended only by the arrival of the Nightwatchman. Under cover of the confusion, Sachs takes Walther into his house.

Act III takes place the following morning, midsummer's

Above: in 1956 Wieland Wagner produced and designed Die Meistersinger at Bayreuth. This is medieval Nuremberg in Act II. Left: Act II of Nathaniel Merrill's production at the Met in 1962, designed by Robert O'Hearn. From left to right are Sandor Konya (Walther), Ingrid Bjoner (Eva), Karl Dönch (Beckmesser), Otto Wiener (Sachs). Opposite: (below left) Act III, scene 1, as designed by Nicola Benois for a production by Otto Erhardt at La Scala, 1952; (below right) Act I as seen in Tokyo, 1960. This was the opera's first production in Japan, staged by Wolfram Humperdinck, son of the composer of *Hänsel und Gretel.*

day. Sachs helps Walther with the composition of his song for the contest, allows Beckmesser to steal a copy of it (since he realizes that the Town Clerk will never be able to interpret it correctly), and promotes David to the rank of journeyman. In the second scene of the act, set in the meadow where the midsummer festival is being held, Beckmesser makes a fiasco of his song, after which he angrily accuses Sachs of being its composer. Walther interprets the song to perfection, is acclaimed the winner, and happily accepts the hand of Eva. He is about to reject with contempt the golden chain of the Guild when Sachs persuades him of the wisdom of building upon tradition instead of rejecting it. In a stirring address, Sachs preaches the virtue of honouring German art and rejecting foreign influences. He is enthusiastically acclaimed by the citizens of Nuremberg.

In *Die Meistersinger*, Wagner made a complete change from his preoccupation with the old myths, with the gods and goddesses of his *Ring* libretto, and with the symbolic personifications of *Tristan und Isolde.* To read the libretto of the opera without the music in one's ears is to realize that the composer was concerned, perhaps for the first time since the *Holländer*, to write about real people in a real, recognizable historical setting, although his Hans Sachs was never claimed to be a faithful portrayal of the historical Sachs, the Nuremberg poet and craftsman. Wagner used the medieval Mastersingers' Guild and its members as pegs on which to build what he considered to be a comedy.

His libretto might have worked reasonably well as the basis of a light opera, which is what Wagner thought he was writing, had not the composer's intransigent racial theories crept into it, and had not his musical genius insisted on going its own way. No one coming to a performance of *Die Meistersinger* for the first time could possibly mistake the opera for the light comedy which Wagner insisted it was. A sense of artistic discretion, never one of his strongest attributes, is considerably less evident in *Die Meistersinger* than in *Der fliegende Holländer* or *Tristan und Isolde.* In a sense, Wagner the composer set to music the true libretto

Above: Act III of Wieland Wagner's second postwar production of DIE MEISTERSINGER at Bayreuth in 1963.
Right: Act III of the 1968 Sadler's Wells production, with sets by Motley and costumes by David Walker.
Opposite: (far right) David Walker's costume design for Walther in the same production; (centre) Norman Bailey (Sachs) and Alberto Remedios (Walther).

of *Die Meistersinger* which exists between the lines of the printed text: a hymn to artistic compromise with, in its final scene, an irrelevant aside appealing to racial prejudice and the baser aspects of nationalism. The knight Walther von Stolzing begins as an artist answerable only to himself and his art. He is shown by wise, kindly old Sachs how to curry favour with his audience and thus win the hand of Eva by compromise, by giving the people what they want. '*Am stillen Herd*', which Walther sings at his first attempt to gain admission to the Guild in Act I, is the finer song, but it is '*Morgenlich leuchtend in rosigem Schein*' which wins the prize in Act III.

The blatant appeal to German nationalism of Hans Sachs's speech to the citizens of Nuremberg is a stunning example of Wagner the politician dominating Wagner the artist. At the time of the opera's premiere it must have sounded like a clear invitation to launch a racial war against the impure Latins. Not only is '*heilige deutsche Kunst*' upheld as the great ideal, but the means of achieving and maintaining it are spelt out as clearly as Wagner elsewhere in his writings spelt out how to get rid of the Jews. The people, to whose judgement, as the libretto makes clear, art must in the end bow, are exhorted to obliterate the influence of French culture with its ephemeral and un-Germanic values: a project which was eventually to be implemented by Hitler, who also took action on one or two of Wagner's other hints. The passage from Sachs's address to the crowd in *Die Meistersinger* quoted below aroused that first Munich audience to a frenzy of enthusiasm, and led a Bayreuth audience in the 'thirties to rise to its feet and stand with hands raised in the Nazi salute throughout the chorus to the end of the opera two minutes later:

Hab't Acht! Uns dräuen üble Streich':
zerfällt erst deutsches Volk und Reich,
in falscher wälscher Majestät
kein Fürst bald mehr sein Volk versteht;
und wälschen Dunst mit wälschem Tand
sie pflanzen uns in deutsches Land;
was deutsch und echt wüsst' keiner mehr,
lebt's nicht in deutscher Meister Ehr'.
D'rum sag' ich euch: ehrt eure deutschen Meister,
dann bannt ihr gute Geister!
Und gibt ihr ihrem Wirken Gunst,
zerging' in Dunst
das heil'ge röm'sche Reich,
uns bliebe gleich
die heil'ge deutsche Kunst!

(Beware! Evil deeds are threatening us. Once the German people and kingdom have been submerged by false French majesty, soon

Opposite: (above) Gerd Brenneis (Walther) and Dietrich Fischer-Dieskau (Sachs) at the Deutsche Oper, Berlin, 1976; (below) Marilyn Richardson (Eva), Norman Bailey (Sachs) and Allen Cathcart (Walther) in the Australian Opera's production in Sydney, 1978. Above: Geraint Evans as Beckmesser begins to sing his song in the Act III contest in Die Meistersinger at the Royal Opera House, Covent Garden in 1969; Rudolf Hartmann's production was designed by Barry Kay. Overleaf: the Karajan production in Salzburg, Easter, 1974, designed by Günther Schneider-Siemssen: (main picture) Act III, scene 2; (inset, left) the quintet in Act III, scene 1; (inset, right) Act II.

no prince will understand his people, and they will plant ephemeral French taste and French vanity in German soil. That which is German and true will no longer be recognized, unless it lives on in the honour of German masters. Therefore I say to you, honour your German masters. Then you will conjure up good spirits. And if you nourish their endeavours, though the Holy Roman Empire should dissolve into nothingness, holy German art would still remain to us.)

Two years before the premiere of *Die Meistersinger* in Munich, Wagner had written to Bülow that he wanted his opera staged in Nuremberg, the city it celebrated, because he saw this ancient German city as a bulwark against Jewish influences. He was highly indignant to discover that, opposite the monument to Hans Sachs in Nuremberg, 'an imposing synagogue in purest Oriental style' had been built. (The Nazis were to demolish the synagogue, and to choose to mount *Die Meistersinger* in Nuremberg to celebrate their annual Party Day.)

One would have to be either naive or disingenuous to adopt a high moral tone towards *Die Meistersinger* simply because it was taken up by the Nazis. On the other hand, to claim that art cannot affect morality is to belittle art. There can be no denying that the music of Hans Sachs's great address at the end of *Die Meistersinger* is of an extraordinary emotive force, of the kind that was peculiarly Wagner's own and that has probably never been equalled by any other composer. The question that it presents is whether the unpleasant taste of the words is redeemed by the beauty and power of the music, or whether these very qualities in the music render more dangerously effective a message which, left in Wagner's raw words, would surely have less appeal, for words speak primarily to the intellect and music to the emotions. It is a question which has never been satisfactorily answered, and one which is far removed from the comparatively simple matter of having to accept the fact that artistic genius does not necessarily reside only in the breasts of those human beings of the most impeccable moral purity.

There can be no doubt that Wagner conceived *Die Meistersinger* as a nationalistic work, and as such it was recognized and used in Germany, at least until 1944, the year Furtwängler conducted it at Bayreuth for the last time before the closure of the theatres, when Hitler's war entered its last phase. The period of its genesis left its mark upon the opera: in 1862, the year in which most of the libretto was written, Bismarck became Minister President of Prussia, and in 1868,

the year of its first performance, Prussia had defeated Austria and was preparing for war against France.

In a letter to the scenic designer Joseph Hoffmann, Wagner confessed that he had perhaps been guilty in the stage directions he wrote into his libretti, and presumably also in his own Munich productions of *Tristan und Isolde* and *Die Meistersinger*, of thinking too much in terms of the old established theatrical and scenic conventions. Nevertheless, in her production of *Die Meistersinger* at Bayreuth in 1888, five years after Wagner's death, Cosima Wagner was content to place on the stage as faithful a reproduction of the original staging as possible. Adolphe Appia saw it, and wrote: 'A living thing is being presented in an atmosphere without life, because on the one hand a means of expression, acting, is exploited exhaustively, while on the other hand the most effective means of expression – light, without which there can be no depth – is ignored.'

Opposite: the Houston Grand Opera production of Meistersinger, 1980, designed by Carl Toms, and directed by Patrick Bakman: (above) Act I, in the church of St Catherine; (below) Act III, scene 1, with (left to right) Diane Kesling (Magdalene), James Atherton (David), Patricia Wells (Eva), William Johns (Walther) and Thomas Stewart (Sachs).

Over the years, Bayreuth productions of *Die Meistersinger* kept cautiously abreast of the conventional styles of the day. In 1933, Heinz Tietjen transformed the chorus from a crowd of individual citizens of Nuremberg to a series of stylized groups, but Rudolf Hartmann in 1951 reverted to a more individualistic approach to the chorus. It was not until 1956 that *Die Meistersinger* was subjected, not altogether happily, to the Wieland Wagner method, in a production which threw out the baby of old Nuremberg and its houses and citizens along with the bathwater of an outmoded scenic style. No festive merry-making by the populace was permitted in the final scene; that Wagner's opera is a comedy can never have been less apparent. Fortunately, Wieland Wagner modified his ideas about *Die Meistersinger* when he produced it for the second time, in 1963. The current Bayreuth production by Wolfgang Wagner in 1981, is traditional but lacking in atmosphere.

None of the earlier stagings of the opera abroad can be said to have contributed significantly to the history of Wagnerian production style. London first heard *Die Meistersinger* at the Theatre Royal, Drury Lane, in 1882, and New York at the Met in 1886. From then until 1939, it was a

Above: Act I of Die Meistersinger at the Teatro Colón, Buenos Aires, 1980, produced by Paul Hager and designed by Roberto Oswald.

Die Meistersinger at Covent Garden, 1982. For this revival of the 1969 production, Barry Kay re-designed his final scene and the opera was rehearsed by Hans Hartleb. Right: Act II. Above: Geraint Evans as Beckmesser, in rehearsal (top) and in performance (above).

Above and opposite: the 1981 Bayreuth Meistersinger, produced and designed by Wolfgang Wagner (above, Act I; opposite, Act III).

succession of distinguished Wagner singers and conductors, rather than stage directors, who added to our knowledge of *Die Meistersinger* through their interpretations; conductors such as Hans Richter, Wilhelm Furtwängler and Bruno Walter, singers such as Friedrich Schorr, Leo Slezak, Lauritz Melchior, Lotte Lehmann and Tiana Lemnitz.

The Metropolitan Opera production of 1962, directed by Nathaniel Merrill with décor by Robert O'Hearn, proved that a staging based on Wagner's instructions, in sets which look like medieval Nuremberg, can still be viable, and may even be the only sensible way to present the work. In the late 'sixties, both of London's opera houses mounted new productions of *Die Meistersinger*, and both attempted to place the historical Nuremberg on the stage. The Sadler's Wells production, sung in English, was directed by Glen Byam Shaw and John Blatchley. Nuremberg, as designed by the team called Motley, looked like a window-dresser's idea of the Middle Ages, but the costumes (by David Walker) contrived to appear both authentic and attractive. It was, however, the conductor, Reginald Goodall, and the baritone Norman Bailey as Hans Sachs, who lent real distinction to these performances. The following year, at Covent Garden, Norman Bailey saved the first night of the Royal Opera's new production by stepping in to sing Sachs (this time in German) at short notice when a Viennese baritone became ill. Rudolf Hartmann's production had the virtue of being unobtrusive, and Barry Kay's scenery did no damage to the work until the final scene, when he was defeated by the festive meadow.

A notable production in which a representational approach to staging and décor was infused with a rare and delicate poetry was that of Herbert von Karajan at Salzburg in 1974. Karajan acted both as producer and conductor, and the décor was by Günther Schneider-Siemssen, one of the most successful of today's Wagner designers. *Die Meistersinger* needs to be firmly placed in its historical setting: in this sense, it is the odd-opera-out in the Wagner canon, not really susceptible to abstraction or symbolism. The best of modern, post-Wieland Wagner productions of the opera not only accept that this is so but make the most of it.

Above: Act III, scene 2 of the 1982 Covent Garden Meistersinger.
Opposite: in Das Rheingold the Nibelungs bring the gold for Freia's ransom. Cartoon by Carl Emil Doepler, who designed the costumes for the Bayreuth Ring of 1876.

VIII
DER RING DES NIBELUNGEN

It was in 1848, when he was in his mid-thirties, that Wagner first put on paper his ideas for the project which was to come to fruition in 1876 at Bayreuth as *Der Ring des Nibelungen* (The Nibelung's Ring). The prose sketch, which he wrote in October 1848, is a re-telling of the old Nibelung myth, with some material drawn from the medieval German epic *Das Nibelungenlied*, and some from the older Scandinavian *Edda*, mythological stories of the old Norse gods and heroes. Wagner's intention at this stage seems to have been to use the earlier parts of the story as pre-history, and to compose an opera about the last days of Siegfried, *Siegfrieds Tod* (The Death of Siegfried). He wrote a verse libretto for *Siegfrieds Tod* but found, when he began to compose the music in 1850, that he needed to begin at an earlier point in the narrative. He therefore broke off from working on the music, and in 1851 wrote a second libretto on the subject of the young Siegfried (*Der junge Siegfried*). This in turn led him to the realization that he would have to begin at the very beginning, and so the libretti of, first, *Die Walküre* (The Valkyrie), and then *Das Rheingold* (The Rhine Gold) were written in 1852.

Though the libretti of what was now to be a tetralogy of four operas had been written in reverse order, the operas themselves were composed in proper chronological sequence. *Das Rheingold* occupied Wagner in 1853–4, and *Die Walküre* from 1854 to March 1856. He began *Siegfried* (formerly *Der junge Siegfried*) in 1856, but put it aside to work on *Tristan und Isolde* for two years and *Die Meistersinger* for five. He returned to *Siegfried* in 1864, and completed it in 1871. The last work of the tetralogy, its title no longer *Siegfrieds Tod* but *Götterdämmerung* (Twilight of the Gods), was composed between 1871 and 1874.

The first opera, *Das Rheingold*, was produced in Munich on 22 September 1869, and the second, *Die Walküre*, followed on 26 June 1870. Wagner was present on neither occasion. He had at first been enthusiastic about the projected Munich performances, but his attempt to interfere with the arrangements and to have the conductor dismissed in favour of himself led to his being refused admittance to the rehearsals. He stayed away from the premieres of both operas, and tried

Above: Carl Emil Doepler's costumes for three of the Valkyries, Bayreuth, 1876. Below: Therese Vogl (Sieglinde) and Heinrich Vogl (Siegmund) in Act I of Die Walküre in the first performance of the opera, in Munich on 26 June 1870. Opposite: engraving after a drawing by Theodor Pixis, 1869, representing Das Rheingold.

C. E. Doepler

Opposite: Doepler's costume designs for the Rhinemaidens, Bayreuth, 1876.
Above: the Rhinemaidens in Das Rheingold at Bayreuth in the 1896 revival of Der Ring
(left to right, Frl. von Arhus, Katharina Rosing, Olive Fremstad).
Below: the machine used at Bayreuth in 1876 to help the Rhinemaidens with their swimming.

Above: design model by Joseph Hoffmann for Act I of DIE WALKÜRE, Bayreuth, 1876.
Opposite: the fight between Siegmund and Hunding, watched by Sieglinde. Drawing by Knut Ekwall, based on the 1876 Bayreuth production of DIE WALKÜRE and published in a Leipzig newspaper in September of that year.

to dissuade his friends and admirers from attending. The operas, nevertheless, were acclaimed by press and public alike. By 1871, with the third opera completed and the fourth under way, Wagner came to the conclusion that *The Ring* and any future works of his would never be staged as he wanted them to be until he could control a theatre of his own, a theatre so designed that it would both project his imaginative creations and, in turn, inspire them. Further thought on this subject led Wagner to decide that a theatre would have to be specially built, in which *Der Ring des Nibelungen* could be staged not as part of the ordinary operatic repertory of a busy theatre but under the ideal conditions which such a huge and unique work required.

Wagner's choice fell upon the small Bavarian town of Bayreuth, and he and as many of his supporters as he could muster began the task of stimulating local interest in the idea of developing the town as a centre of Wagnerian music-drama. Having gained the goodwill of the mayor of Bayreuth, Wagner then began fund-raising in earnest. Subscribers were found, and a thousand 300-thaler shares issued. The site, an excellent one on a small hilltop just outside the town, was donated by the municipality, and King Ludwig was persuaded to part with a sum of money to enable the composer to build a suitable residence for himself and his family in the town.

A temporary theatre was to be erected. When the subscription scheme failed, Wagner appealed once more to Ludwig, for the entire enterprise was already so heavily in debt that, unless a large amount of money could immediately be raised, it would collapse. The King instructed his finance

Left: Max Brückner's design for Act III of Siegfried, Bayreuth, 1876.
Above: costume design by Doepler for Siegfried, Bayreuth, 1876.

minister to negotiate a loan, and Wagner's theatre was saved. The temporary structure opened in 1876 with the first complete performance of the entire *Ring* tetralogy, on 13, 14, 16 and 17 August. That temporary structure is still in use as the Festival Theatre, for the permanent theatre was never built.

The four operas trace the consequences of the theft of the Rhine gold from the river, first by the dwarf Alberich, who forges from the gold a magic ring, and then from Alberich by the god Wotan. The curse placed by Alberich on all who strive for possession of the ring is finally lifted by its return to the element of water from which it came.

DAS RHEINGOLD

Although the music of the opera's single act is continuous, there are four scenes. The first takes place at the bottom of the Rhine, where three Rhinemaidens cavort around the gold which they guard. The dwarf Alberich, one of the race of Nibelungs who inhabit Nibelheim, a subterranean realm under the Rhine, attempts to make advances to the Rhinemaidens who respond by mocking him. Learning from them that whoever renounces love, and fashions a ring from the gold, will become ruler of the world, Alberich proceeds to forswear love forever. He seizes the gold and departs as the Rhinemaidens lament their loss.

The scene changes to a mountain summit. The gods Wotan and his spouse Fricka are obliged to offer Freia, goddess of eternal youth, to the giants Fasolt and Fafner in return for the giants having built Valhalla, a castle for the gods. Loge, god of fire and cunning, advises Wotan to gain possession of the Rhine gold and use it to buy off the giants and ransom Freia. In the third scene Wotan and Loge have descended to Nibelheim, where Alberich has intimidated his brother Mime into making him a magic helmet from part of the Rhine gold. With the aid of this helmet, Alberich can assume any form at will. The cunning Loge taunts the dwarf into turning himself first into a huge serpent and next into a minute toad, in which form Wotan and Loge are able to capture him and bear him away.

In the final scene, on the gods' mountain summit, Alberich is forced to give up the gold, the Tarnhelm or magic helmet, and also the magic ring. The giants return Freia to the gods in return for the gold, but also demand the ring which Wotan had intended to keep. Erda, the earth-mother, warns Wotan that his lawless actions will have disastrous consequences, and he reluctantly relinquishes the ring to the giants. They immediately begin to quarrel over it, and Fasolt is killed by Fafner. As the gods ascend, across a rainbow bridge, into their fortress, Valhalla, the voices of the Rhinemaidens can be heard lamenting the loss of their gold.

DIE WALKÜRE

Act I takes place in the hut belonging to Hunding. Siegmund, completely exhausted, stumbles into the hut in a state of exhaustion, and Hunding's wife, Sieglinde, gives him a reviving drink. Siegmund says he is being pursued by enemies, and is about to leave again, so as not to bring misfortune to the house, when Sieglinde begs him to stay. Hunding returns and questions Siegmund about himself. Siegmund reveals that he is of the race of Wälsungs: he does not realize that his father, Wälse, was in reality Wotan. He also tells Hunding of his recent fight when he tried to defend a woman who was being ill-treated.

Hunding reveals himself as one of Siegmund's enemies. He will give him hospitality for the night, but tomorrow they must fight. Hunding and Sieglinde retire, but not before Sieglinde has attempted to draw Siegmund's attention to the ash-tree which grows through the centre of the hut, and in the trunk of which is embedded a sword. Later, Sieglinde returns and tells Siegmund how, during the ceremony of her betrothal to Hunding, a stranger placed the sword in the tree-trunk, saying that it would belong to the hero who was able to withdraw it. Sieglinde senses that Siegmund is to be that hero. The door of the hut flies open at the sudden advent of spring, and Siegmund tells Sieglinde his name as he triumphantly draws forth the sword. She recognizes him as her brother, and they embrace passionately before rushing out into the night.

Acts II and III take place in a mountainous landscape. Wotan orders Brünnhilde, his daughter and one of the sisterly band of Valkyries or warrior-maidens, to protect Siegmund in his fight with Hunding, but Fricka demands that the victory be given to Hunding. Wotan accepts that Fricka is upholding a law of nature, and withdraws his instruction to Brünnhilde. However, when Brünnhilde announces to Siegmund his imminent death, he rejects a hero's afterlife with the gods in Valhalla if it means losing Sieglinde. Moved by his love for Sieglinde, Brünnhilde attempts to protect Siegmund in the fight, but Wotan intervenes and Siegmund, his sword shattered, is killed. Seizing the pieces of the sword, Brünnhilde flees with Sieglinde. After despatching Hunding to his death with a contemptuous gesture, Wotan sets out in pursuit of his disobedient daughter.

In the third act, the other Valkyries attempt to protect Brünnhilde and Sieglinde from Wotan's wrath. However, Brünnhilde barely has time to encourage Sieglinde to escape

Above: Götterdämmerung revived at Bayreuth, 1896, designed by Max Brückner: the Hall of the Gibichungs.

Siegfried and Fafner.

in order to bear Siegmund's child before Wotan terrifies the Valkyries into abandoning their sister to his rage. Reluctantly, Wotan punishes Brünnhilde, the daughter whom he most loves, by placing her in a magic slumber from which she will be awakened to belong to whichever man has found her. He grants Brünnhilde's wish that only a hero may awaken her, by invoking Loge, god of fire, who surrounds her with a ring of flame.

SIEGFRIED

The son of Siegmund and Sieglinde, Siegfried has grown to young manhood, having been found and brought up by the Nibelung Mime. Wotan, disguised as a traveller, visits their cave in the forest and questions Mime. Siegfried successfully forges together the broken pieces of his father's sword, while Mime makes a futile attempt to kill the young hero with a poisoned drink.

In Act II, Siegfried approaches the lair of Fafner who, with the aid of the Tarnhelm, has transformed himself into a dragon in order to guard his gold. While he rests before doing battle with Fafner, Siegfried is fascinated by the sound of a forest bird. When the sleeping Fafner awakens, Siegfried kills him; before he dies, Fafner warns the young hero against Mime.

Sucking a little of the dragon's blood from his finger, Siegfried finds he can now understand the song of the bird, who advises him to take the ring and the Tarnhelm from the dead Fafner. As Siegfried goes into the dragon's cave to do so, Mime is about to follow him but is stopped by his brother Alberich who has been hiding nearby. Siegfried is warned

Opposite: drawing from the *Illustrated London News*, 7 June 1913, showing Siegfried after he has slain the dragon Fafner; based on the Covent Garden performance of SIEGFRIED which was seen as part of the complete RING cycle performed twice at the Royal Opera House in April and May.

Below: drawing by Georges Redon showing how Siegfried's slaying of the dragon was staged at the Paris Opéra in 1902. An assistant conductor directs the singer of Fafner, who is seated before a megaphone.

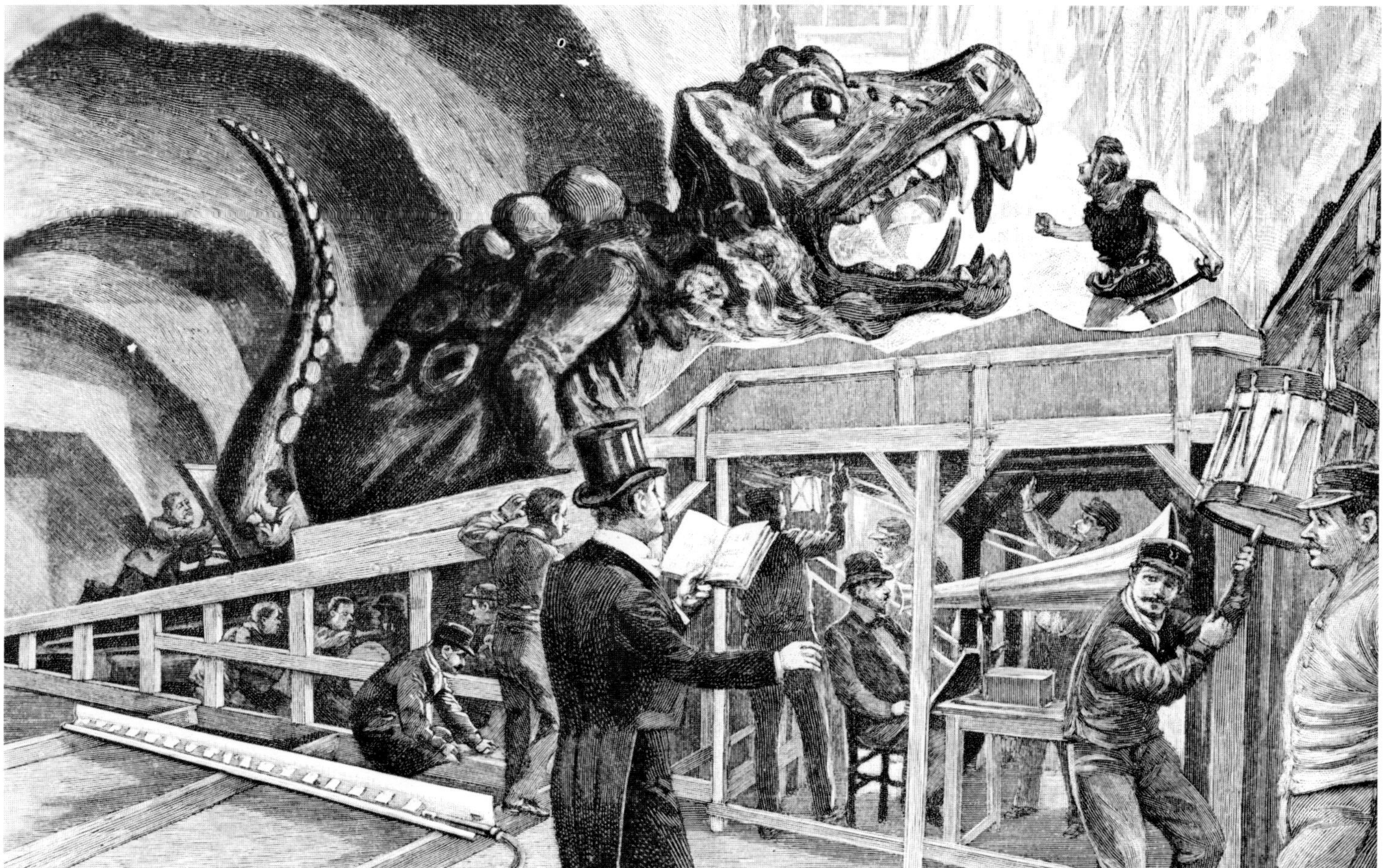

Rheingold Scene I

Der Ring at the Metropolitan Opera, New York, in 1912. Opposite: (above) Das Rheingold, scene 1; (below left) Götterdämmerung, Act III, scene 1; (below right) Alberich and Mime in Das Rheingold. Above: the gods in Das Rheingold. Overleaf: scenes from a silent film, Siegfried, based on the Nibelung saga, made by the German company UFA and directed by Fritz Lang. Siegfried (1923) was followed by a sequel, Kriemhilde's Revenge. (Wagner's Ring used material from parts of the Nibelung saga.) Left: (top) Siegfried and Alberich; (centre) Siegfried and Brunhild; (bottom) Kriemhilde and Brunhild with the corpse of Siegfried. Right: King Etzel and the children at the blossoming tree.

by the bird to be on his guard against Mime, and can now hear the dwarf's unspoken thoughts behind his lying words. He kills Mime, and is led by the bird to the beautiful woman who sleeps upon a mountain-top, surrounded by fire.

In Act III, Wotan summons Erda, who refuses to tell him what the future holds. Wotan is now willing to relinquish his authority to the hero, Siegfried, who must, however, win it in his own right and by his own unaided strength. Siegfried approaches in search of Brünnhilde, and Wotan attempts to prevent him from going further. When Siegfried's sword shatters Wotan's spear, the god realizes that he has lost his power, and steps aside. Siegfried breaks through the magic circle of fire, awakens the sleeping Brünnhilde, and claims her as his own. At first humiliated and reluctant, Brünnhilde is soon overcome by Siegfried's passion, and joyfully surrenders herself to him.

Götterdämmerung

In a Prologue, the three Norns or fates are seen weaving the thread of destiny. As they prophesy the destruction of the gods, the thread snaps and they disappear.

On their mountain summit, Brünnhilde and Siegfried

„Ross" Berlin SW 68

SW 68

Etzel und die Kinder am Blütenbaum

emerge from a cave. Leaving the gold ring with Brünnhilde, Siegfried sets forth in search of new adventures. He journeys down the Rhine and arrives at the Hall of the Gibichungs where Alberich's son, Hagen, lives with his half-brother Gunther and Gunther's sister Gutrune. By drugging Siegfried's drink, Hagen is able to make him forget Brünnhilde, promise to marry Gutrune, and agree to fetch back for Gunther the sleeping woman protected by magic fire. In this manner, Hagen hopes to gain possession of the ring.

Brünnhilde is visited on the mountain summit by her sister, Waltraute, who tries in vain to persuade her to return the ring to the Rhinemaidens. Disguised as Gunther through the magic of the Tarnhelm, Siegfried breaks through the circle of fire again, overcomes Brünnhilde, seizes the ring from her, and forces her to accompany him back to the Hall of the Gibichungs, where preparations are in hand for the double wedding of Brünnhilde to Gunther and Siegfried to Gutrune. When she sees Siegfried, now in his own form, wearing the ring, Brünnhilde accuses him of treachery. With Hagen and Gunther, she plots Siegfried's death.

In the final act, the Rhinemaidens plead with Siegfried to return the ring to them. He is about to do so when Hagen, Gunther and their huntsmen arrive. Siegfried is speared in the back by Hagen. His body is borne to the Hall of the Gibichungs, where Gunther and Hagen quarrel over the ring and Gunther is killed. As Hagen attempts to take the ring from Siegfried's finger, the dead hero's arm rises threateningly.

Brünnhilde enters, having been made aware by the Rhinemaidens of what has really happened, and orders a funeral pyre to be constructed for Siegfried. Taking the ring from him, she places it on her own finger, and rides her horse into the blazing pyre. As the Hall collapses in flames, Hagen attempts to snatch the ring from Brünnhilde but is dragged

Opposite: Kirsten Flagstad sings Brünnhilde's battle cry in a Paramount film entitled THE BIG BROADCAST OF 1938. Flagstad sang Brünnhilde at the Met on several occasions between 1935 and 1941.

Below: Act III of GÖTTERDÄMMERUNG at Bayreuth in 1927, when Kurt Söhnlein's sets were still being used.

Der Ring at Bayreuth in Wieland Wagner's production, which was performed every year from 1951 to 1958; (above) Siegfried, Act III; (right) Siegfried, Act II.

down by the Rhinemaidens into the river, which now overflows its banks. The ring is returned to the water whence it came, on earth the fire rises to destroy the gods' Valhalla, and the sins of the past are redeemed by the love of Brünnhilde for Siegfried as the old order disappears and a new world dawns.

Composed over a period of more than a quarter of a century, the music of *The Ring* is stylistically hybrid, though echoes in it of Wagner's earlier operas are few. Such climaxes as the final scenes of *Die Walküre* and *Götterdämmerung*, the awakening of Brünnhilde in *Siegfried* and the dead hero's

At Bayreuth, the Wagner brothers alternated as producers of Der Ring. Right: Act II of Wolfgang Wagner's Götterdämmerung (1960–64). Below: Act I, scene 1 of Götterdämmerung in Wieland's production, first staged in 1965.
Opposite: (below) the final scene of Wieland Wagner's 1965 Rheingold; (above) Act III of Die Walküre when, in 1970, a new production of Der Ring by Wolfgang replaced his brother's 1965 Ring.

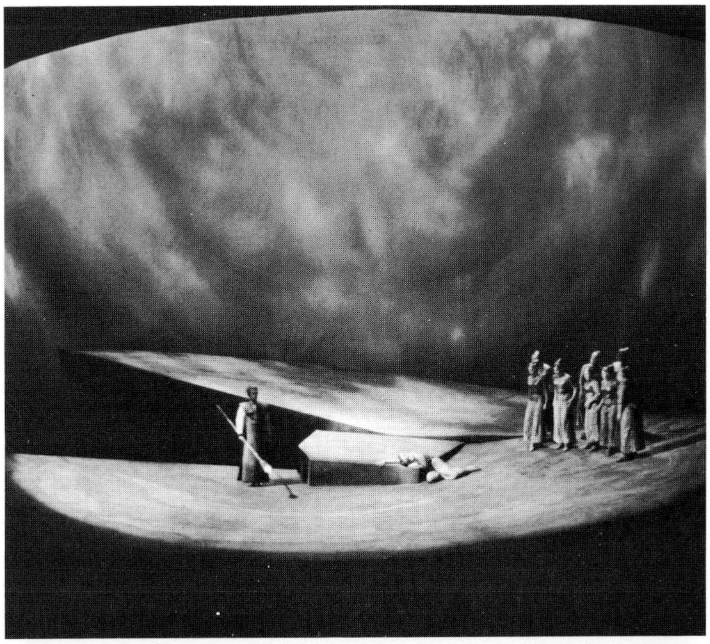

funeral march in *Götterdämmerung* are what make the huge cycle an artistic and emotional experience of unique force. But the lyrical genius of Wagner is no less impressive, as in the entire first act of *Die Walküre*, and much of Act II of *Siegfried*. Seen and heard individually, each of the four separate music-dramas has its occasional *longueurs*, but the effect of the total work is one of remarkable power.

Ideally, the four parts of *The Ring* should be heard complete and consecutively: the entire work demands a greater degree of concentration from the listener than any other opera by Wagner, or by anyone else. This is not simply because of the vast system of nearly two hundred leitmotifs woven into the giant work, but because of the complex nature of the ideas inherent in it, and because of the variety of interpretations to which it is susceptible. Considered as an old Norse saga of gods, heroes, dwarfs, dragons and giants, reworked by Wagner into frequently bad and occasionally repetitive verse, *The Ring* is obviously a flawed and unsatisfactory affair. However, its power to move an audience lies elsewhere, in the ability of Wagner's music to bypass its listeners' intellectual and aesthetic responses and to communicate directly with the deepest recesses of the psyche. The naive absurdities of the plot, the antiquated trappings of the old saga, all fade into insignificance before the force of Wagner's music. In a sense, *The Ring* fails as a vindication of its composer's theory of the *Gesamtkunstwerk*, or total work of art, for its message is delivered by the music alone: not even, to any significant extent, by the voices, but by Wagner's orchestra. Whether *The Ring* is completely successful as theatre or as music-drama may be debatable. What is beyond question, however, is that it provides the listener with a great musical experience, and one that in some mysterious way transcends the art of music alone to become almost a spiritual or psychical experience.

It is by no means easy to describe the effect of this masterwork upon the receptive intelligence, and one takes grateful refuge in Wagner's reply to a disciple, August Röckel, who had requested elucidation of certain ambiguities in *The Ring*: 'You must feel that something is being enacted that is not to be expressed in mere words – and it is wrong of you to challenge me to explain it in words.' Elsewhere in the same letter, however, Wagner comments on the meaning, for him, of the myth of the Ring:

The development of the whole poem sets forth the necessity of

Overleaf: Act II of Götterdämmerung at the Salzburg Easter Festival, 1970, produced and conducted by Herbert von Karajan, and designed by Günther Schneider-Siemssen.

Between 1962 and 1964, a new production of DER RING was built up at Covent Garden. Hans Hotter directed and sang Wotan, and the operas were designed by Günther Schneider-Siemssen. Above: Michael Langdon (Fafner) and Forbes Robinson (Fasolt) in DAS RHEINGOLD. Right: Act I of DIE WALKÜRE with Ernst Kozub (Siegmund) and Claire Watson (Sieglinde).

recognizing and yielding to the change, the many-sidedness, the multiplicity, the eternal renewing of reality and of life. Wotan rises to the tragic height of *willing* his own destruction. This is the lesson that we have to learn from the history of mankind: *to will what necessity imposes*, and ourselves bring it about. The creative product of this supreme, self-destroying will, its victorious achievement, is a fearless human being, one who never ceases to love: Siegfried. That is the whole matter. As a matter of detail, the mischief-making power, the poison that is fatal to love, appears under the guise of the gold that is stolen from Nature and misapplied – the Nibelungs' Ring, never to be redeemed from the curse that clings to it until it has been restored to Nature and the gold sunk again in the depths of the Rhine. But it is only quite at the end that Wotan realizes

The Ring was performed in English by the Sadler's Wells Opera at the London Coliseum in 1973, and has been revived in more recent years.
Opposite: the three Norns in the Prologue to The Twilight of the Gods.
Above: Derek Hammond-Stroud (Alberich) and Gregory Dempsey (Mime) in Act II of Siegfried.
The sets were designed by Ralph Koltai.

this, when he himself has reached the goal of his tragic career; what Loge had foretold to him at the beginning with a touching insistence, the god consumed by ambition had ignored. Later in Fafner's deed he merely recognized the power of the curse; it is only when the Ring works its destroying spell on Siegfried himself that he realizes that only by restoration of what was stolen can the evil be annulled, and he deliberately makes his own destruction part of the conditions on which must depend the annulling of the original mischief.

Experience is everything. Moreover, Siegfried alone (man by himself) is not the complete human being: he is merely the half; it is only along with Brünnhilde that he becomes the redeemer. To the isolated being not all things are possible; there is need of more than one, and it is woman, suffering and willing to sacrifice herself, who becomes at last the real, conscious redeemer: for what is love itself but the "eternal feminine" (*das ewig Weibliche*)?

The first complete performance of *Der Ring des Nibelungen* was given at the Wagner Festival Theatre, Bayreuth, in August 1876: *Das Rheingold* on 13 August, *Die Walküre* (14 August), *Siegfried* (16 August) and *Götterdämmerung* on 17 August. The composer, who directed the staging, had chosen his singers with the greatest care, and had worked with several of them for weeks on end at various times in the two years preceding the 1876 performances. The conducting of the performances he entrusted to Hans Richter and the stage designs were commissioned from Joseph Hoffmann, whose sketches were then turned over to the Brückner brothers for practical realization. The costumes were designed by Emil Doepler. A number of technical problems were solved with the use of stage machinery designed and built by Karl Brandt. The swimming of the three Rhinemaidens in *Das Rheingold* necessitated the invention of a 'swimming machine', with two stagehands allotted to each singer as well as a choreographer to devise swimming movements.

Even those who did not succumb completely to the spell of Wagner's music responded to the composer's staging of his vast work. Tchaikovsky wrote an account of it for a Russian newspaper:

... Whether Richard Wagner was right in serving his idea to the extent he has done, whether he neglected the principles of artistic and aesthetic balance and whether Art will now progress from his work as a point of departure or whether *The Ring* will mark a point at which a reaction will set in – who would wish to pronounce on that today? One thing is certain, that something has happened

Scenes from the English National Opera's Ring. Opposite: Clifford Grant (Fafner) and Robert Lloyd (Fasolt) in The Rhinegold. Right: Derek Hammond-Stroud (Alberich) and Gwynne Howell (the Wanderer) in Siegfried; (above) Ann Howard (Fricka) in The Rhinegold.

Left: Act III of Siegfried in the English National Opera production at the London Coliseum.
Above: Jon Weaving (Siegfried) and Paul Crook (Mime) in a 1976 revival of the ENO Siegfried.
Below: Don Garrard as Wotan in the ENO production of The Rheingold, a role he undertook when the production went on tour in 1973.

at Bayreuth, something which our grandchildren and great-grandchildren will remember.

If I, as a professional musician, had the feeling of total mental and physical exhaustion after the performance of each of the parts of *The Ring* – how great must be the fatigue of the amateurs! It is true that the latter concern themselves far more with the wonders which take place on the stage than with the orchestra or the singers – but one must assume that Wagner wrote the music for it to be listened to and not to be secondary to the drama. The musician, then, judges the actual music whereas the amateur-dilettante enjoys the scenery and transformations, the dragon and the snakes, the swimming Rhinemaidens and the rest . . . For the present I say quite honestly that *The Ring* made an overwhelming impression on me not so much through its musical beauty (which it possesses in perhaps too great an abundance) but rather through its gigantic proportions.

I brought away the impression that *The Ring* contains many passages of extraordinary beauty, especially symphonic beauty, which is remarkable, as Wagner has no stated intention of writing an opera in the style of a symphony. I feel a respectful admiration for the immense talents of the composer and his wealth of technique, such as has never been heard before. I will, however, continue the study of the music – the most complicated which has hitherto been composed. Yet, if *The Ring* bores one in places, if much of it is incomprehensible and vague, if Wagner's harmonies are at times open to objection as being too complicated and artificial, and his theories false, even if the results of his immense work should eventually fall into oblivion, and the Bayreuth Theatre drop into an eternal slumber, yet the *Ring of the Nibelungs* is an event of the greatest importance to the world, an epoch-making work of art.

The ENO RING. Below: Rita Hunter (Brünnhilde) with Raimund Herincx (Wotan) and the Valkyries in Act III of THE VALKYRIE.
Right: Rita Hunter (Brünnhilde) and Elizabeth Connell (Waltraute) in THE TWILIGHT OF THE GODS Act I.

Above: the final scene of DAS RHEINGOLD as performed by Scottish Opera in 1971, in sets by Michael Knight. Opposite: the Met's new production of DER RING in 1975 was based on the Karajan Salzburg staging, designed by Günther Schneider-Siemssen and conducted by Karajan; (above) GÖTTERDÄMMERUNG; (below) Act I of DIE WALKÜRE with Janis Martin (Sieglinde) and James King (Siegmund).

Overleaf: the Götz Friedrich production of DER RING at Covent Garden began with DAS RHEINGOLD in 1974. The designer was Josef Svoboda. Main picture: George Shirley as Loge. Above left: the Rhinemaidens. Opposite: (left) Donald McIntyre as Wotan; (right) Donald Shanks as Fafner.

To his brother Modeste, Tchaikovsky wrote more bluntly: '*The Ring* may be actually a magnificent work, but it is certain that there never was anything so endlessly and wearisomely spun out ...'

The Viennese critic Eduard Hanslick, after a detailed and not unsympathetic discussion of the work itself, concluded his long review with an interesting and useful, though not necessarily unbiased, description of the staging:

With whatever hopes and fears one may have made the pilgrimage to Bayreuth, we were all united at least in our anticipation of an extraordinary theatrical event. But even this expectation was only partially fulfilled. I have duly acknowledged Wagner's imaginative innovations in the arrangement of his theatre, including, as regards the mechanical side, the scene of the swimming Rhinemaidens in *Rheingold*. From there on there is a gradual descent. That the very first change of scene failed mechanically, that everything went generally awry, is not something to which I can attach much importance. That sort of thing can happen in any theatre, although it would have been better had it not happened in this widely heralded and elaborately prepared "model production" at Bayreuth. There were examples aplenty of incorrect and deficient mounting, and in decisive places. The rainbow, over which the gods proceed to Valhalla, was set so low that one could have taken it for a painted bridge in a flower garden. The struggle between Siegmund and Hunding, and Wotan's intervention, took place in such remote darkness that none of the listeners got any idea of what was going on. The Valkyries never appeared on horseback – they simply moved across the horizon in ineffective and indistinct dissolving views. In Munich they had young stable boys dressed as Valkyries jumping back and forth on thick carpets; their riding, uncannily rapid and noiseless, was remarkably effective. What was possible for such a humble court theatre should certainly be possible for the model stage at Bayreuth. The wall of fire which should surround Brünnhilde was visible only behind her; on three sides she was perfectly free and approachable. The Munich Theatre, years ago, showed how this too should be done. I shall pass over Fricka's ludicrous team of rams and the ageing nag which Brünnhilde did not ride but which was led by the bridle and held fast by a cord beneath the stage: likewise the many unsuccessful scenic effects. I shall mention only the final scene of *Götterdämmerung* in which the scenic art of the Wagner Theatre should have reached its height. Who could not have looked forward eagerly to the moment when Brünnhilde, according to the explicit assurance of the libretto, would "leap impetuously upon the steed and with one impulse vault into the flaming fire"? Instead of this, she led her miserable Rosinante calmly off into the wings. There was no thought of leaping or vaulting. Hagen, who should throw himself as if crazed

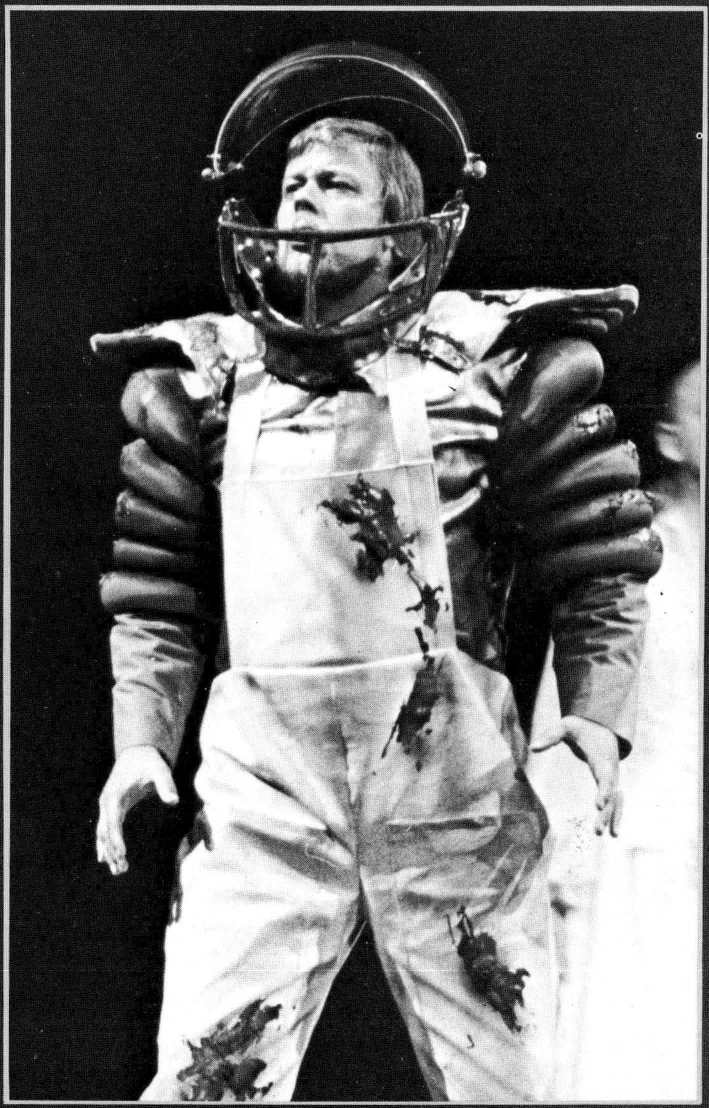

Above: Act II of the Svoboda-Friedrich Siegfried at Covent Garden. Right: the second scene of Das Rheingold in the Svoboda-Friedrich staging.

into the river, strolled into the wings on the right, and turned up a few seconds later in the middle of the Rhine. And finally, the Rhine, which should "burst its banks in a mighty flood", wobbled – like the Red Sea in a provincial production of Rossini's *Moses*. If in such a principal scene a performance cannot achieve what Wagner expressly prescribes in the libretto and promises to the spectator, then there is little further occasion to speak of a "model production". By far the most successful were the sets by Joseph Hoffmann, as well painted as they were original in conception; with faithful execution and more purposeful lighting they could have been even more effective. The painter of the scenery can only account for a half of the total effect; the other half rests with the lighting, which corresponds to the instrumentation of a musical idea. This second half was not fully carried out in Bayreuth, and Hoffmann's ideas appear more melodiously conceived in the photographs than they appeared in the Festival Theatre.

In 1896, thirteen years after the composer's death, Cosima Wagner had the *Ring*'s scenery completely redesigned by Max Brückner, with new costumes by Hans Thoma. She also personally supervised the staging of the work, but her authoritarian attempts to insist upon the letter rather than the spirit of Wagner's intentions were not sufficiently grounded in knowledge or experience to be really successful. Bernard Shaw wrote:

> The plain truth is that Madame Wagner does not know what acting can and cannot do, or how much the imagination of the audience will do when the situation goes beyond the resources of acting. Over and over again ... we find the Bayreuth artists making the most violent demonstration, striking the most overcharged attitudes, and trying to look ineffable things at the very moment, in short, when the slightest betrayal of any share on their part in the excitement of the audience must mar the whole effect – the moment,

consequently, when a skilled actor allows the play itself, helped by the imagination of the spectators, to do all the work. This is the whole secret of the amateurishness of Bayreuth. Madame Wagner is beyond question a very clever lady, and a most able woman of business; but she knows so little how dramatic effects are produced technically that at the very points where her husband's genius and the emotions to which it appeals are producing their most searching effects she assumes that no effect will be produced at all if the prima donna does not exhibit the most demonstrative consciousness of it. I call this amateurish, but from the Bayreuth point of view it is even worse than amateurish: it is heretical, being the most foolish characteristic of Italian operatic acting. I do not say that Wagner himself was free from it.

Clearly, in his original Bayreuth production of 1876, Wagner was not free from it, if one is to believe Hanslick. Nor was the basically conventional *Ring* production at Bayreuth greatly altered by the Wagners' son and Cosima's successor, Siegfried Wagner, until 1924; and then only by the substitution of solid three-dimensional sets for the painted flats of his father's and mother's time.

During the Nazi period, the Bayreuth *Ring* was newly produced by Heinz Tietjen, and a note of grandiose pomposity was brought into the staging – and into the musical performance: Tietjen sometimes conducted his own productions, and under him the chorus of Gibichungs in *Götterdämmerung* was increased from Richard Wagner's twenty-six to 101. Of Tietjen, Siegfried Wagner's daughter Friedelind wrote: 'As a stage director, I considered him great, although I was sorry when he fell a victim to the lavishness of the Reinhardt school. He was no longer satisfied unless he had at least eight hundred people and a dozen horses milling around on the stage. Comparing his manner with father's, I was finally convinced that many of his productions were too elaborate and a departure from the inner meaning of the music dramas.'

There were, of course, political reasons in the 'thirties for the lavishness of the Bayreuth style. It was not until 1951 and the 'new Bayreuth' that much thought was again to be given by stage directors to the inner meaning of Wagner's music-dramas, and specifically *The Ring*.

However, though directors may not have been thinking deeply about the meaning of *The Ring*, critics and Wagner commentators continued to discuss and to expound. *Der Ring des Nibelungen* is, for all its unevenness and disproportionate length and shape, the composer's most important work, and the one on which most critical theories of Wagner are based.

The Götz Friedrich Covent Garden Ring. Right: Donald McIntyre as Wotan in Siegfried. Opposite: Gwyneth Jones as Brünnhilde in Die Walküre. Overleaf: Götterdämmerung, from the same sequence.

Above: the Rhinemaidens in Friedrich's Götterdämmerung. Opposite: the Norns in the same production.

So vast and wide-ranging are its scale and its references that it is possible to interpret *The Ring* in terms of sociology, politics, economics, history, psychology and moral philosophy. One useful key to its understanding lies in Bernard Shaw's *The Perfect Wagnerite*. Shaw, having noted that, at the point where *The Ring* changes from music-drama into opera, it also ceases to be philosophic and becomes didactic, continues:

The philosophic part is a dramatic symbol of the world as Wagner observed it. In the didactic part, the philosophy degenerates into the prescription of a romantic nostrum for all human ills. Wagner, only mortal after all, succumbed to the panacea mania when his philosophy was exhausted, like any of the rest of us.

In the 1960s, Robert Donington interpreted *The Ring* from the point of view of Jungian psychology. By this time the stage directors, led by Wieland Wagner at Bayreuth, had begun to reinterpret Wagner's tetralogy in the light of several theories, aesthetic, socio-political and moral. It was Wieland Wagner's 1951 Bayreuth production which led the way. Wieland's Appia-influenced designs, his stripping away of all but the bare essentials of staging, which are space and light, seemed somehow less revolutionary when applied to *The Ring* than when imposed upon other Wagner operas, and the Wieland Wagner *Ring* remained in the Bayreuth repertoire until 1958, though it underwent several modifications and revisions.

When Covent Garden staged its first really new post-war *Ring* in 1954, it was not to the new Bayreuth style that it looked, but back to the traditional past. Rudolf Hartmann was entrusted with the production, and the settings were by Leslie Hurry, who was less at home in Wagner's world than in that of romantic ballet. Something of balletic frivolity affected Hartmann's normally high-minded conventionality, and led to a production which lacked both the confidence of traditionalism and the excitement of innovation. When this production was replaced in the early 'sixties, it was by one which had a foot in both camps. The director was Hans Hotter, a great Wotan who was approaching the end of his singing career. Though he may not have been wise to combine the functions of singer and producer, it is likely that Hotter's production would have been no more firmly based if he had not also been singing in it. Günther Schneider-Siemssen's sets were evocative, and even did something to bridge the gap

Opposite: the Seattle RING, DAS RHEINGOLD in 1981: (above) Froh (Augusto Paglialunga) shows Wotan (Franz Ferdinand Nentwig) and Fricka (Diane Curry) and the bridge to Valhalla; (below) scene 1, in John T. Naccarato's set.

Above: (left) the final scene of DAS RHEINGOLD at the Bavarian State Opera, Munich, in a 1975 production by Günther Rennert, designed by Jan Brazda; (right) the same scene at the San Francisco Opera in 1977, in a production by Ghita Hager.

between the realism of the past and the symbolism of the future.

Meanwhile, at Bayreuth, Wieland Wagner's *Ring* had been replaced, in 1960, by a production staged by his brother Wolfgang. The result was not a return to the unsymbolic past but another uneasy compromise. The huge tilted saucer-shape space on which most of the action was played dominated the four evenings and the producer's thoughts as well, for no overall view of the work emerged.

Considerably more impressive was the *Ring* production by Herbert von Karajan at the Vienna State Opera, which was given its first performance in June 1960. In sets by Preetorius which successfully blended the realistic and the symbolic, poetically and imaginatively lit by the producer, Karajan set *The Ring* before his audience with clarity and purpose. His later stagings of the operas at Salzburg, given separately with even more impressive sets by Schneider-Siemssen, necessarily lacked the unity of vision of his Vienna production which interposed nothing between the work and the imaginative response of its audience.

Wolfgang Wagner's 1960 *Ring* at Bayreuth was replaced, in 1965, with a new production by Wieland, who announced some of his intentions in advance to the critic Walter Panofsky:

Once upon a time I tried to enlarge the force of the acting in *The Ring* by concentrating it in a small space – the ring-disc – and to stylize the Nature which encircles this acting space. This acting platform which substitutes for the *cothurnus* of the Ancients I shall retain in future, as it has proved itself scenically, particularly in *The Ring*. On the other hand I shall try to find analogies for the musical ciphers of *The Ring*'s score in archetypal scene-pictures: Wagner himself called his scenic visions dream-pictures. The translations of these Wagnerian visions of Nature would indeed be a task worthy of the leading artists of our day. It is disappointing that sculptors of genius like Moore and Lipschitz who have indeed found the path back to archaic fields, to an art of archetypes, are completely estranged from the archaic realm of *The Ring* and the world of Wagnerian creation altogether. The path which I began to take in 1951, as seen from today, hesitantly and with many compromises, leads me necessarily from the empty stage, lit by diffused light, to abstract, sculptural forms and "contemporary" colour.

When his new production was seen at Bayreuth, it became clear that Wieland Wagner was attempting to find his way back from abstraction to a real world, while resisting the real world of his grandfather. The result was a staging which was, on a superficial level, more interesting to spectators than his 1951 production had been, and certainly busier in movement and more complex in the relationship of one character to another, but which, in its specific references, did not always sound the right note. As the Editor of *Opera* noted, 'This approach of Wieland's made for a dark, claustrophobic *Ring*, in which the vast open spaces and magic lighting of his previous production were replaced by projections and

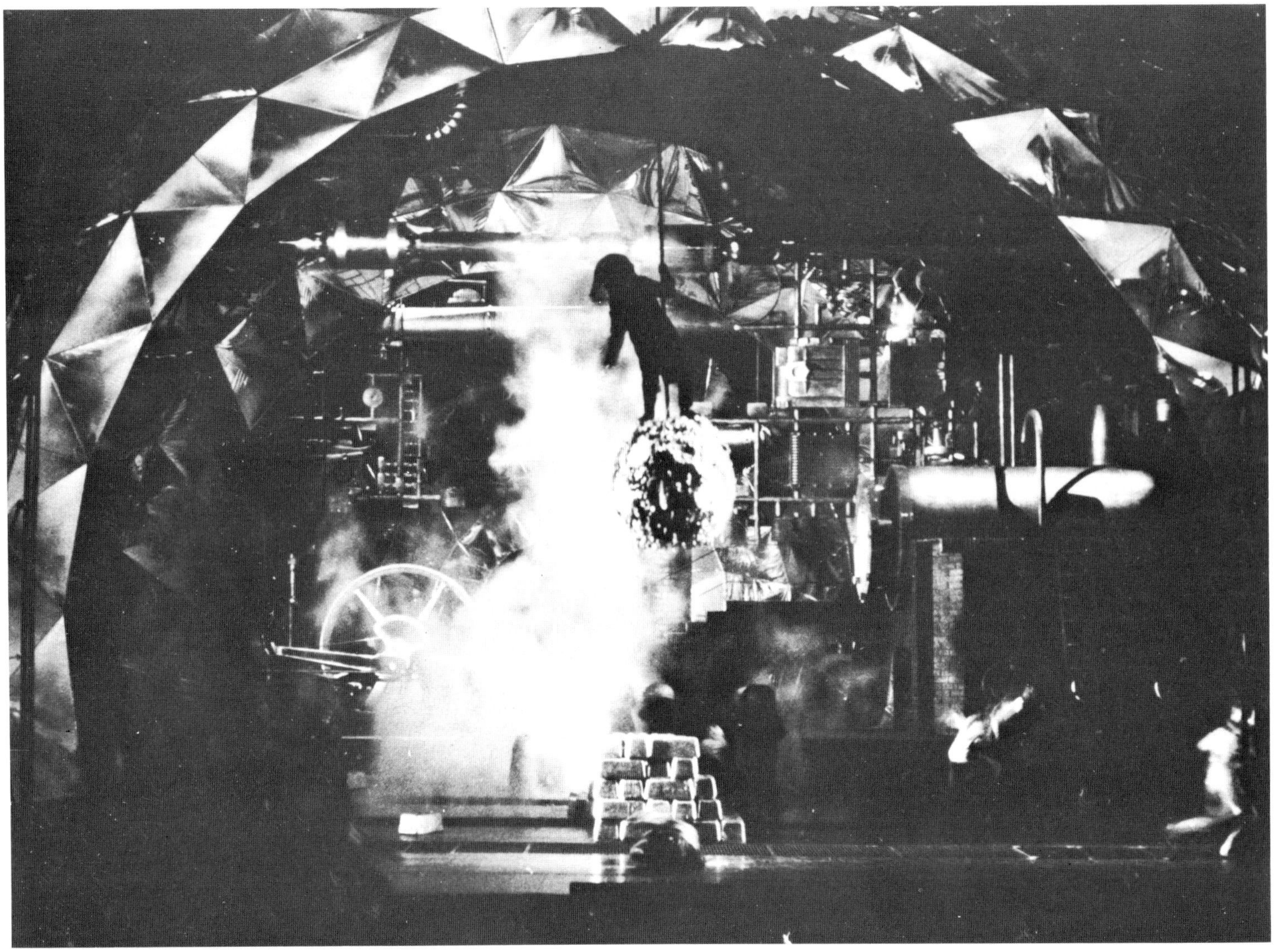

costumes which seemed to stem from the Far East or Mexican civilizations.'

In 1970, it became Wolfgang's turn again to stage *The Ring* at Bayreuth. Back came the 1960 saucer for some of the scenes, but for others Wolfgang had decided to 'take a cautious step towards realism', as John Warwick wrote in *Opera*. The overall result was, he thought, incongruous, and was not helped by 'costumes that hit a new low in hideousness'. This was, surely, the least effective, and least interesting of any post-war Bayreuth staging of the tetralogy. It was also, memory insists, the darkest: frequently, the spectator simply could not see what was happening on stage!

During the 1960s, Scottish Opera had slowly been assembling, one opera at a time, a production of *The Ring* which was given its first complete performance in Glasgow in 1971. Peter Ebert's staging made up in theatrical effectiveness what it may have lacked in intellectual penetration; the style, in general, could be described as modified Bayreuth. A more considerable achievement was English National Opera's production, first given complete at the London Coliseum in 1973. The sets by Ralph Koltai, aggressively modernistic, both literally and metaphorically 'flashy', and tending to suggest outer space in the year 2001 rather than Europe in primeval times, were not generally liked as the cycle was being built up, but by the time it was performed complete audiences had become used to the look of this *Ring*, and appreciated the intelligence and dramatic restraint of the joint producers, Glen Byam Shaw and John Blatchley.

Since the mid-'seventies, there have been at least four important *Ring* productions in various parts of the world, three of which have been revived on several occasions. Two of them are more controversial than the others. The relatively uncontroversial productions, both American, are those of the New York Metropolitan Opera, and the Pacific Northwest Festival in Seattle.

The Met's staging, directed by Herbert von Karajan and designed by Schneider-Siemssen and Wakhewitch, was based on Karajan's Salzburg productions of the operas, one by one, at his Easter Festivals. Expensive to mount, requiring a great many technical rehearsals, the production was enthusiastically received in 1975 when all four operas were seen in the latter part of the season, though the two-month span over which the performances ranged militated against audiences being able to experience the cumulative effect of the cycle. Seattle's production by George London, in sets by John T. Naccarato, though generally considered to be naively old-fashioned in its neo-romanticism, is nevertheless the kind of staging best suited to the Pacific Northwest Festival. To quote an American critic, Martin Kirschen, 'Seattle's association with the Alaskan gold rush can still be felt. Mount Rainier towers in majesty to the South, and the Cascade and Olympic mountains frame Seattle on the West and East with godlike splendour. The history and surroundings fit in well with a cycle dwelling on the fate of the gods in their Olympian fortress Valhalla and on that of dwarfs within the mountains forging and coveting golden hoards.'

London's Royal Opera House production of *The Ring* by Götz Friedrich, designed by Josef Svoboda, is nothing if not controversial. Relentlessly Germanic in his intellectualizing of the aesthetic process, Friedrich might therefore be thought to be the ideal Wagner producer. But, although Friedrich's various statements of his intentions make fascinating reading, those intentions are clarified only rarely in his staging. Svoboda's bleakly unpoetic décor sometimes illuminates but sometimes obscures the significance of the work, and Friedrich's determination to treat *Der Ring des Nibelungen* not as a unified work but as four separate operas each of which, even within a production of the complete cycle, is to be approached and interpreted individually, leaves the spectator finally unable to experience Wagner's vast tetralogy as a unity. What one might consider to be a valid criticism of his production – that it looked as though it was happening nowhere but on the stage of the opera house – is something which Friedrich himself, in a note in the Covent Garden programme, virtually claimed as his conscious intention:

If the place of action must be stated, it is the Stage of Covent Garden. The ground plan and size of aperture, measurements of the under-, side-, and back-stage offer the outline of a stage area which, supported and moved by a single mighty piston, becomes a changeable platform portraying the realm of the Gods, the nether world, earth and water, buildings and rocky mountains, forest and palace. The world: the theatre. The stage: a world. The movements seem almost unlimited; peaceful, circling, quickly turning, rising and sinking (by sharply tipping showing the mirrored underside), jutting up into the sky (through different positioning), creating sharp and bizarre slants. Yet, as varied as the movement possibilities are, they always follow recognizable rules. They are centralized by the hydraulic piston that holds and moves the platform – a symbol of constantly changing and self-generating energy. Such a stage allows and demands solutions which extend far beyond a normal production. The gestures of the singing actors can be better

Opposite: (above) DAS RHEINGOLD at Cassel. Cassel's 'space-age' RING, as audiences called it, was first seen in its entirety in 1974. The producer was Ulrich Melchinger, and the designer Thomas Richter-Forgách; (below) DAS RHEINGOLD as designed by Jürgen Rose for Götz Friedrich in Hamburg, 1980.

Above and right: scenes from the 1976 Bayreuth Rheingold, designed by Patrice Chéreau, from the complete Ring cycle.

The Chéreau RING at Bayreuth, designed by Richard Peduzzi
with costumes by Jaques Schmidt:
(top) scene 2 of DAS RHEINGOLD; (above) SIEGFRIED, Act I.

Chéreau's Bayreuth RING: (top) scene I of DAS RHEINGOLD; (above) GÖTTERDÄMMERUNG, Act III.

Chéreau's Bayreuth Ring:
(above) Die Walküre; (opposite) Siegfried.

illustrated and controlled. From being able to control them one can gain insights. Comic effects are likewise possible, as with the archetypes who cross the line into tragedy. The stage projects inside and outside – it is a geographic and psychic space.

It is, to the spectator who has not read Götz Friedrich on the subject but has merely experienced what has been put on the stage, not a 'geographic and psychic space' but a series of visually and theatrically stunning pictures which do not necessarily relate to Wagner's music-drama. Unfortunately, in concentrating on the Covent Garden stage, Herr Friedrich neglected to consider the Covent Garden auditorium, and in consequence some of his finest effects are simply not visible from certain parts of the house. In this remarkable production, the staging has taken over from the work with a vengeance.

Götz Friedrich's *Ring* is being replaced by the Royal Opera in 1983, on the occasion of the hundredth anniversary of the death of Wagner, just as the Patrice Chéreau production, seen at Bayreuth from 1976 to 1980, was dropped in the latter year to be replaced by Sir Peter Hall's production in 1983.

Chéreau's *Ring* was an achievement on a much higher aesthetic and intellectual level than Friedrich's, and thus managed to shock and outrage a greater number of people. After attending the first performance at Bayreuth in 1976, the Editor of *Opera* wrote:

> It was Pierre Boulez [the conductor] who insisted that Chéreau should be engaged by Bayreuth after his attempts to get both Ingmar Bergman and Peter Stein had failed. Like Götz Friedrich at Covent Garden, Chéreau treats each of the four parts of *The Ring* as separate entities rather than as parts of a complete whole. Unlike Friedrich, however, he does not try to make serious political points, but rather hopes, by treating *The Ring* as a black comedy, to make his points that way. That he must have succeeded to some extent was shown by the hostility of large sections of the audience, especially the German portion of it, who clearly saw some of their rather nastier characteristics mirrored in Chéreau's treatment of certain of the personages on stage – not that we do not all to a greater or lesser extent possess some of those unpleasant traits in our own make-up, whatever our nationality!

Chéreau dressed his characters in costumes of the period of the work's first production, the late nineteenth century, which worked better for the first two operas than the last two. Some of the settings, however, were of the twentieth century. Consistency was not Chéreau's aim; nor, surely, was he trying to avoid making political points. In fact, a more firmly based criticism of his *Ring* would be that it represented only a partial view of Wagner's great work, and a partisan political view at that. Opera audiences are easily shocked by what they see on the stage: an audience from the dramatic theatre would take Chéreau's production in its stride. What opera audiences ought to have objected to was not that Wotan wore a stove-pipe hat, Siegfried a dinner-jacket and Hagen a lounge suit, but that the producer's approach to the work was unmusical, indeed anti-musical. Brian Magee accurately described it in the 1977 Festival issue of *Opera*:

> The first and fundamentally mistaken decision was to present the work predominantly in terms of its stage action and words, when it is a work whose primary medium of expression is (whatever Wagner's conscious intentions) the music. That at once makes it Chéreau's *Ring* more than Wagner's – a fact clearly reflected in the general discussion. The next mistake was to single out one

strand from the intricate pattern of meanings in the text – the strand of revolutionary social comment – and stage the entire work in terms of that solitary thread. The third mistake was to localize the references in time and place, presenting it as if it were 'about' the late-capitalist era in Western European history, when Wagner deliberately refrained from doing any such thing, setting it in a world of epic and legend precisely because he believed that what he was saying was of universal significance. In short, Chéreau's approach has been to reduce, and then reduce, and then reduce again. What he ends up with is a concept that leaves most of the work out of account. He then tries to solve the problem of sustaining this impoverished structure over four evenings by colouring its surface with a cosmetic layer of bright ideas – some of which are indeed bright, and would enhance a better production.

A wider audience will be able to judge these issues for themselves, for the Chéreau production was filmed before being dismantled. Meanwhile, *The Ring* is a resilient masterpiece, and is not likely to lie down under any one interpretation for long. Directors will continue to face the challenges it presents, and the best of them will recognize the problem as one of reconciling the work itself and its presentation on the stage. The work, both words and music, does not change. It is as it was when first fully revealed to audiences in 1876. Styles and tastes in staging, however, do change, have changed several times since 1876, and will continue to change. Productions of *The Ring* and of Wagner's operas in general must satisfy the taste of the time while not betraying the nature of '*das ewige Werk*'.

Chéreau's Bayreuth Ring: (opposite) Peter Hofmann as Siegmund in Die Walküre; (below) Manfred Jung as Siegfried in Götterdämmerung.

Above: Hermann Winkelmann, the first Parsifal, at Bayreuth in 1882.
Opposite: Act I of PARSIFAL at Covent Garden in 1979, designed by Farrah for a production by Terry Hands.

IX
PARSIFAL

The premiere of PARSIFAL, Bayreuth, 1882: costumes for Amfortas (above), Kundry (opposite, above) and Titurel. Below: Klingsor's castle. Opposite: (below right) the Temple of the Grail. Scenery and costumes were by Paul von Joukowsky. His set for the Temple continued to be used at Bayreuth until 1934.

‘*Parsifal* is bound to be another very nasty job’, wrote Wagner to Mathilde Wesendonk in 1859. He had already put on paper his ideas for a libretto some two years earlier, and the opera was to occupy his thoughts intermittently for a good many years to come. A quarter of a century separates the composer's first thoughts on *Parsifal* and its premiere in 1882. His 1857 sketch for a three-act libretto appeared twelve years after Wagner first read the romance *Parzival* by Wolfram von Eschenbach (a character the composer had put into his opera *Tannhäuser*). The Eschenbach work was a lengthy account in verse of the history of the knight who became Lord of the Grail.

In Christian mythology, the Holy Grail is the cup from which Christ drank at the Last Supper, a legend familiar in English literature from the fifteenth-century *Morte Darthur* by Sir Thomas Malory and the nineteenth-century *Idylls of the King* by Tennyson.

The Grail in Wolfram von Eschenbach's poem is a precious stone with no specific Christian significance: Wagner, even in his earliest thoughts about the opera he hoped to write, was determined to restore the Christian element to the story. In that same letter to Mathilde Wesendonk, he explains that ‘the Grail, after *my* reading, is the Cup of the Last Supper, wherein Joseph of Arimathea gathered the blood of the Saviour on the cross’. Wolfram remained his principal source, but the libretto the composer fashioned from the medieval poem, first as a prose scenario in 1865, with a second draft in February 1877, and the entire verse libretto a month or two later, developed not only Parsifal but also the other characters of the story along lines which could never have been envisaged by Eschenbach.

Wagner's attention was diverted from the *Parsifal* project in the years between 1865 and 1877 by his work on other operas (the completion of *Die Meistersinger* and its Munich premiere, the composition of the last act of *Siegfried* and the whole of *Götterdämmerung*) and by the building of his Festival Theatre at Bayreuth and the 1876 premiere of the complete *Ring*. But with his *Parsifal* libretto complete and the Bayreuth Festival Theatre opened, Wagner was now ready to compose the music.

Though the Bayreuth *Ring* performances in 1876 had been artistically successful, they had been a financial disaster, and Wagner was forced to undertake concert engagements in an attempt to reduce the deficit. The composition of *Parsifal*, therefore, proceeded fitfully. Ludwig II came to the composer's aid by transferring Wagner's remaining liabilities to the state of Bavaria on certain conditions, one of which

was that *Parsifal*, described by the composer not as opera or music-drama but as '*Bühnenweihfestspiel*' (sacred festival drama), should be performed only at Bayreuth and 'never desecrated by contact with any profane stage'.

Partly at the Villa Wahnfried, the house Wagner had built in Bayreuth, and partly in Italy, the music of *Parsifal* was slowly urged into existence. By January 1882, it was complete and fully scored. Six months later, on 26 July, the opera was given its first performance at Bayreuth.

The first act of *Parsifal* takes place in medieval times, near, and later in, the temple of the Holy Grail at Montsalvat in Spain. The Grail is guarded by a band of knights, and when the opera begins an elderly knight, Gurnemanz, is describing to two pages how their leader Amfortas, having been seduced by a beautiful enchantress in the magic garden of the evil magician Klingsor, had been stabbed by Klingsor with the sacred spear. The wound will never heal until it is touched again by the spear, which can only be wrested from Klingsor by a 'pure fool made wise through pity'. Meanwhile, Amfortas has to be carried on a litter to the lake at frequent intervals, to have his wound bathed.

Kundry, a strange, wild woman, offers a rare balm for the wound. An unknown youth (Parsifal) is brought in. He has killed one of the sacred swans. Gurnemanz at first thinks the youth may be the promised saviour of Amfortas, and takes him to the temple to witness the unveiling of the Grail at the ceremony of Holy Communion. However, the youth fails to comprehend the significance of what he sees and is angrily dismissed by Gurnemanz.

The second act takes place in Klingsor's magic garden. The beautiful enchantress is revealed to be Kundry, who had laughed at Christ on the cross, and for this has been condemned to seek salvation throughout eternity. She is forced

The Parsifal premiere.
Top: Joukowsky's set for the magic garden.
Above: his costume design for Klingsor.
Opposite: Hermann Winkelmann (Parsifal) and
Amalie Materna (Kundry) in Act II.

by Klingsor to attempt the seduction of Parsifal. The flower-maidens of Klingsor's garden fail to tempt Parsifal, but Kundry calls him by his name and speaks to him of his mother and his childhood. As she kisses him on the lips, a sudden realization of the significance of Amfortas's wound comes to the youth, and he is made 'wise through pity'.

Kundry now appeals to Parsifal to free her from her state of damnation. He rejects her. Klingsor suddenly appears and throws the holy spear at Parsifal, but it remains suspended over the youth's head. Parsifal seizes the spear and makes with it the sign of the cross, at which the magic garden collapses. He hurries away to seek again the temple of the Grail.

In Act III years have passed, Gurnemanz has grown very old, and the repentant Kundry returns to give service and to minister to his needs. Parsifal enters, and at first is recognized only by Kundry. Gurnemanz chides him for carrying arms on Good Friday, but what Parsifal carries is the holy spear and, after Kundry has bathed Parsifal's feet, Gurnemanz consecrates him as King of the Grail. Parsifal gives absolution to Kundry.

The final scene takes place in the temple. The knights urge Amfortas to unveil the Grail, but in despair he refuses and begs them to kill him. Parsifal appears, tells Amfortas that his sin has been pardoned, and heals his wound. He orders the Grail to be unveiled. The holy vessel glows with light, and a white dove hovers over Parsifal as he raises the Grail aloft. Kundry falls lifeless to the ground.

It is possible to view *Parsifal* merely as sickly, *fin-de-siècle* homoerotic fantasy, a slow-moving opera the extreme length of which is disproportionate to its musical and dramatic worth. On the surface, it is a work of pious Christianity; although, as the American critic Robert Gutman has pointed out, Wagner detested Christianity, considering it to be 'Judaic error perpetuated'. But *Parsifal*, whatever else it may be, is a complex work of art. If it can be seen as an attempt to give aesthetic validity to the violent racial prejudice of the composer's contemporaneous articles and essays in the *Bayreuther Blätter*, it can also be seen as the portrait of a soul on its journey towards maturity. Whether it is a 'brooding nightmare of Aryan anxiety' (Gutman's phrase) or a celebration of high-minded homosexuality, *Parsifal* seems now very much of its time, considerably more so than *Tristan und Isolde*, than *The Ring* or even *Die Meistersinger*. Parsifal's purity was threatened both racially and sexually. Is it fanciful to trace a connection between the young knight's monastic homosexuality and what Gutman calls the 'not dissimilar fellowship of Ernst Röhm's troopers'? The simplistic answer is that art is art, life is life, and never the twain shall meet. But *Parsifal* surely deserves to be considered on a more complex level of response than this. Allowing of fewer varieties of interpretation than *The Ring*, it has nevertheless been subjected to many, by critics desirous either of emphasizing Wagner's anti-Semitism or of diverting attention from it. Directors, on the other hand, have tended to be more cautious in their approach to the work, taking it for the most part at its face value.

A study of *Parsifal*'s libretto in relation to Wagner's various prose writings makes it clear that one of the composer-dramatist's main concerns was to 'Aryanize' Christianity by divorcing it from its Jewish beginnings. In his essay '*Heldentum und Christentum*' (Heroism and Christianity), written in 1881 as a polemical appendage to *Parsifal*, he explains how the Aryans, the Teutonic leaders of mankind, sprang from the gods, only the lesser races being descended from the apes. Christianity's worship of a Jewish tribal God, made flesh in

Above: the 'unauthorized' production of Parsifal in 1903, given at the Metropolitan Opera, New York. Scenery designed by the Pach brothers for Act II, scene 1.

the Jewish Christ, appalled him. In *Parsifal* he re-created Christ in his own Gentile image. Parsifal is an Aryan Christ.

In another essay, 'Religion and Art', Wagner voiced his own very strong doubts as to the Jewishness of the original Jesus. In the same essay, God is taken to task not only for being Jewish but also for being anti-vegetarian. The evil Klingsor in *Parsifal*, Wagner informed Cosima, represented not only the tainted blood of the Jew but also the Jesuit. The luxurious, voluptuous garden, which the composer thought of as representing Jewish art, is made to disappear by the magical power of the Aryan cross. In the third act of the opera, the pure blood of an Aryan Jesus glows with desire to rejoin the blood in the sacred cup. Amfortas, who had allowed his blood to mingle with that of the racially inferior Kundry, is redeemed, while Kundry is reduced to that menial grovelling which Wagner sees as her proper condition.

The music of *Parsifal* is, at least intermittently, as powerful and compelling as anything Wagner ever composed. To those who sentimentally equate great art with great morality, the opera stands as an uncomfortable reminder that art and morality are often not on speaking terms. The philosopher Nietzsche described *Parsifal* as 'a work of malice, of vindictiveness ... a bad work ... an outrage on morality'. He also recognized the power and the beauty of much of its music. However, if it is accepted that the arts can influence human behaviour, then presumably they can influence it for evil as well as for good. One is inclined to believe that music, as an art, is essentially innocent, and that only when it is allied to text or drama can it corrupt. But corruption is itself a question-begging concept: it is safer to proceed no further than the declaration that, to some temperaments, *Parsifal* is an uncommonly persuasive work of art.

The first production of *Parsifal* at Bayreuth in 1882 was

directed by the composer himself, and designed, to Wagner's close specifications, by a young Russian painter, Paul von Joukowsky, who had become a member of the Wagner entourage a year or two earlier. Some of Joukowsky's décor remained in use at Bayreuth until 1934. The Viennese critic Eduard Hanslick, he who had been caricatured as Beckmesser in *Die Meistersinger*, was present at the first performances of *Parsifal*, which he reviewed for the Viennese newspaper *Die Neue Freie Presse*. Hanslick was as impressed by the visual aspect of the production as by the music:

Now comes the wonderfully effective Transformation Scene. This masterpiece of scenic art receives only step-motherly musical support. Until their arrival in the Temple of the Grail, Parsifal and Gurnemanz march to heavy, tiresomely monotonous chords. From here on the composition gets under way and rises to significant realization, supported by the magnificent and original impressions of the setting. Admirable in their effect are the solemn unison song of the knights, the chorus of the young men and, finally, floating down from above, the promise, "Durch Mitleid wissend – der reine Tor". In this surprising blend of pure high voices the promise motive makes exactly the desired impression; in itself the rather empty ascending theme in fifths would hardly appear original or interesting.

The Holy Communion of the Knights of the Grail in the vaulted hall, with the three singing groups of knights, youths and boys (above in the cupola), with the heavy ringing of the bells, the strange painting-like walls, the solemn unveiling of the Grail – all this combines to make a wonderful picture. The finale belongs unquestionably among those dazzling musico-scenic achievements in which Wagner has no rival.

The composer himself has left an account of the first Bayreuth *Parsifal*, which includes a description of some of the scenic effects:

As regards the scenery in its widest sense, the first thing to claim our solicitude was a fitness in the costumes and decorations. Here, much had to be invented, needless as it might seem to those accustomed to catering for the love of pomp and entertainment by a skilful combination of all the tried effects of opera. As soon as it came to the question of a costume for Klingsor's magic flower maidens, we found nothing but models from ballet or masquerade: the now so favourite court carnivals, in particular, had betrayed our most talented artists into a certain conventional lavishness of ornament that proved quite futile for our object, which was to be attained only on lines of ideal naturalness. These costumes must completely harmonize with Klingsor's magic garden itself, and we had to be quite sure that, after many attempts, we had found the right motive for this floral majesty, unknown to physical experience, before we could introduce into it living female forms that seemed to spring quite naturally from out its wizard wealth. Then with two of those giant flower bells that decked the garden in their rich profusion we had the costume for our magic maiden: to give the last touch to her attire, she had only to snatch up one of the glowing flower cups all strewn around, to tilt it childlike on her head – and, forgetting each convention of the opera ballet, we might take the thing as done.

Though our utmost diligence was spent on giving the height of solemn dignity to the ideal temple of the Grail, whose model could be taken only from the noblest monuments of Christian architecture, yet the splendour of this sanctuary of a divinest halidom was by no means to be extended to the costume of its knights themselves: a noble Templar-like simplicity arrayed their figures with a picturesque severity, yet human grace. The significance of the kingship of this brotherhood we sought in the original meaning of the word 'king' itself, as head of the race, a race here chosen to protect the Grail: nothing was to distinguish him from the other knights, save the mystic import of the lofty office reserved for him alone, and his sufferings understood by none.

Above: Ludwig Sievert's design for Act I of PARSIFAL at Frieberg in 1912, before it could officially be staged outside Bayreuth.

Cosima Wagner was legally empowered to prevent staged performances (though not concert versions) of *Parsifal* from taking place anywhere in Europe other than Bayreuth until 31 December 1913. She was, however, unable to prevent the Metropolitan Opera, New York, from staging the opera in 1903. This was the first non-Bayreuth production of *Parsifal*, a lavish affair with singers from Bayreuth and scenery which

Above: PARSIFAL costumes designed by Charles Ricketts in 1910.
Opposite: (top) Kurt Söhnlein's design for the
magic garden in PARSIFAL, as seen at Bayreuth, 1928.
The production was by Siegfried Wagner;
(below) Klingsor's castle designed by Wieland Wagner, Bayreuth, 1951.

looked like Bayreuth's. The *New York Times* thought that it was 'without doubt the most perfect production ever made on the American lyric stage'.

European opera companies rushed to stage *Parsifal* as soon as it came out of copyright, Barcelona getting in first with a performance which began at midnight on 31 December 1913. There had, however, been a few other stage performances in Europe even before this, managements having discovered various ways of bypassing Cosima's ban: a private performance for members of a Wagner society in Amsterdam; a charity production in Monte Carlo; a public production in Zurich, the Swiss copyright having expired earlier. London stayed within the law, and *Parsifal* was first produced at Covent Garden in February 1914, though an abbreviated arrangement of the opera, without voices, had been conducted by Sir Henry Wood at the London Coliseum in 1913, accompanying a series of 'living tableaux' designed by Byam Shaw.

Something of the piety which was discerned in the work transferred itself to *Parsifal* productions, for no one dared to stage the opera in anything other than a copy of the 'authentic' Bayreuth production until Bayreuth itself broke the spell in 1951. The authentic production of Richard Wagner was, nevertheless, continually undergoing modification throughout the years. In 1934, the great Viennese stage designer Alfred Roller was engaged to replace Joukowsky's sets and costumes. The results were considered to be disappointing, the reason usually given being that Roller was old and in ill health (he died the following year). Unfortunately, no pictorial record of the Alfred Roller *Parsifal* has survived. It was superseded in 1937 by a new staging which utilized the first designs of Wieland Wagner, then aged twenty. Wieland modified the Joukowsky style in the direction of simplicity, and replaced the old rolling scenery in the transformation scene with cinematic projections, which considerably shocked the old guard of Bayreuth.

Those among them who survived were even more shocked when, in 1951, the mature Wieland Wagner presented his own production of *Parsifal*, a defiant proclamation of the direction the new Bayreuth was to take. Geoffrey Skelton described it, in *Wagner at Bayreuth*:

> No leafy wood and lake for the first scene, but the bare shadow of great tree trunks in a cool grey morning light; no richly decorated temple interior with pillars and cupola, only four plain columns and a bare round table and bench dimly discernible in a vast gloom; no battlements for Klingsor, but a projection of light, white on black, which seemed at first to be a spider's web with Klingsor's head and shoulders brilliantly lit at the centre, but could be rationalized as a round tower up which one looks from the base; no flower garden of bright colours, but a mauve-lit vagueness peopled with graceful fluttering wraiths; no Good Friday meadow-carpet, but a bare desert landscape in which hope seemed lost and only endurance remained; and then back to the sombreness of the great temple, where at the end fulfilment was reached and the darkness yielded to a rich red glowing.

In other words, Adolphe Appia had arrived posthumously at Bayreuth. Though Wieland Wagner was never keen to admit the influence of Appia (in fact, he denied that he had been influenced by anyone!), his and Appia's ideas about staging and, in particular, about *Parsifal*, coincided at many

Above: (left) Act I of PARSIFAL in Wieland Wagner's Bayreuth production, first seen in 1951; (right) Sandor Konya (Parsifal), Boris Christoff (Gurnemanz) and Rita Gorr (Kundry) at La Scala, 1960. The production was by Frank de Quell and the décor by Nicola Benois.

Opposite: Act II at Covent Garden, 1959. The production by Herbert Graf was designed by Paul Walter. Parsifal (Karl Liebl) is seen with the Flowermaidens.

points and diverged at few. 'In *Parsifal*', Appia had written in 1897,

> the visual aspect consists of a series of diverse scenes which are there for the sole purpose of working a miraculous transformation in the hero's pure and unconscious soul; Parsifal through them becomes conscious of himself, and by means of his chastity is able at the same time to extend his knowledge to all living things: supreme unity is thus revealed to him.

This is echoed in Wieland Wagner's letter in 1951 to the conductor Hans Knappertsbusch, quoted in the 1973 Bayreuth *Parsifal* programme-book: 'Strictly speaking, the scenery in *Parsifal* is nothing but the expression of the changing moods of Parsifal's soul, whose "path to salvation" ... it is the director's job to reveal.' And, of his design for the Good Friday meadow, Wieland wrote in another letter that the essential point of his production was that this scene would represent the achievement 'of ultimate spiritual clarity and an understanding of the ultimate condition of the world, rather than a romantic experience of nature, which of course would be far better represented by means of a few birches and Gurnemanz's hut'.

Wieland Wagner's *Parsifal* in 1951 was thought by the distinguished Wagnerian Ernest Newman, writing in the London *Sunday Times*, to be 'not only the best *Parsifal* that I have ever seen or heard, but one of the three or four most moving spiritual experiences of my life'. 'We were conscious', he continued, 'for the first time, of the characters as Wagner must have seen them in his creative imagination, and the music, with nothing intruding now between it and us, spoke to us with a poignancy beyond the power of words to express.' It is, surely, the ability to allow the music to speak 'with nothing intruding', a much rarer quality than that simple phrase would suggest, which is the hallmark of the great

Above: Act I of PARSIFAL in Wolfgang Wagner's Bayreuth production of 1975; (inset, top) Act III at Florence, in 1966, when the opera was designed by Tina Sestini Palli and produced by the conductor Lovro von Matacic. Parsifal (Ernst Kozub) is seen with

Kundry (Herta Fischer) and Eduard Wollitz (Gurnemanz); (inset, above) Act I of PARSIFAL at the Met in 1970, with Norman Bailey as Amfortas. The opera was staged by Nathaniel Merrill, with sets and costumes by Robert O'Hearn.

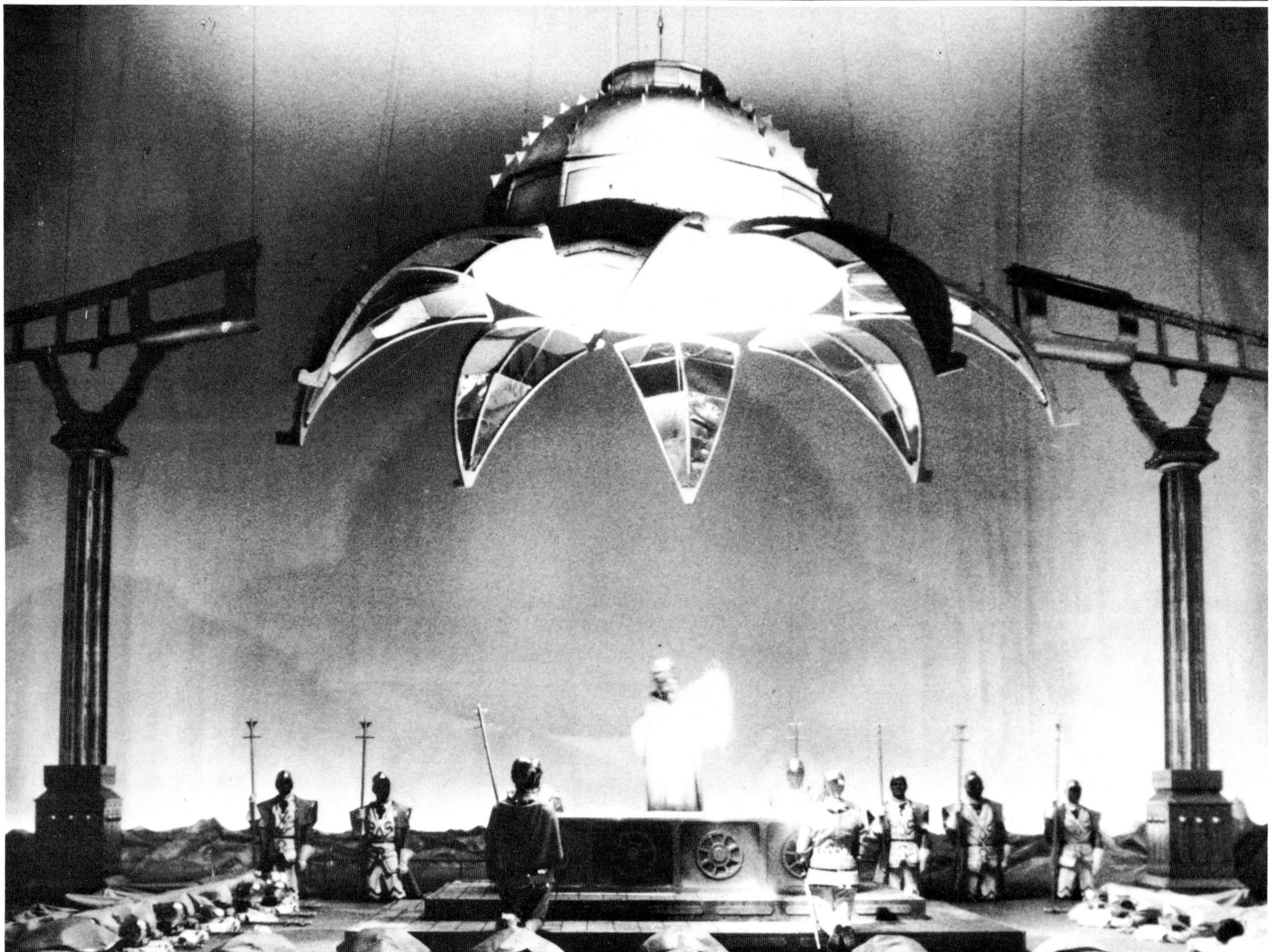

directors of opera, men of the calibre of Wieland Wagner, Peter Hall and, at his best, Herbert von Karajan. The belittling polemicists are revealed in all their tawdriness by the contrast between their several partial (rarely impartial) views of the music-dramas of Wagner's maturity and the productions by freer-ranging spirits which allow the music to speak with nothing intruding.

Wieland Wagner continued to work on and to alter and adjust his 1951 *Parsifal* until the end of his life. 'What is left of the 1951 production now?', he asked in an interview in 1964, and went on to answer: 'The disc, the temple of the Grail, the holy lake. Otherwise everything is different.' Wieland died in 1966, but his production continued to be revived at Bayreuth until it was replaced in 1975 by a new production by his brother Wolfgang, a production which reverted to a semi-naturalism, an impure compromise adulterating Wieland's vision with a more mundane view of what constitutes a theatrical experience. At its 1980 revival, Wolfgang's production had dwindled into being, in the words of *Opera*'s critic, 'currently the most traditional of the productions to be seen at Bayreuth: innocent of innovation, the performances are both satisfying and enjoyable'.

Outside Bayreuth, just as most productions had earlier followed the original staging by the composer, so now producers tended to follow Wieland Wagner and the new Bayreuth, though often in a modified form. Herbert Graf at Covent Garden in 1959, using scenery and costumes by Paul Walter (to whom the lighting was also credited), attempted a compromise between pre-war tradition and 'new Bayreuth' simplification with only partial success. At Cassel, in 1970, the meaning of the work was obscured in an ugly, 'space-age', surrealistic production by Ulrich Melchinger, whose designer was Thomas Richter-Forgách. 'Imagine', wrote the critic of *Opera*, 'that the world has been destroyed by some nuclear catastrophe, and that a small band of dedicated men has gathered on a remote mountain plateau surrounded by snowy peaks to preserve the ancient and everlasting laws of mankind. The Grail temple is a golden, globular space-ship supported in the air by rays from four cylindrical sources on columns, concealed at first by a "wood" of surrealistic machine-age debris which later rolls away. The colours are of our time, pale green and fuchsia for the sky, white with silver trim, bright orange capes and gold helmets for the knights, and a "papal" crown for Amfortas during

Above: Japan saw Parsifal for the first time in 1967, when the Nikikai Opera Group presented the opera in Tokyo. Toshitaka Mori (Parsifal) is seen with Yonako Nagano (Kundry).

Opposite: the team of Ulrich Melchinger (producer) and Thomas Richter-Forgách, also responsible for Cassel's 'space-age' Ring, presented Parsifal in Cassel in similar style in 1970: (above) the opening scene; (below) the Temple of the Grail.

Scenes from the 1979 Covent Garden PARSIFAL, produced by Terry Hands and designed by Farrah. The principals included Peter Hofmann (Parsifal), Yvonne Minton (Kundry), Norman Bailey (Amfortas), Kurt Moll (Gurnemanz) and Franz Mazura (Klingsor).

Above: Gerd Brenneis (Parsifal), Martti Talvela (Gurnemanz) and Janis Martin (Kundry) at the Deutsche Oper, Berlin, 1975. Opposite: Act I of August Everding's production, designed by Ernst Fuchs at the Staatsoper, Hamburg, in 1976.

Overleaf: Karajan's 1980 production of PARSIFAL at the Salzburg Easter Festival was revived the following year: this scene shows the forest, designed by Günther Schneider-Siemssen.

the Grail scene during which the "space-ship" peels open to form a mirrored dome.'

At the Deutsche Oper, Berlin, in 1975, Filippo Sanjust as director, stage designer and costume designer placed an Appia- and Wieland Wagner-like emphasis on lighting, with constant changes in the intensity of the light, but to considerably less effect than had been achieved by Wieland's intense discipline of the imagination at Bayreuth. Götz Friedrich and his designer Gunther Uecker staged a *Parsifal* in Stuttgart in 1976 with neon lighting and abstract sets which effectively drained Wagner's *Bühnenweihfestspiel* of most of its qualities. The scenery was almost geometrically stylized, with white poles to represent trees and the acting area surmounted by a huge, mirror-glass ceiling. A desperate poverty of the imagination lay like a shroud over the entire enterprise.

Worse, however, was to come. Covent Garden in 1979 engaged as producer of *Parsifal* someone from the dramatic theatre who had never seen a Wagner opera, let alone *Parsifal*. This 'pure fool' proceeded to divert attention from his inexperience and lack of ideas relevant to the work by extracting from his designer sets which were both ugly and impractical, and by directing his performers as though they were acting in a play by Galsworthy. Critical response was unanimously unfavourable, and a reader of *Opera* was moved to write a letter of protest. He could tolerate the furry logs and the *al fresco* celebration of the ceremony of the Grail, but 'the masks worn by the knights (reminiscent of *Ballo in maschera* or even *Die Fledermaus*), the unsuitably clad chorus and the nightclub hostesses who accompanied Kundry in the second act were a positive deterrent to enjoyment of the opera'. He ended with the suggestion that the Covent Garden management take a sabbatical and 'scour the world for reliable

and experienced producers and designers for Wagner operas'.

At Salzburg in 1980, Herbert von Karajan as director (though perhaps not as conductor, for his reading of the score was curiously cold-hearted – at least by the time it was committed to record) came close to perfection, aided by the redoubtable Günther Schneider-Siemssen as designer. The myth was humanized again, the settings were both beautiful and appropriate, and the drama was rendered faithfully.

The 1882 Bayreuth production by the composer was, unlike the 1876 Bayreuth *Ring*, exemplary. Clearly, future directors of *Parsifal* cannot be bound to it by fetters of the imagination, for the work must continually be subjected to re-interpretation. However, it would be as well for them to study the libretto carefully and in conjunction with the original designs before arbitrarily imposing their own ideas upon an opera which is probably not in need of such ideas.

Audiences used to be asked not to applaud at performances of *Parsifal*, it being widely held that the work was too sacred. However, the following note was printed in the 1967 Bayreuth programme book of the opera:

As many complaints have been made that a part of the audience attempts by hissing to prevent the applause after the acts of *Parsifal*, the Committee think it advisable to publish the wishes of the Master himself in this respect. The quiet finish of the first act precludes, of course, any applause; but the Master himself wished that after the second and third acts the audience might show their thanks to the artists by applause. The re-opening of the curtain has been arranged by the Master's desire, and it will, therefore, be continued.

Opposite: portrait of Wagner by Jager.

X
BIOGRAPHICAL DICTIONARY

Adam, Theo (b. Dresden, 1 Aug. 1926) German bass-baritone. He made his Bayreuth début in 1952, and sang his first important roles there in 1954, beginning with King Henry in *Lohengrin*. His other Bayreuth roles include the Dutchman, Amfortas and Hans Sachs. He made his first appearance at Covent Garden in 1967 as Wotan, and his first appearance at the Metropolitan Opera as Hans Sachs in 1963. Since the retirement of Hans Hotter (q.v.), Adam has been regarded as the leading Wotan and Sachs. He is an intelligent artist with a sympathetic, though less than ideally steady voice.

Alvary, Max (b. Düsseldorf, 3 May 1856; d. Grosstabarz, Thuringia, 7 Nov. 1898) German tenor. His most celebrated Wagner role was Siegfried in the third of the four *Ring* operas. It was in *Siegfried* that he made his American début at the Metropolitan Opera in 1887. He sang Tristan and Tannhäuser at Bayreuth in 1891 and, when in 1892 he made his London début in *The Ring*, conducted by Mahler, the order of the operas was changed so that Alvary could first be heard in his favourite role. He was the outstanding Wagner tenor of his day, and made a break with tradition by performing the heroic tenor roles without a beard.

Appia, Adolphe (b. Geneva, 1 Sept. 1862; d. Lyon, 29 Feb. 1928) Swiss stage designer and theatrical theorist. His ideas on stage design are set out in several books, the most important of which are *La mise en scène du drame wagnérien* (1895) and *Die Musik und die Inszenierung* (1899). He made his first sketches for a production of *The Ring* in 1892, after having visited Bayreuth and been appalled at the visual standard of the productions. In 1923, at the invitation of Toscanini (q.v.) he designed *Tristan und Isolde* at La Scala, Milan.

Austral, Florence (b. Melbourne, 26 Apr. 1894; d. Newcastle, NSW, 16 May 1968) Australian soprano. After study in Australia and the USA, Austral made her début with the British National Opera Company at Covent Garden as Brünnhilde in *Die Walküre*, and during the season added the role of Brünnhilde in *Siegfried* and *Götterdämmerung* to her repertoire. She was also a greatly admired Isolde. Possessor of a dramatic soprano voice of consistently beautiful timbre, she sang, mainly in Great Britain, until the outbreak of World War II. She also appeared in Berlin, where she survived comparison with the reigning favourite Brünnhilde, Frida Leider (q.v.).

Norman Bailey as the Dutchman.

Bahr-Mildenburg, Anna (b. Vienna, 29 Nov. 1872; d. Vienna, 27 Jan. 1947) Austrian soprano. She made her début in Hamburg in 1895 as Brünnhilde, and quickly became one of the leading Wagner sopranos of her time. Mahler (q.v.), who conducted the Hamburg performance, engaged her for Vienna where she remained until 1916. She excelled in all the great Wagner roles, including Kundry, which she sang in Bayreuth as well as Vienna. She sang Isolde and Elisabeth at Covent Garden in 1906. As a friend of the Wagner family, she often assisted Cosima Wagner (q.v.) with productions at Bayreuth. She was as renowned for the dramatic force of her interpretations as for the splendour of her voice. She married the Viennese author Hermann Bahr and was co-author with him of *Bayreuth und das Wagner-Theater* (1910).

Bailey, Norman (b. Birmingham, Warks., 23 Mar. 1933) English baritone. Brought up in South Africa, he studied there and in Vienna, and made his operatic début in Vienna in 1959. After performing with various provincial German companies for nearly a decade, he joined the Sadler's Wells Opera in London, and soon became renowned for his Wagner roles, the first of which was Hans Sachs in *Die Meistersinger*. He sang Sachs, Wotan and the Dutchman at Covent Garden, and was soon invited to appear at Bayreuth in most of the Wagner baritone repertory. It is Bailey's intelligence and humanity which make his Sachs and Wotan in particular such memorable interpretations.

Beecham, Sir Thomas (b. St. Helen's, Lancs., 29 Apr. 1879; d. London, 8 Mar. 1961) English conductor. The son of a wealthy industrialist, Beecham had no formal musical education, but acquired a practical knowledge of opera by travelling abroad and attending performances. In 1910, backed by his father, he mounted an opera season at Covent Garden, and during World War I launched the Beecham Opera Company. During the 'thirties he was chief conductor at Covent Garden, and was instrumental in introducing a number of distinguished international singers to London audiences. In the concert hall, he was renowned as a Mozart conductor. In opera, he favoured Strauss rather than Wagner, but was responsible for a fine *Meistersinger* at Covent Garden in 1951.

Berglund, Joel (b. Torsäker, 4 June 1903) Swedish bass-baritone. He was in demand in the Wagner roles in Europe and North and South America in the 'thirties, and in 1942 sang the Dutchman at Bayreuth. A versatile artist, Berglund was director of the Stockholm Opera from 1949 to 1952, and continued to sing until 1970.

Bispham, David (b. Philadelphia, 5 Jan. 1857; d. New York, 2 Oct. 1921) American baritone. He studied in Milan and made his opera début in London as Kurwenal in *Tristan und Isolde*. Joining the Metropolitan

Opera, New York, during the 1896–7 season, Bispham sang most of the Wagner baritone roles there and at Covent Garden. He was a staunch advocate of opera in the vernacular, and for many years gave recitals only in English, whatever the original language of the arias or songs he sang. His voice was powerful, with strong nasal resonance (something he appears to have passed on to his most famous pupil, the baritone Nelson Eddy). As Kurwenal and as Beckmesser, Bispham is said to have been the equal of any of his contemporaries.

Bjoner, Ingrid (b. Kraakstad, 8 Nov. 1927) Norwegian soprano. She studied in Frankfurt, and was engaged by Kirsten Flagstad (q.v.) for the Norwegian National Opera after a 1956 radio broadcast in which she had sung Gutrune in *Götterdämmerung* to Flagstad's Brünnhilde. She appears regularly in the Wagner dramatic soprano roles in Munich, and at Covent Garden has been particularly effective as Senta and Sieglinde. Her voice is both powerful and beautiful, and her performances have great intensity. She was much admired as Isolde in the hundredth anniversary performance of *Tristan und Isolde* in Munich.

Bockelmann, Rudolf (b. Bodenteich, nr. Lüneberg, 2 Apr. 1892; d. Dresden, 9 Oct. 1958) German bass-baritone. He made his début in Leipzig in 1921 as the Herald in *Lohengrin*, and remained with the Leipzig Opera singing leading roles until 1926. From 1928, he sang regularly at Bayreuth as the Dutchman, Gunther, Kurwenal, Sachs and Wotan. A dignified and authoritative artist with a rich, sympathetic voice, he was one of the finest interpreters of the role of Hans Sachs. His Nazi sympathies made it difficult for Bockelmann to resume his career after World War II, so he taught singing in Dresden.

Bodanzky, Artur (b. Vienna, 16 Dec. 1877; d. New York, 23 Nov. 1939) Austrian conductor. At the age of 18, he became a violinist at the Vienna Opera, and eight years later became assistant conductor there to Mahler. He conducted the first London performance of *Parsifal*, and the following year was appointed chief conductor of the German repertory at the Metropolitan Opera, New York. He made his American début with *Götterdämmerung*. Although he conducted a wide range of music, Bodanzky was best known as a Wagnerian. His heavily cut performances of the *Ring*, however, attracted criticism from the more fervent Wagnerians.

Böhm, Karl (b. Graz, 28 Aug. 1894; d. Salzburg, 14 Aug. 1981) Austrian conductor. After studying in Vienna, Böhm made his début in Graz, before being called to the Munich Opera by Bruno Walter, who was a strong influence on Böhm's Wagner interpretations. Böhm's operatic reputation was based on Wagner, Strauss and Mozart. Swift tempi and a skilful blend of sound characterized his performances of Wagner in Munich, Bayreuth and Vienna, especially of the *Ring* and *Tristan und Isolde*.

Böhme, Kurt (b. Dresden, 5 May 1908) German bass. He studied in Dresden, and was a member of the opera company there from 1930 to 1950, after which he joined the Bavarian State Opera. A beloved Baron

Ingrid Bjoner as Isolde.

Ochs in Strauss's *Der Rosenkavalier*, Böhme's Wagner roles included Hunding and Hagen, roles in which he was heard at Covent Garden between 1956 and 1960.

Brandt, Marianne (b. Vienna, 12 Sept. 1842; d. Vienna, 9 July 1921) Austrian mezzo-soprano. She studied in Vienna and in Baden-Baden with Pauline Viardot and made her début at Olmütz as Halévy's *La Juive*. She sang Waltraute in the first Bayreuth performance of *Götterdämmerung* in 1876, and Kundry in the second Bayreuth performance of *Parsifal* (1882), in which year she was the first London Brangaene in *Tristan und Isolde*, a role which she also introduced to Berlin and New York. Her extensive vocal range enabled her to sing both soprano and mezzo-soprano parts.

Branzell, Karin (b. Stockholm, 24 Sept. 1891; d. Altadena, Calif., 15 Dec. 1974) Swedish mezzo-soprano. After having been a member of the Stockholm Royal Opera and the Berlin Staatsoper, she came to the Metropolitan Opera, New York, as Fricka in *Die Walküre* in 1924, and sang such roles as Fricka, Brangaene and Waltraute with the Met until 1944. She also appeared at Bayreuth and Covent Garden in the 'thirties, and was a notable Kundry in Vienna.

Brilioth, Helge (b. Wäxjo, 7 May 1931) Swedish tenor. Originally a pianist, then a baritone, he made his début as a tenor in 1965. He first sang at Bayreuth as Siegmund in 1969, and subsequently added most of the other Wagner *Heldentenor* roles to his repertoire. He has sung Tristan, Siegfried and Parsifal at Covent Garden, and made his Met début as Parsifal in 1971. An intelligent artist and musician, Brilioth is in demand as a Wagner tenor and in recent years has turned to character roles in the operas of other composers.

Brouwenstijn, Gré (b. Den Helder, 26 Aug. 1915) Dutch soprano. Although she never specialized in Wagner, this distinguished singer whom London knew mainly as an intelligent and stylish interpreter of Verdi was greatly admired in Bayreuth in the mid-'fifties as Elisabeth, Gutrune, Eva and Sieglinde.

Jean Cox as Siegfried.

Buesst, Aylmer (b. Melbourne, 28 Jan. 1883; d. St Albans, Herts., 25 Jan. 1970) Australian conductor. His studies included a period in Leipzig with Nikisch. After engagements at German opera houses, he came to England, and became one of the founders of the British National Opera Company, many of whose performances, especially of Wagner, he conducted to great acclaim. He was the author of an excellent analysis, *Richard Wagner: the Nibelung's Ring: an Act by Act Guide to the Plot and Music* (1932; revised 1952).

Bülow, Hans von (b. Dresden, 8 Jan. 1830; d. Cairo, 12 Feb. 1894) German conductor. After initial musical training, he intended to take up the law as a profession, but was so overwhelmed by Liszt's production of *Lohengrin* at Weimar that he went to Zurich to study with Wagner. He married Liszt's daughter, Cosima, became in 1864 chief conductor at the Royal Opera, Munich, and there conducted brilliant first performances of *Tristan und Isolde* (1865) and *Die Meistersinger* (1868). When Cosima deserted him for Wagner, he left Munich to take up engagements abroad.

Bumbry, Grace (b. St Louis, Missouri, 4 Jan. 1937) American mezzo-soprano and soprano. After studying in Boston, she was taken up by Lotte Lehmann (q.v.), who coached her for some years and was responsible for her musical education at Santa Barbara. Bumbry changed to soprano roles after making her international reputation as a mezzo. Though not a Wagner specialist, she made an impressive Bayreuth début in 1961 as Venus, and was the first black singer to appear there.

Burian, Karel (b. Rousinov, 12 Jan. 1870; d. Senomaty, 25 Sept. 1924) Czech tenor. Known generally outside Czechoslovakia as Carl Burrian, he sang with the Prague National Theatre and then with the Dresden

Opera. In the years preceding World War I he was greatly in demand as a Wagner *Heldentenor* excelling as Tristan, Tannhäuser and Lohengrin at Covent Garden and virtually all of the Wagner tenor roles at the Metropolitan Opera, New York. He was praised for the golden quality of his tone and also for his electrifying dramatic ability.

CASSILLY, RICHARD (b. Washington DC, 14 Dec. 1927) American tenor. After studying in Baltimore and appearing in opera in the USA, Cassilly made his European début in 1965. He has sung such roles as Siegmund and Tannhäuser in London, Vienna, Paris and elsewhere, and is the possessor of a large, somewhat unwieldy voice and an impressive physical presence.

CHÉREAU, PATRICE (b. 2 Nov. 1944) French producer. He began his career as a director for the non-lyric theatre. When he leapt to international fame with his controversial production of *Der Ring* at Bayreuth in 1976, his only experience of producing opera had been with Rossini's *L'Italiana in Algeri* in Spoleto, and Offenbach's *Les Contes d'Hoffmann* at the Paris Opéra. A perfectionist, Chéreau has returned to Bayreuth from year to year to adapt and modify his *Ring* production.

COATES, ALBERT (b. St Petersburg, 23 Apr. 1882; d. Cape Town, 11 Dec. 1953) English conductor (and composer). Born in Russia of English parents, Coates was artistic director of the St Petersburg Opera for some years, after conducting a successful performance of *Siegfried* there in 1911. He had studied in Leipzig, and conducted there and elsewhere in Germany. He first appeared at Covent Garden to conduct *Tristan und Isolde* in 1914, and was also responsible for English-language performances of *The Ring* staged by the British National Opera Company in the 'twenties. At that time, he made recordings of excerpts from Wagner operas, mainly with British singers.

COATES, JOHN (b. Girlington, nr. Bradford, Yorks., 29 June 1865; d. Northwood, Middx., 16 Aug. 1941) English tenor. After

Marcelle Demougeot as Elisabeth.

beginning in light opera, he became known as a fine Wagner tenor. He was one of the best British Tristans and Siegfrieds, and sang these roles with success also in Germany.

COX, JEAN (b. Gadsden, Alabama, 14 Jan. 1922) American tenor. He studied in America and then in Rome, and made his début in opera in 1951. He first appeared at Bayreuth in 1956 as the Steersman in *Tristan und Isolde*, and became a sought-after Wagner interpreter in the 'sixties and 'seventies, appearing as Lohengrin, Parsifal, Siegfried, and Walther in *Die Meistersinger* in European and American opera houses. Though he may have lacked sufficient vocal stamina for Siegfried, he looked more convincing in the part than most of his rival tenors.

CRESPIN, RÉGINE (b. Marseilles, 23 Feb. 1927) French soprano. She made her Paris début as Elsa in *Lohengrin* and went on to become an admired interpreter of other Wagner roles as well, including Kundry, which she sang at Bayreuth in 1958, and Sieglinde. She was persuaded by Herbert von Karajan (q.v.) to undertake Brünnhilde in *Die Walküre* at Salzburg (1967), but this role proved too heavy for her vocal resources.

DALMORÈS, CHARLES (b. Nancy, 31 Dec. 1871; d. Hollywood, 6 Dec. 1939) French tenor. He made his stage début in Rouen in 1899 as Siegfried, and after making a special study of Wagner he sang Lohengrin in Bayreuth in 1908. He was admired in Wagner roles in America, as well as in Germany and Austria where he toured between 1908 and 1914, and was particularly successful in Chicago as Tristan.

DAMROSCH, WALTER (b. Breslau, 30 Jan. 1862; d. New York, 22 Dec. 1950) German-American conductor. His father, Leopold Damrosch, had conducted the first American *Walküre*. Walter was responsible for the American premieres of the other three *Ring* operas together with *Rienzi, Meistersinger* and *Tristan und Isolde*. With the Damrosch Opera Company, which he formed in 1894, he toured Wagner operas in the USA from coast to coast.

DAVIS, SIR COLIN (b. Weybridge, Surrey, 25 Sept. 1927) English conductor. Davis has conducted with great success a number of Wagner operas at Sadler's Wells Theatre and Covent Garden, as a consequence of having been music director of the two leading English opera companies. Though he came later to Wagner than, for instance, Mozart, of whose operas he is a leading interpreter, Davis has proved an impressive Wagner conductor, especially for the dramatic intensity and the well-judged and essentially non-ponderous tempi he brings to *The Ring*. He has conducted at Bayreuth with great success.

DEMOUGEOT, MARCELLE (b. Dijon, 18 June 1871; d. Paris, 24 Nov. 1931) French soprano. She sang Fricka at the first Paris Opéra performances of *Rheingold* and *Die Walküre* in 1909, and went on to become the leading French Wagner soprano of her generation, achieving her greatest successes as Brünnhilde, Elisabeth and Kundry.

DEMUTH, LEOPOLD (b. Brno, 2 Nov. 1861; d. Czernowitz, 4 Mar. 1910) Austrian baritone. He studied in Vienna, was engaged by Mahler for the Vienna Opera in 1898, and remained there until his death. Renowned for his Wagner performances, he sang Hans Sachs and Gunther at Bayreuth in 1899. He was the possessor of a voice of great beauty and was a fine musician as well.

DE RESZKE, ÉDOUARD (b. Warsaw, 22 Dec. 1853; d. Garnek, 25 May 1917) Polish bass, brother of Jean (q.v.). It was only late in a career based on Italian opera that De Reszke turned to Wagner. He sang such roles as Hans Sachs, King Mark and Hagen, at first in Italian and later in German, in London, Chicago and New York. His huge voice and stature made him an imposing Wanderer in *Siegfried*.

DE RESZKE, JEAN (b. Warsaw, 14 Jan. 1850; d. Nice, 3 Apr. 1925) Polish tenor, brother of Édouard (q.v.). He sang for some years as a baritone before being persuaded by his brother to re-train as a tenor. His early successes were in the French repertory, but he later turned to Wagner and in 1889 sang Walther in *Die Meistersinger* at Covent Garden with great success. He made his American début in Chicago in 1891 as Lohengrin, and then progressed to the heavier roles of Tristan and Siegfried. He was blessed with a superb voice, fine musicianship and a handsome stage appearance.

DERNESCH, HELGA (b. Vienna, 3 Feb. 1939) Austrian soprano. She studied in Vienna, sang small roles at Bayreuth in the mid-'sixties and scored a huge success as Eva at Bayreuth in 1968. For Herbert von Karajan at his Salzburg Easter Festival between 1969 and 1974 she undertook the heavier roles of Brünnhilde and Isolde. A beautiful woman with a rich and freely produced voice, she is perhaps more suited to the lyric-dramatic roles than to those she was persuaded to assume at Salzburg.

Jean de Reszke as Siegfried.

DE SABATA, VICTOR (b. Trieste, 11 Apr. 1892; d. Santa Margherita Ligure, 11 Dec. 1967) Italian conductor. De Sabata is one of that small group of Italian conductors who have distinguished themselves as much in Wagner as in the Italian repertory. After his performances of *Tristan und Isolde* at La Scala in 1930–31, he came to be regarded as an outstanding interpreter of that opera, which he conducted at Bayreuth in 1939. His incandescent performances of Wagner and Verdi were thought by many to equal those of Toscanini (q.v.).

DESTINN, EMMY (b. Prague, 26 Feb. 1878; d. České Budějovice, 28 Jan. 1930) Czech soprano. As much at home in Italian opera as in Wagner, Destinn was chosen to sing Senta in the first Bayreuth performance of *Der fliegende Holländer* in 1901. Greatly acclaimed in this role, she found herself much sought after by international opera houses as a result. In later years, she used exclusively the Czech form of her name, Ema Destinnová.

DOWD, RONALD (b. Sydney, 23 Feb. 1914) Australian tenor. An impressive and versatile dramatic tenor, Dowd sang a very large repertory of roles in Australia and Great Britain. He was a most poetic Lohengrin in Melbourne in the early 'fifties, and a memorable Walther in *Die Meistersinger* at his Covent Garden début in 1960.

DOWNES, EDWARD (b. Birmingham, Warks., 17 June 1926) British conductor. An experienced opera conductor who has avoided the dangers of specialization, Downes brings to his Wagner performances, especially to *The Ring*, a fresh, unteutonic and essentially lyrical style, and a regard for the voice which is not always met with in conductors too rigidly geared to the Bayreuth tradition.

DVOŘÁKOVA, LUDMILA (b. Kolin, 11 July 1923) Czech soprano. After studies in Prague, and appearances in Vienna and Berlin, she was engaged for Bayreuth, and between 1965 and 1971 sang Brünnhilde, Venus, Kundry and Gutrune there. In the same years, Covent Garden heard her as Brünnhilde and Isolde. Her exciting voice, attractive appearance and warmth of temperament more than compensated for a less than ideally secure vocal technique.

DYCK, ERNEST VAN (b. Antwerp, 2 Apr. 1861; d. Berlaer-les-Lierre, 31 Aug. 1923) Belgian tenor. He made his début in 1887 as Lohengrin in the first performance of that opera in France. The following year he was engaged to sing Parsifal in Bayreuth, and continued to appear at Bayreuth until 1912. Though he sang other Wagner roles, it was as Parsifal and Lohengrin (his two Bayreuth roles) that he was most admired.

EAMES, EMMA (b. Shanghai, 13 Aug. 1865; d. New York, 13 June 1952) American soprano. Possessor of a lyric soprano voice of pure and beautiful quality, Eames sang the Wagner lyric-dramatic roles such as Elisabeth, Elsa, Eva and Sieglinde with success, especially at Covent Garden and the Metropolitan Opera, New York. She was also admired in Mozart and Verdi.

Easton, Florence (b. Middlesbrough, Yorks., 25 Oct. 1884; d. New York, 13 Aug. 1955) British soprano. One of the most versatile sopranos of the inter-war years, Easton included Brünnhilde among her most successful roles. She sang Isolde at Covent Garden, Brünnhilde there, in Chicago and at the Metropolitan Opera, and made her farewell appearance at the Met in 1936 as Brünnhilde in *Die Walküre*.

Edelmann, Otto (b. Vienna, 4 Feb. 1917) Austrian bass-baritone. Edelmann sang Hans Sachs at the first two Bayreuth Festivals after World War II, in 1951 and 1952, and was also admired in this role in New York and at the Edinburgh Festival. He has sung both Gurnemanz and Amfortas in *Parsifal*, the former a bass and the latter a baritone role, and also numbered King Henry in *Lohengrin* among his Wagner roles. He was also a famous Baron Ochs in Richard Strauss's *Der Rosenkavalier*.

Elmendorff, Karl (b. Düsseldorf, 25 Oct. 1891; d. Hofheim am Taunus, 21 Oct. 1962) German conductor. A distinguished Wagnerian, he conducted at Bayreuth every year from 1927 to 1942, in which year he succeeded Karl Böhm (q.v.) as musical director at Dresden. He fostered a reciprocal interest in German and Italian opera by conducting Wagner at the Florence Maggio Musicale and elsewhere in Italy, and by introducing a number of Italian operas to German audiences.

Erede, Alberto (b. Genoa, 8 Nov. 1909) Italian conductor. One of the few really first-rate Italian conductors of Wagner, he made his opera début in Turin with *The Ring* in 1935. In 1968, with *Lohengrin*, he became the third Italian (after Toscanini and De Sabata, q.q.v.) to conduct at Bayreuth.

Ernster, Deszö (b. Pécs, 23 Nov. 1898) Hungarian bass. He made his Bayreuth début in 1931, and sang a number of Wagner roles at the Metropolitan Opera, New York, in the post-war years. He sang Hagen at Covent Garden in 1949 and 1954.

Ershov, Ivan (b. Novocherkassk, 20 Nov. 1867; d. Leningrad, 21 Nov. 1943) Russian tenor. After studying in Russia, he appeared in Italy and then returned to Russia where he appeared regularly between 1895 and 1929. As well as Russian and French roles, he sang several Wagner roles: Siegfried, Siegmund, Tristan, Lohengrin and Tannhäuser.

Evans, Sir Geraint (b. Pontypridd, 16 Feb. 1922) Welsh baritone. A lyric baritone, Evans has limited his Wagner roles to the Nightwatchman in *Die Meistersinger*, with

Ernest van Dyck as Lohengrin.

Kirsten Flagstad as Isolde and Max Lorenz as Tristan.

which he made his Covent Garden début in 1948, and Beckmesser in the same opera, of which role he was one of the leading exponents for many years. He is an accomplished actor, especially in comedy parts.

Everding, August (b. Bottrop, 31 Oct. 1928) German director and administrator. After several years as administrator of a theatre company in Munich, he became the Intendant of the Hamburg Opera in 1972, and of the Munich Opera in 1976. He directed Bayreuth productions of *Der fliegende Höllander* in 1969, and *Tristan und Isolde* in 1974, and is regularly in demand to direct opera.

Fassbaender, Brigitte (b. Berlin, 3 July 1939) German mezzo-soprano. Daughter of the lyric baritone Willi Domgraf-Fassbaender, she studied with her father in Nuremberg. She has been a member of the Bavarian State Opera since 1961 and also sings regularly at Salzburg Festivals. In 1973 she sang Fricka in *Das Rheingold* at the Salzburg Easter Festival, to great success.

Fassbender, Zdenka (b. Děčin, 12 Dec. 1879; d. Munich, 14 Mar. 1954) Czech soprano. She studied in Prague, and was a leading soprano in Munich from 1906 to 1932. Her dramatic voice and temperament suited her especially to the Wagner roles, and she was greatly acclaimed as Isolde, a role which she also sang in London under Sir Thomas Beecham in 1910 and 1913. At a performance of *Tristan und Isolde* in Munich in 1911 in which she was singing, her husband Felix Mottl (q.v.), who was conducting, collapsed and died.

Fischer, Emil (b. Brunswick, 13 June 1838; d. Hamburg, 11 Aug. 1914) German bass-baritone. He studied with his parents, both of whom were singers, and made his début in Graz in 1857. He was Covent Garden's Hans Sachs in 1884, and then went to the Metropolitan Opera, New York. He sang Sachs in the first American performances of *Die Meistersinger*, and was also the first American Stefano (in *Rienzi*), King Mark, Wotan (in *Rheingold*), Wanderer and Hagen. He settled in New York, and after retiring from opera became a teacher.

Fischer-Dieskau, Dietrich (b. Berlin, 28 May 1925) German baritone. Though not a Wagner specialist, or even primarily an opera singer, Fischer-Dieskau sang at the Bayreuth Festival, in 1954/5/6, as the Herald in *Lohengrin*, Kothner in *Die Meistersinger*, Amfortas, and Wolfram in *Tannhäuser*, scoring his greatest success as Wolfram. He has recorded the heavier Wagner roles, such as Wotan, for which his voice is not suited in the opera house, though he also appeared at the Deutsche Oper, Berlin, as Hans Sachs during the 1975–6 season.

Fisher, Sylvia (b. Melbourne, 18 Apr. 1910) Australian soprano. After studying in Melbourne, she took up a concert career, and did not make her professional opera début until she left Australia and went to London in 1949. She was Covent Garden's leading dramatic soprano in the 'fifties, her finest Wagner role being Sieglinde. She also undertook Isolde and Brünnhilde. She had a radiant soprano voice and a stage presence of great warmth.

Flagstad, Kirsten (b. Hamar, 12 July 1895; d. Oslo, 7 Dec. 1962) Norwegian soprano. Until her late thirties she appeared only in Norway and mainly in operetta and musical comedy. Engaged to sing small parts at Bayreuth in 1933, she progressed to Sieglinde and Gutrune the following year. This led to an engagement at the Metropolitan Opera, New York, in 1935, and it was her American performances as Sieglinde, Brünnhilde and Kundry which led to Flagstad's being recognized as one of the leading Wagner sopranos of her day, along with Leider and Lehmann (q.q.v.). In 1936 and 1937 she repeated her success at Covent Garden, as Isolde, Brünnhilde and Senta. She spent the war years in Norway with her husband, a Nazi sympathizer, and this led to difficulties when she attempted to resume her American career after 1945. She was, however, warmly received again at Covent Garden where she continued to sing her

Olive Fremstad as Kundry.

Wagner roles until 1951. Never a very exciting actress, Flagstad triumphed by virtue of the radiant splendour of her powerful voice.

Fleischer-Endel, Katherina (b. Mühlheim, 27 Sept. 1873; d. Dresden, 18 July 1928) German soprano. Although she sang at Covent Garden and the Metropolitan Opera, New York, her career was mostly based in Germany. At Bayreuth between 1904 and 1908, she appeared with success as Elisabeth, Elsa, Sieglinde and Brangaene.

Formichi, Cesare (b. Rome, 15 Apr. 1883; d. Rome, 21 July 1949) Italian baritone. He made his début in Milan in 1911, and sang at Covent Garden in the 'twenties and 'thirties. Outside Italy he was in demand for Verdi and Puccini, but in Italy he was also admired for his Wagner interpretations.

Frantz, Ferdinand (b. Kassel, 8 Feb. 1906; d. Munich, 26 May 1959) German bass-baritone. He made his début in Kassel in 1927 in the small part of Ortel in *Die Meistersinger*. In the 'thirties he sang in the German provinces, and was a member of the Bavarian State Opera, Munich, from 1943 till his death. After World War II, he was greatly in demand in the Wagner *Heldenbariton* roles, Wotan, Sachs and the Dutchman, but such was his range that he also undertook such unequivocally bass roles as Mark (in *Tristan*), Daland (in *Der fliegende Holländer*), the Landgrave (in *Tannhäuser*) and King Henry (in *Lohengrin*).

Franz, Paul (b. Paris, 30 Nov. 1876; d. Paris, 20 Apr. 1950) French tenor. He made his début at the Paris Opéra in 1909 as Lohengrin, and remained a leading tenor there until 1938, when he became Professor of singing at the Paris Conservatoire. He was the first Paris Parsifal in 1914. He was admired for his fine stage presence as well as for his large voice with its rich middle register.

Fremstad, Olive (b. Stockholm, 14 Mar. 1871; d. Irvington, NY, 21 Apr. 1951) Swedish-American soprano. Of illegitimate birth, she was adopted and taken to live in Minnesota. After studying in Minneapolis and New York, she went to Germany and made her début as a mezzo-soprano in 1895 in Cologne. She sang minor roles in *The Ring* in Bayreuth in 1896, and then assumed such roles as Ortrud, Venus, Isolde, Brünnhilde and Kundry, which she sang at Covent Garden, the Metropolitan Opera and elsewhere. At her farewell appearance at the Met, she sang Elsa, and was given nineteen curtain calls in a remarkable demonstration of audience affection.

Fretwell, Elizabeth (b. Melbourne, 13 Aug. 1923) Australian soprano. She made her début in Australia in 1947 as Senta, and was a leading soprano with Sadler's Wells Opera in London from 1955 until the mid-'seventies. She was not primarily a Wagner soprano, but was very much admired as Senta in London.

Frick, Gottlob (b. Olbronn, 28 July 1906) German bass. He made his début in Coburg in 1934 as Daland, was with the Dresden Opera throughout the 'forties, and subsequently became a member of the Vienna State Opera. Small of stature, he possessed a large, dark bass voice, which made him admirably suited to such roles as Hagen, Hunding, Daland and Fasolt. He sang these roles, and Pogner, until his retirement in 1970, not only in Vienna and Bayreuth but also at Covent Garden and the Metropolitan Opera. One of his most successful roles was Gurnemanz.

Friedrich, Götz (b. Naumberg, 4 Aug. 1930) German director. Assistant to Walter Felsenstein at the Komische Oper, East Berlin, from 1953 to 1962, Friedrich then succeeded him as director of the company. It was not until he was invited to direct *Tannhäuser* at the Bayreuth Festival of 1972, a production which ended irrelevantly and inappropriately with a clenched-fist salute from a chorus of modern workers, that he became thought of as a Wagner director. He was responsible for Covent Garden's new *Ring* production in the mid-'seventies, and was appointed director of productions of the Royal Opera. A committed Marxist, Friedrich's main interest in opera is in what he has referred to as its social relevance.

Fuchs, Marta (b. Stuttgart, 1 Jan. 1898; d. Stuttgart, 22 Sept. 1974) German soprano. One of the finest dramatic sopranos of her time, she sang Kundry in Bayreuth from 1933 to 1937, and gradually took over from Frida Leider (q.v.) the roles of Isolde and Brünnhilde between 1938 and 1942. She retired in 1945.

Furtwängler, Wilhelm (b. Berlin, 25 Jan. 1886; d. Baden-Baden, 30 Nov. 1954) German conductor. After the usual apprenticeship in provincial German theatres, Furtwängler came to prominence in Berlin and Vienna in the 'twenties and 'thirties, primarily as an interpreter of the symphonic repertoire, but also in opera. He conducted at Bayreuth for the first time in 1931 and during the Nazi era became Bayreuth's chief conductor. His spontaneous, highly individual interpretations of *The Ring* and *Tristan und Isolde* have been preserved on gramophone records.

Josef Greindl as the Dutchman.

Gadski, Johanna (b. Anklam, 15 June 1872; d. Berlin, 22 Feb. 1932) German soprano. After making her début in Berlin, she went to the USA where she became famous for her Wagner roles with the Metropolitan Opera, especially Elsa and Senta. In 1899 she sang Eva at Bayreuth. She brought an unusual purity of voice and style to Wagner, at a time when these qualities were rare outside the Italian repertoire.

Goodall, Reginald (b. Lincoln, Lincs., 13 July 1905) English conductor. After having been on the musical staff at Covent Garden for many years, during which time he was allowed to conduct only an occasional performance, Goodall suddenly became accepted as a major Wagnerian when he conducted *The Mastersingers* at Sadler's Wells Theatre in 1968. This led to his being invited to conduct the first Sadler's Wells *Ring*. He has also conducted *Tristan and Isolde* with great success, first for the Welsh National Opera and then, in 1981, for the English National Opera. His tempi are generally spacious: in this he is the opposite of Karl Böhm (q.v.).

Gorr, Rita (b. Zelzaete, 18 Feb. 1926) Belgian mezzo-soprano. She made her début in Antwerp in 1949 as Fricka, a role she subsequently sang at Bayreuth in 1958. Her other Wagner roles were Ortrud and Kundry.

Graf, Herbert (b. Vienna, 10 Apr. 1904; d. Geneva, 5 Apr. 1973) Austrian (later naturalized American) director. Son of the Viennese music critic Max Graf, he studied in Vienna. He worked as a director in German theatres but emigrated to America during the Hitler years, and directed productions first for the Philadelphia Opera and then for the Metropolitan Opera. After the war he returned to Europe and worked in Switzerland. As a Wagner director, he is remembered for his Salzburg production of *Die Meistersinger* in 1936, conducted by Toscanini, and for his Covent Garden *Parsifal* in 1958.

Greindl, Josef (b. Munich, 23 Dec. 1912) German bass. After studying in Munich, he made his début in Krefeld as Hunding in 1936. His first Bayreuth appearance was as

Pogner in 1943. He sang leading bass roles at Bayreuth from its re-opening in 1951 until 1970. He also sang the baritone role of Hans Sachs at Bayreuth. In 1973 he became a professor at the Vienna Hochschule für Musik.

Grob-Prandl, Gertrud (b. Vienna, 11 Nov. 1917) Austrian soprano. She studied in Vienna and was a leading dramatic soprano at the Vienna State Opera from 1947 till 1964. She was noted for her Brünnhilde, Isolde and Ortrud.

Grümmer, Elisabeth (b. Niederjeutz, 31 Mar. 1911) German soprano. She made her début in Aachen in 1940 as First Flowermaiden in *Parsifal.* A lyric soprano, she specialized in Mozart and Strauss and the lyrical Wagner roles such as Eva and Elsa. She sang both these roles in Bayreuth, and was a very effective and moving Elsa.

Gudehus, Heinrich (b. Altenhagen, 30 Mar. 1845; d. Dresden, 9 Oct. 1909) German tenor. One of the second generation of Wagner tenors, he was leading tenor at Dresden from 1880 to 1890, making his début there as Lohengrin. During the 1880s he was at Bayreuth where, in 1882, he sang *Parsifal* at the second performance and also appeared as Tristan (1886) and Walther (1888). He was Covent Garden's first Tristan and Walther, and sang in the first London *Parsifal*, which was a concert performance held at the Royal Albert Hall in 1884.

Gura, Eugen (b. Pressern, 8 Nov. 1842; d. Aufkirchen, 26 Aug. 1906) German bass-baritone. He created the roles of Donner and Gunther in the first complete performance of *The Ring* at Bayreuth in 1876, and returned there to sing Amfortas, King Mark and Hans Sachs in the 1880s. He made his London début at Drury Lane in *Der fliegende Holländer* in May 1882, and the following week sang Hans Sachs and King Mark in the first London performances of *Die Meistersinger* and *Tristan und Isolde.* His voice was really baritone (he was a noted Wolfram), but he had no difficulty in encompassing most bass roles.

Hans Hotter as Wotan.

Hafgren, Lily (b. Stockholm, 7 Oct. 1884; d. Berlin, 27 Feb. 1965) Swedish soprano. She began her career as a pianist. When Wagner's son Siegfried heard her sing, he advised her to become a professional singer. She made her Bayreuth début in 1908 as Freia, and went on to sing Eva, Isolde and Brünnhilde.

Hall, Sir Peter (b. Bury St Edmunds, Suffolk, 22 Nov. 1930) English director. The director of Great Britain's National Theatre, Peter Hall has also made a reputation as a director of opera, principally at Glyndebourne and Covent Garden. His *Tristan und Isolde* in 1971 at Covent Garden was intended to inaugurate his appointment there as co-director, but he resigned almost immediately, finding the routine of opera house administration irksome and the 'star system' uncongenial. He was engaged to direct the Bayreuth production of *The Ring* in 1983, on the occasion of the hundredth anniversary of the death of Wagner.

Harper, Heather (b. Belfast, 8 May 1930) Irish soprano. She studied in London, and sang frequently at Covent Garden in the 'sixties and 'seventies. Her only two Wagner roles of any importance were Eva and Elsa. Her Eva at Covent Garden under Josef Krips (q.v.) was praised by the conductor himself, who thought her the finest Elsa he had worked with since Lotte Lehmann; her Elsa was admired at Bayreuth in 1967 and 1968.

Harshaw, Margaret (b. Narberth, Penn., 12 May 1912) American soprano, originally mezzo-soprano. After singing at the Metropolitan Opera, New York, from 1942 to 1950 as a mezzo, she undertook the roles of Senta (1951) and the *Götterdämmerung* Brünnhilde (1952) and established herself as a leading Wagner soprano. She sang Brünnhilde in *The Ring* at Covent Garden for three seasons from 1953 to 1956 and again in 1960. She retired in 1964 to teach in Bloomington, but came out of retirement to sing Brünnhilde there in 1970.

Hartmann, Rudolf (b. Ingolstadt, 11 Oct. 1900) German director and administrator. He spent most of his working life in Munich, but has directed operas throughout Europe. A traditional director, he was responsible for an excellent *Ring* at Covent Garden in 1954.

Helm, Anny (b. Vienna, 20 July 1903) Austrian soprano. She studied in Vienna, sang Brangaene and Venus at Bayreuth between 1927 and 1931, and was heard at Covent Garden as Venus in 1939. Her repertory also included Brünnhilde and Isolde.

Hertz, Alfred (b. Frankfurt, 15 July 1872; d. San Francisco, 17 Apr. 1942) German (later naturalized American) conductor. After working in Germany, he went to the Metropolitan Opera, New York, in 1902, and conducted the first American *Parsifal* in 1903. This so infuriated Wagner's widow, Cosima, who had forbidden performances of *Parsifal* outside Bayreuth, that Hertz was unable ever to appear again in a German opera house.

Herz, Joachim (b. Dresden, 14 June 1924) German director. After working as an assistant to Felsenstein in East Berlin in the mid-'fifties, Herz became director of the Leipzig Opera, and also began to accept

Walter Hyde as Siegmund.

engagements abroad. He directed a film version of *Der fliegende Holländer* in 1963.

Hoengen, Elisabeth (b. Gevelsberg, 7 Dec. 1906) German mezzo-soprano. She made her début in Wuppertal in 1933, and joined the Vienna State Opera in 1943. An impressive singing-actress, she was an especially imposing Ortrud.

Hoffman, Grace (b. Cleveland, Ohio, 14 Jan. 1925) American mezzo-soprano. She studied in New York with Friedrich Schorr (q.v.), and made her début in 1951. From 1957 to 1970 she was regularly heard at Bayreuth as Brangaene, Fricka and Waltraute. She also sang frequently in Vienna.

Hofmann, Ludwig (b. Frankfurt, 14 Jan. 1895; d. Frankfurt, 28 Dec. 1963) German bass-baritone. Between 1935 and 1955 he was heard frequently in Vienna and Bayreuth in the Wagner bass and baritone roles. In 1935, he sang King Mark in *Tristan und Isolde* in Salzburg, under Toscanini.

Holm, Richard (b. Stuttgart, 3 Aug. 1912) German tenor. A lyric tenor, Holm's Wagner roles were David and Loge. In 1953, he sang David at Covent Garden under Beecham, and returned to London as Loge in 1958–60 and 1964–6. He appeared in Vienna, Bayreuth and other principal opera houses, and was a member of the Munich ensemble from 1948 until he became a professor of singing at the Munich Hochschule für Musik in 1967.

Homer, Luise (b. Pittsburgh, 30 Apr. 1871; d. Winter Park, Florida, 6 May 1947) American contralto. Born Louise Beatty, she married the composer Sidney Homer. After studying in America and in Paris, she made her début in Vichy in 1898. She sang most of the leading Wagner contralto and mezzo-soprano roles, and was particularly admired as Ortrud. She had a long and successful career at the Metropolitan Opera from 1900 to 1929.

Hopf, Hans (b. Nuremberg, 2 Aug. 1916) German tenor. He sang at Bayreuth from 1951 to 1966, as Walther, Siegfried, Tannhäuser and Parsifal, and was also heard in the Wagner repertory at Covent Garden and the Metropolitan Opera. He was a useful rather than an especially noteworthy *Heldentenor*, but flourished at a time when the genuine article was difficult to find.

Hotter, Hans (b. Offenbach-am-Main, 19 Jan. 1909) Austrian bass-baritone of German birth. From 1940 until his retirement in the early 'seventies, he was a member of the Munich company, and also sang regularly in Vienna. He was a stalwart of the Bayreuth ensemble in the post-war years, and was that period's most notable exponent of the *Heldenbariton* roles. Vocally he had his superiors, but dramatically and interpretatively Hotter had no equals as Wotan, the Dutchman, Gurnemanz or Hans Sachs. A great favourite at Covent Garden, he directed a production of *The Ring* there, in 1961–4.

Hunter, Rita (b. Wallasey, Cheshire, 15 Aug. 1933) English soprano. She joined the Sadler's Wells chorus in 1954, and two or three years later graduated to leading roles.

Her first great success was as Senta. With her Brünnhilde in the English National Opera production of *The Ring* in the vernacular, she became recognized as a major Wagner singer, and began to receive invitations to sing abroad. Her first Brünnhilde in German was at the Metropolitan Opera, New York, in 1972.

HÜSCH, GERHARD (b. Hanover, 2 Feb. 1901) A lyric baritone who specialized in Mozart and Verdi, and a distinguished lieder-singer, Hüsch was acclaimed as an outstanding Wolfram at Bayreuth in 1930 and 1931.

HYDE, WALTER (b. Birmingham, Warks., 6 Feb. 1875; d. London, 11 Nov. 1951) English tenor. After beginning his career in musical comedy and operetta, he was engaged to sing Siegmund in an English-language *Ring* at Covent Garden in 1908 under Richter (q.v.). This led to his appearing regularly at Covent Garden until 1924. He also sang Siegmund at the Metropolitan Opera in 1909–10.

JADLOWKER, HERMANN (b. Riga, 5 July 1877; d. Tel Aviv, 13 May 1953) Latvian tenor. He studied in Vienna, and began his career in the provincial German theatres, graduating to Berlin in 1907. Between 1910 and 1913 he also sang in Boston and New York. The creator of Bacchus in Strauss's *Ariadne* at Stuttgart in 1912, his Wagnerian roles included Lohengrin and Parsifal. Jadlowker was admired especially for his technique. After 1929, he returned to Riga as chief cantor in the synagogue, and in 1938 emigrated to Tel Aviv where he taught singing.

JANOWITZ, GUNDULA (b. Berlin, 2 Aug. 1937) German soprano. A discovery of Herbert von Karajan, she began her career in Vienna in 1960, in which year she also made her Bayreuth début. She was chosen by Karajan to sing Sieglinde at Salzburg in 1967, and was enthusiastically received in the same role in 1967 in New York. Possessor of a rich, strong voice, she is an impressive Elisabeth in *Tannhäuser*.

JANSSEN, HERBERT (b. Cologne, 22 Sept. 1895; d. New York, 2 June 1965) German baritone. He made his début in Berlin in 1924, sang for the first time at Covent Garden two years later, and was a popular favourite in London for most seasons until 1939, when he went to live in America, and sang at the Metropolitan Opera regularly until 1951. The Wagner roles in which his warm lyric baritone was most admired in Bayreuth, as well as London and New York, were Amfortas, Wolfram, Gunther and Kurwenal.

Siegfried Jerusalem as Parsifal.

JERITZA, MARIA (b. Brno, 6 Oct. 1887) Czech soprano. After her first appearance in Vienna in 1911, she became a great favourite with Viennese audiences. She sang there until the Anschluss and again after the war. She created roles in two Strauss operas. Her most successful Wagner role was Elsa.

JERUSALEM, SIEGFRIED (b. Oberhausen, 1940) German tenor. He studied violin, piano and bassoon in Essen, and began his professional career as a bassoonist in the Swabian Symphony Orchestra. He began to study singing in 1972, and in 1975 was engaged by the Stuttgart Opera. Jerusalem made his

Bayreuth début in relatively small parts in 1977, achieved his first big success as a Wagner tenor with the role of Lohengrin in 1978 in Hanover and Munich, and the following year was acclaimed as Parsifal, first in Vienna and then at Bayreuth. Now regarded as one of the leading Wagner tenors, although his voice is essentially lyrical rather than heroic, he made his Metropolitan Opera début as Lohengrin in 1980.

JONES, GWYNETH (b. Pontnewynydd, 7 Nov. 1936) Welsh soprano. She began her career as a mezzo, but quite soon switched to soprano roles. Her London début was as Leonora in Verdi's *Il trovatore*, but her successes in Wagner roles in Bayreuth and Vienna led to her being invited to sing elsewhere primarily as a Wagner specialist. Her Wagner roles include Sieglinde, Senta, Kundry, Venus and Elisabeth. She has also sung Brünnhilde, although the role is thought by some critics to be too heavily dramatic for her voice. An exciting performer, she possesses an impulsively generous and sympathetic stage personality.

KAPPEL, GERTRUD (b. Halle, 1 Sept. 1884; d. Munich, 3 Apr. 1971) German soprano. She studied piano with Nikisch, and made her singing début in 1906 in Hanover. In the 'twenties and mid-'thirties, in New York as well as in German theatres, she was highly regarded as a Wagner dramatic soprano, and was thought by many to be superior to Frida Leider (q.v.) and Kirsten Flagstad (q.v.). Her finest roles were Brünnhilde and Isolde.

KARAJAN, HERBERT VON (b. Salzburg, 5 Apr. 1908) Austrian conductor and producer. After studying in Salzburg and Vienna, Karajan made his début in Salzburg at the age of nineteen, conducting *Fidelio*. His career until the outbreak of World War II was mainly in Germany; later, though he became the conductor of the Berlin Philharmonic Orchestra, he also assumed a leading role in Salzburg, not only in the summer festival, but also in the Easter Festival which he himself founded in 1963, for the purpose of presenting the operas of Wagner in Salzburg under the finest conditions. Though his interpretations have aroused controversy, in purely musical terms Karajan can have few equals as a conductor.

Ernst Kraus as Siegfried.

KEMPE, RUDOLF (b. Niederpoyritz, 14 June 1910; d. Zurich, 11 May 1976) German conductor. He studied in Dresden with Fritz Busch, and made his début as a conductor in Leipzig. After World War II, he began to be known internationally, especially in the operas of Strauss and Wagner. He conducted the 1960 production of the *Ring* at Bayreuth, and *Lohengrin* there in 1967. At Covent Garden, his interpretation of the *Ring*, more lyrical, less grandiose than that of many other conductors, was greatly appreciated.

KIPNIS, ALEXANDER (b. Zhitomir, 13 Feb. 1891; d. Westport, Conn., 14 May 1978) Russian bass. He studied in Warsaw and Berlin, and made his début in Hamburg in 1915. Until 1933, he was a leading bass in German opera houses, distinguishing himself especially in such Wagner roles as Gurnemanz, Hagen and Mark. He sang at Bayreuth from 1927 to 1933, and frequently at the Metropolitan Opera after he emigrated to the USA in the latter year.

KLEIN, PETER (b. Zündorf, 25 Jan. 1907) German tenor. He specialized in '*Spieltenor*' or second-tenor roles, and sang in German houses, at Covent Garden and the Metropolitan Opera regularly until the mid-'sixties. His two important Wagner roles were Mime in *Rheingold* and *Siegfried* and David in *Die Meistersinger*.

KLEMPERER, OTTO (b. Breslau, 14 May 1885; d. Zurich, 6 July 1973) German conductor. One of the last of the great conductors of his generation, Klemperer conducted at a number of provincial German houses before becoming music director at the Kroll Opera, Berlin, in 1927. Forced to leave Germany in 1933, he went to America, and conducted little opera thereafter except for a period in Budapest from 1947 to 1950, and at Covent Garden in the early 'sixties. A superb Wagner conductor, his *Lohengrin* at Covent Garden was vitiated by a poor stage production.

KLOSE, MARGARETE (b. Berlin, 6 Aug. 1902; d. Berlin, 14 Dec. 1965) German mezzo-soprano. Though she occasionally sang elsewhere, most of Klose's career was in Berlin, where she was regarded as one of the most distinguished singers of a first-rate ensemble, and especially admired in Wagner and Verdi. She was a very effective Brangaene and a memorable Fricka.

KNAPPERTSBUSCH, HANS (b. Elberfeld, 12 Mar. 1888; d. Munich, 25 Oct. 1965) German conductor. Appointed General Music Director at Munich in 1922, he left in 1936 under pressure from the Nazis, and conducted at the Vienna Opera from 1936 to 1950, after which he became a mainstay of the new Bayreuth ensemble. He excelled in the operas of Wagner, and his *Parsifal* is generally considered to be one of the finest interpretations of the work in living memory.

KOLLO, RENÉ (b. Berlin, 20 Nov. 1937) German tenor. The son of an operetta composer, he made his début as a pop singer,

René Kollo as Lohengrin.

turning to opera in 1965. He specializes in the Wagner operas, and has sung most of the leading tenor roles at Bayreuth and elsewhere since 1969. Lohengrin, Parsifal, Walther and Siegfried are the roles with which he has been most successful, although his voice lacks the weight of the true dramatic tenor.

KONETZNI, HILDE (b. Vienna, 21 Mar. 1905; d. Vienna, 20 Apr. 1980) Austrian soprano. She remained a member of the Vienna Opera for most of her career, and was still singing, though in small roles, in her late sixties. A popular Viennese favourite, she had a beutiful voice and was especially successful as Sieglinde (often with her sister Anny as Brünnhilde).

KONYA, SANDOR (b. Sarkad, 23 Sept. 1923) Hungarian tenor. He studied in Budapest, and sang in a number of German companies in the 'fifties. His Bayreuth début was in 1958 as Lohengrin, his finest Wagner role.

KRAUS, ERNST (b. Erlangen, 8 June 1863; d. Waldstadt, 6 Sept. 1941) German tenor. A leading tenor in Berlin from 1898 to 1924, he appeared at every Bayreuth Festival from 1899 to 1909. His major roles were Siegmund, Siegfried, Walther and Erik (in *Die Meistersinger*). After his retirement in 1924, he taught singing.

KRAUSS, CLEMENS (b. Vienna, 31 Mar. 1893; d. Mexico City, 16 May 1954) Austrian conductor. He studied in Vienna, and conducted there and in major German opera houses. He gave the first performances of a number of Strauss operas, and was highly regarded in Wagner, especially for *Die Meistersinger* and *Tristan und Isolde*, both of which operas he conducted at Covent Garden in the 1950s.

KRAUSS, FELIX VON (b. Vienna, 3 Oct. 1870; d. Munich, 30 Oct. 1937) Austrian bass. He made his stage début as Hagen at Bayreuth, and appeared at Bayreuth for the following ten years as Gurnemanz, Mark, and the Landgrave. His wife, the contralto Adrienne Krauss-Osborne, also sang at Bayreuth

Lilli Lehmann as Isolde.

during the same period, as Erda and Waltraute.

KRIPS, JOSEF (b. Vienna, 8 Apr. 1902; d. Geneva, 13 Oct. 1974) Austrian conductor. He studied with Weingartner in Vienna, and began his career there at the Volksoper. From 1933 to 1938 he was a chief conductor at the Vienna State Opera until dismissed by the Nazis. He conducted the first opera performance in Vienna after the war in 1945. An outstanding interpreter of the Viennese classical repertory and of the operas of Strauss and Mozart, Krips also excelled in the middle-period operas of Wagner, *Der fliegende Holländer, Lohengrin, Tannhäuser* and *Die Meistersinger*.

KUNZ, ERICH (b. Vienna, 20 May 1909) Austrian baritone. He studied in Vienna, and has been a member of the Vienna State Opera since 1940. An accomplished comedian and the possessor of a warm, lyric baritone, Kunz made the Mozart roles of Leporello, Figaro, Guglielmo and Papageno his speciality. His one Wagner role of any importance was Beckmesser, which he sang with great success at Bayreuth as well as in Vienna. He also appeared with the Metropolitan Opera and other American companies. He is still active in Vienna.

LARSÉN-TODSEN, NANNY (b. Hagby, 2 Aug. 1884) Swedish soprano. She made her début in Stockholm in 1906, and was a leading soprano with the Stockholm Opera until 1933, first as a lyric soprano and later in dramatic roles. She specialized in Wagner, and sang at Bayreuth between 1927 and 1931, and also at Covent Garden and the Metropolitan Opera in the 'twenties. Her roles included Isolde, Brünnhilde, Kundry and Fricka.

LAWRENCE, MARJORIE (b. Dean's Marsh, Victoria, 17 Feb. 1909; d. Little Rock, Arkansas, 10 Jan. 1979) Australian soprano. After studying in Paris, she made her début in Monte Carlo as Elisabeth in *Tannhäuser*. She sang leading roles at the Paris Opéra, among them Brünnhilde and Ortrud, until 1938, after which she was engaged mostly at the Metropolitan Opera where she shared such roles as Brünnhilde and Isolde with Flagstad (q.v.). She was stricken with poliomyelitis during a performance of *Die Walküre* in Mexico City in 1941, after which she was unable to walk unaided. She continued to appear in concert performances of opera, and in recitals, and even sang Venus and Isolde in specially staged performances in which she was either not required to move (Venus) or was carried on and off the stage (Isolde). She possessed a dramatic soprano voice of great beauty and power, and would undoubtedly have been recognized as one of the great Wagner sopranos of the century had it not been for her illness.

Max Lorenz as Siegfried.

LEHMANN, LILLI (b. Würzburg, 24 Nov. 1848; d. Berlin, 17 May 1929) German soprano. She sang a Rhinemaiden, a Valkyrie and the Woodbird in the first Bayreuth *Ring* in 1876, and later became internationally known as a dramatic soprano in the Wagner operas. She sang Isolde under Hans Richter at Covent Garden in 1884, and was the first American Isolde and Brünnhilde in *Götterdämmerung*. In 1896 she returned to Bayreuth as Brünnhilde. She later became a distinguished teacher.

LEHMANN, LOTTE (b. Perleberg, 27 Feb. 1888; d. Santa Barbara, 26 Aug. 1976) German soprano. She studied in Berlin, and made her début in Hamburg. From 1914 to 1938 she was one of the most popular stars of the Vienna Opera. In Vienna, she sang a wide repertory which included French and Italian as well as German roles, but abroad she was known and admired chiefly for her performances in the operas of Strauss and Wagner. She created roles in three Strauss operas. Her Wagner roles were Eva, Elsa, Elisabeth and Sieglinde. After the Anschluss, she emigrated to America and sang at the Metropolitan Opera until 1945 and in recitals until 1951. From then until her death she taught, and was responsible for passing on her knowledge to a new generation of singers, several of whom are now internationally known.

LEIDER, FRIDA (b. Berlin, 18 Apr. 1888; d. Berlin, 4 June 1975) German soprano. After studying in Berlin and Milan, she made her début in Halle in 1915, as Venus. A leading Wagner dramatic soprano in Berlin in the 'twenties and 'thirties, she also appeared at Covent Garden during this period, and at Bayreuth. She sang in America, but restricted her appearances to Europe after 1934. She was a performer of great dramatic intensity with a beautiful voice, and was widely regarded as an outstanding Brünnhilde and Isolde.

LIST, EMANUEL (b. Vienna, 22 Mar. 1890; d. Vienna, 21 June 1967) Austrian bass. He began singing as a boy chorister in Vienna, and made his adult début there in 1922. He sang in Vienna, Berlin, Bayreuth and Covent Garden until 1933, in such roles as Hunding, Hagen, Pogner and King Mark. After the arrival of the Nazis, he went to America, and sang at the Metropolitan Opera until 1950. He possessed a voice of great richness and depth.

LJUNGBERG, GÖTA (b. Sundsvall, 4 Oct. 1893; d. Lidingö, 28 June 1955) Swedish soprano. She made her début in Stockholm in 1918 as Gutrune, was an admired Sieglinde at Covent Garden in the 'twenties and

Amalie Materna as Brünnhilde.

sang Isolde and Brünnhilde with success in New York in the early 'thirties. After her retirement she taught in New York for several years.

London, George (b. Montreal, 20 May 1920) Canadian bass-baritone. After beginning his career in America in 1941, in small roles in opera, and touring in concert groups and operettas, he auditioned for Karl Böhm in 1949 and was engaged for the Vienna Opera. In the 'fifties and early 'sixties he sang with success in Vienna, Bayreuth and New York such roles as the Dutchman and Amfortas. He was an impressive actor, with a rich and flexible voice. After retiring from singing, he became a director and opera administrator in America. In the 'seventies, he staged productions of *The Ring* in Seattle and San Diego.

Lorenz, Max (b. Düsseldorf, 10 May 1901; d. Vienna, 1975) German tenor. He made his début in Dresden in a small role (Walther von der Vogelweide) in *Tannhäuser*. From the late 'twenties until the end of the war, he sang in Vienna, Berlin and Bayreuth, and was generally regarded as one of the finest Wagner tenors of his day. He appeared at Covent Garden in 1934 as Walther (*Meistersinger*) and in 1937 as Siegfried and as Erik (*Holländer*).

Lubin, Germaine (b. Paris, 1 Feb. 1890; d. 27 Oct. 1979) French soprano. She sang at the Paris Opéra from 1914 to 1944, her great roles being Kundry and Isolde. She became the first French artist to sing these roles at Bayreuth, and appeared in them in London in 1939. As she had been found guilty of collaborating with the Germans, it became impossible for her to continue her career after the war.

Mahler, Gustav (b. Kalischt, 7 July 1860; d. Vienna, 18 May 1911) Austrian composer and conductor. As a young conductor, he gave a notable performance of *The Ring* in Prague in 1885. He was artistic director of the Vienna Opera for ten years from 1897 to 1907, during which time he staged and conducted a number of highly acclaimed opera productions, among them *The Ring* and *Tristan und Isolde*. He was the conductor of Covent Garden's first *Ring* in 1892.

Materna, Amalie (b. St Georgen, 10 July 1844; d. Vienna, 18 Jan. 1918) Austrian soprano. She began her career in Austria in operetta and light opera, but became Bayreuth's first Brünnhilde in 1876, and in 1882 its first Kundry. She also sang under Wagner's baton in concerts in London in 1877. She was Brünnhilde in the Metropolitan Opera's first *Walküre*, and was generally regarded as the finest Wagner soprano of her day. After her retirement, she taught singing in Vienna.

Maurel, Victor (b. Marseilles, 17 June 1848; d. New York, 22 Oct. 1923) French baritone. Although more famous for his Verdi roles, Maurel was Covent Garden's first Telramund (in 1875), Wolfram (1876) and Dutchman (1877).

Mayr, Richard (b. Henndorf, 18 Nov. 1877; d. Vienna, 1 Dec. 1935) Austrian bass-baritone. He is remembered most as a superb Baron Ochs in *Der Rosenkavalier*, but was equally renowned in his own day as Gurnemanz in *Parsifal*, and was successful in a number of other Wagner bass roles. He made his Bayreuth début in 1902, as Hagen.

Melchior, Lauritz (b. Copenhagen, 20 Mar. 1890; d. Santa Monica, 19 Mar. 1973) Danish tenor. He began his career in 1912 as a baritone, but made a second début in 1918 as a tenor, in the role of Tannhäuser. He became the leading Wagnerian heroic tenor of his time, singing at Bayreuth from 1924 to 1931, after which his base became the Metropolitan Opera, New York, where he continued to appear until 1950. He sang virtually all the leading tenor roles in Wagner, and appeared as Tristan more than 200 times. He had a large and ringing voice, of seemingly inexhaustible vigour, and an exuberant stage personality more fitted to the young Siegfried than to Parsifal, though he encompassed both roles with great success. Towards the end of his opera career, he appeared in a number of American films, in which he sang a wide range of music from opera to popular song.

Mödl, Martha (b. Nuremberg, 22 Mar. 1912) German soprano. She began to sing as a mezzo-soprano, but later added soprano roles to her repertory, and after 1950 sang only as a soprano. She was Kundry in the first Bayreuth post-war season in 1951, and later went on to sing Isolde, Sieglinde, Brünnhilde and Gutrune there. She had a warm and beautiful voice, and was an exciting and impulsive performer. In recent years she has sung small roles in Munich.

Mottl, Felix (b. Unter-Sankt-Veit, 24 Aug. 1856; d. Munich, 2 July 1911) Austrian conductor and composer. One of Wagner's assistants at the first Bayreuth Festival, he subsequently conducted there between 1888 and 1902. He edited the vocal scores of all of Wagner's operas for publication. In 1907 he became music director in Munich, and died there in 1911 while conducting a performance of *Tristan und Isolde*, in which his wife Zdenka Fassbender (q.v.) was singing.

Muck, Karl (b. Darmstadt, 22 Oct. 1859; d. Stuttgart, 2 Mar. 1940) German conductor. He conducted the first performances of *The Ring* in Moscow and St Petersburg in 1889, and was a favourite conductor at Bayreuth from 1901 to 1930. He was generally regarded as the finest *Parsifal* interpreter of his generation.

Birgit Nilsson as Isolde, for a festival performance of *Tristan*.

Neidlinger, Gustav (b. Mainz, 21 Mar. 1910) German bass-baritone. He studied in Frankfurt, and made his début in Mainz in 1931. Specializing in Wagner roles, among them Telramund and Alberich, he was a Bayreuth stalwart from 1952 to 1975, and also sang at Covent Garden and the Metropolitan Opera, New York.

Newman, Ernest (b. Liverpool, 30 Nov. 1868; d. Tadworth, 6 July 1959) English critic. He studied music and philosophy, and published his first book on Wagner, *A Study of Wagner*, in 1899. He was music critic of *The Manchester Guardian* from 1905 to 1919, and then, after a short spell on *The Observer*, became music critic of *The Sunday Times* from 1920 to 1958. Opera in general and Wagner in particular were his special loves; his *Life of Richard Wagner* is still regarded as the most authoritative in English, and his *Wagner Nights* is an extremely useful introduction to the major operas. He also translated most of Wagner's operas for performance in English.

Nilsson, Birgit (b. Karup, 17 May 1918) Swedish soprano. She made her début in Stockholm in 1946; it was after she sang Brünnhilde in Munich in the 1954–5 season that she quickly established herself as the major Wagnerian soprano of the time. She has sung Brünnhilde, Isolde and other roles in London, Vienna, Bayreuth, New York, and a number of other major opera houses. Her large, bright, seemingly inexhaustible soprano voice (with temperament to match) is more suited to the Valkyrie than to Isolde.

Nordica, Lilian (b. Farmington, Conn., 12 May 1857; d. Batavia, 10 May 1914) American soprano. She was the first American artist to be engaged at Bayreuth, where she first appeared in 1894 as Elsa. Later, she became a famous Brünnhilde and Isolde.

Jaro Prohaska as Wotan.

She was remarkable for being able to encompass roles as different musically as, on the one hand, the Wagner heroines, and, on the other, Verdi's Violetta or Gounod's Marguerite.

Ohms, Elisabeth (b. Arnhem, 17 May 1888; d. Marquardstein, Germany, Dec. 1974) Dutch soprano. She studied in Amsterdam and Berlin, and became known as a Wagner soprano in Munich, where she remained a member of the company from 1922 to 1936. She appeared at Covent Garden during this period as Venus, Ortrud, Brünnhilde and Isolde, and also sang at the Metropolitan Opera, New York. She was Bayreuth's Kundry in 1931, and was chosen by Toscanini to sing Kundry at La Scala.

Onegin, Sigrid (b. Stockholm, 1 June 1889; d. Magliaso, 16 June 1943) Swedish contralto, of German-French parentage. Possessor of a voice of enormous range and power, she was not a Wagner specialist but was heard to great effect as Fricka and Brangaene.

Osten, Eva von der (b. Insel, Heligoland, 19 Aug. 1881; d. Dresden, 5 May 1936) German soprano. Leading soprano at Dresden for a quarter of a century from 1902 to 1927, she was London's first Kundry, in 1914. Her farewell to the stage in 1927 was as Brünnhilde, with her husband, Friedrich Plaschke, as Wotan.

Perron, Karl (b. Frankenthal, 3 June 1858; d. Dresden, 15 July 1928) German bass-baritone. He made his début in Leipzig in 1884 as Wolfram, and sang at Bayreuth from 1889 to 1904 as Amfortas, Wotan, Mark and Daland. He also created roles in three operas by Strauss at Dresden.

Preetorius, Emil (b. Mainz, 21 June 1883; d. Munich, 27 Jan. 1973) German stage designer. He began his career as a book illustrator, but was recommended by Thomas Mann to Bruno Walter as designer for an opera in Munich. He became Bayreuth's designer in 1932, and designed virtually all the Bayreuth productions until 1941: *Der Ring, Meistersinger, Tristan, Lohengrin* and *Der fliegende Holländer*. He designed sets for *Der fliegende Holländer* at Covent Garden, twice: in 1937 and in 1950. An impressive, traditional designer, he was most highly regarded in Nazi Germany.

Albert Reiss as Hunding.

Prey, Hermann (b. Berlin, 11 July 1929) German baritone. Possessor of a most mellifluous baritone voice, heard at its best in ardently romantic roles, Prey's Wagner roles are few. He made a most impressive Bayreuth début as Wolfram in *Tannhäuser* in 1965, and in 1981 at Bayreuth added the role of Beckmesser to his repertory, again with great success.

Prohaska, Jaro (b. Vienna, 24 Jan. 1891; d. Munich, 28 Sept. 1965) Austrian bass-baritone. He was, as a child, a member of the Vienna Boys' Choir, and as an adult studied in Vienna. He was active at Bayreuth from 1933 to 1942, and continued to sing in Berlin until 1953. His most impressive roles were Wotan, Sachs, the Flying Dutchman and Amfortas.

Ralf, Torsten (b. Malmö, 2 Jan. 1901; d. Stockholm, 27 Apr. 1954) Swedish tenor. He studied in Stockholm, and made his début abroad, in Stettin. He was a leading tenor in Dresden from 1935 to 1944, and sang at Covent Garden both before and after World War II and at the Metropolitan Opera, New York, from 1945 to 1948. A dramatic tenor of style and musicianship, he was especially admired as Parsifal, Lohengrin and Walther.

Reinmar, Hans (b. Vienna, 11 Apr. 1895; d. Berlin, 7 Feb. 1961) Austrian baritone. He studied in Vienna and Milan. One of the finest singing actors of his day, he appeared mainly in Germany and Austria. At Bayreuth between 1939 and 1941 he sang Donner, Gunther and Amfortas.

Reiss, Albert (b. Berlin, 22 Feb. 1870; d. Nice, 19 June 1940) German tenor. He began his career as an actor, but at the age of 27 made his operatic début in Königsberg. He specialized in character roles not requiring beauty of tone. Engaged for the Metropolitan Opera in 1901, he remained there until 1920, and was thought to be particularly fine as Mime and as David.

Rethberg, Elisabeth (b. Schwarzenburg, 22 Sept. 1894; d. New York, 6 June 1976) German soprano. She studied in Dresden, where she made her début in 1915. A lyric-dramatic soprano with a voice of great beauty and purity, she sang both German and Italian roles, becoming as renowned for her Verdi as for her Strauss and Wagner interpretations. Her most successful Wagner roles were Elsa, Elisabeth and Sieglinde. She was a great favourite at the Metropolitan Opera between 1922 and 1942, during which time she was also occasionally heard at Covent Garden.

Richter, Hans (b. Györ, 4 Apr. 1843; d. Bayreuth, 5 Dec. 1916) Austro-Hungarian conductor. He studied in Vienna, and in 1866–7 assisted Wagner in making a fair score of *Die Meistersinger*. He was recommended by Wagner to von Bülow as chorus-master in Munich. In 1868 he even sang, at short notice, the role of Kothner in a Munich performance of *Die Meistersinger*. Richter conducted the first *Ring* at Bayreuth in 1876, and continued to conduct there until 1912. He was generally regarded as the leading Wagner conductor of the time.

RIDDERBUSCH, KARL (b. Recklinghausen, 29 May 1932) German bass. Since 1957, Ridderbusch has been greatly in demand for those Wagner roles in which he specializes: Fasolt, Hunding, Hagen, the Landgrave and Daland. He has also sung Hans Sachs. He has appeared at Covent Garden and the Metropolitan Opera as well as Bayreuth and the Salzburg Easter Festival.

RODE, WILHELM (b. Hanover, 17 Feb. 1887; d. Munich, 2 Sept. 1959) German bass-baritone. He made his début in Erfurt in 1908 as the Herald in *Lohengrin*, and sang at most of the leading European opera houses until the outbreak of World War II. He continued to sing in Berlin until 1944. He was considered by many to be the finest Wagner baritone of the inter-war period, his principal roles being Hans Sachs, Wotan and the Dutchman.

ROLLER, ALFRED (b. Vienna, 10 Feb. 1864; d. Vienna, 21 June 1935) Austrian painter and stage designer. His designs for operas produced and conducted by Mahler in Vienna were very much in advance of their time, but managed to find acceptance with the Viennese public and critics. His *Tristan und Isolde* designs were particularly admired.

ROOY, ANTON VAN (b. Rotterdam, 1 Jan. 1870; d. Munich, 28 Nov. 1932) Dutch bass-baritone. He made his début as Bayreuth in 1897 as Wotan, and was soon recognized as a leading Wagner interpreter. After he sang Amfortas in the 'unauthorized' New York *Parsifal* in 1903, Cosima Wagner banned him from Bayreuth from then on. He was thought to be the finest Sachs, Kurwenal and Wotan of his time, and was also an admired exponent of the title-role in *The Flying Dutchman*.

ROSWAENGE, HELGE (b. Copenhagen, 29 Aug. 1897; d. Munich, 19 June 1972) Danish tenor. He joined the Berlin State Opera in 1929, and remained with the company until 1944, distinguishing himself in Italian as well as German roles. His voice had a magnificent heroic ring, and it maintained its quality for a remarkably long period. In his sixties, Roswaenge was still appearing in Berlin and Vienna in leading roles. He was greatly admired at Bayreuth in the mid-'thirties as Parsifal.

RYSANEK, LEONIE (b. Vienna, 14 Nov. 1926) Austrian soprano. She studied in Vienna, and has been a leading soprano there since 1954. She is also popular at the Metropolitan Opera and in San Francisco. A lyric-dramatic soprano with a voice of rich beauty,

Leonie Rysanek as Senta.

she excels in Strauss and Verdi as much as in Wagner. At Bayreuth and elsewhere, she has been greatly admired as Sieglinde (many claiming her to be the finest Sieglinde since Lotte Lehmann), as Elsa, and as Senta.

Saltzmann-Stevens, Minnie (b. Bloomington, Indiana, 17 Mar. 1874; d. Milan, 25 Jan. 1950) American soprano. She studied in Paris, and made her début in London in 1909 as Brünnhilde in an English-language *Ring*. At Bayreuth, she was heard as Sieglinde and Kundry in the years before World War I, but her highly successful career was cut short by illness and she made no stage appearances after 1918.

Sawallisch, Wolfgang (b. Munich, 26 Aug. 1923) German conductor. General Music Director of the Bavarian State Opera, Munich since 1971, Sawallisch has appeared at Bayreuth with great success. He conducted new productions there of *Tristan und Isolde* (1957), *Der fliegende Holländer* (1959) and *Tannhäuser* (1961).

Scaria, Emil (b. Graz, 18 Sept. 1838; d. Blasewitz, 22 July 1886) Austrian bass. He created the role of Gurnemanz in *Parsifal* at Bayreuth in 1882, and was also a notable Wotan. He died insane.

Scheidemantel, Karl (b. Weimar, 21 Jan. 1859; d. Weimar, 26 Jan. 1923) German baritone. He made his début in Weimar in 1871 as Wolfram, and sang there until 1886, in which year he first appeared at Bayreuth. He was greatly admired at Bayreuth as Amfortas, Hans Sachs and Wolfram. He also wrote books on singing and translated opera libretti into German.

Schipper, Emil (b. Vienna, 19 Aug. 1882; d. Vienna, 20 July 1957) Austrian bass-baritone. After studying in Vienna, he made his début in Prague in 1904 as Telramund. He was said to excel in the Wagner baritone and bass-baritone roles. His wife, the mezzo-soprano Maria Olczewska, was also greatly admired in the Wagner repertory, especially as Fricka.

Schlusnus, Heinrich (b. Braubach, 6 Aug. 1888; d. Frankfurt, 18 June 1952) German baritone. Although Schlusnus made his début in Hamburg in 1915 as the Herald in *Lohengrin*, it was as Germany's leading Verdi baritone in the inter-war years that he was to become famous. However, he is also remembered for the *bel canto* approach he brought to the role of Wolfram in *Tannhäuser* at Bayreuth in 1933.

Schmedes, Erik (b. Gjentofte, 27 Aug. 1866; d. Vienna, 23 Mar. 1931) Danish tenor. He made his début in Wiesbaden in a baritone role, the Herald in *Lohengrin*, and sang as a baritone until 1897. His tenor début was as Siegfried. He was a member of the Vienna Opera from 1898 to 1924, and was one of the most admired artists in Gustav Mahler's team of singers in Vienna. His great roles were Parsifal and Siegfried. After his retirement in 1924, Schmedes taught singing in Vienna.

Schneider-Siemssen, Günther (b. Augsburg, 7 June 1926) German stage designer. He studied in Munich with Emil Preetorius (q.v.), and has been a leading designer in Vienna since 1962, and also in Salzburg where he has designed all of Herbert von Karajan's Wagner productions. His Wagner designs have also been seen at the Metropolitan Opera, Covent Garden and in many other leading opera houses. He combines the traditional approach of his teacher Preetorius with something of the theories of Appia, and is probably the finest designer of Wagner operas now currently at work.

Schnorr von Carolsfeld, Ludwig (b. Munich, 2 July 1836; d. Dresden, 21 July 1865) German tenor. The leading dramatic tenor of the Dresden Opera between 1860 and 1865, he was heard as Lohengrin by Wagner, who insisted that he create the role of Tristan in the Munich premiere performances of *Tristan und Isolde*. Shortly after the performances, Schnorr von Carolsfeld died of a heart disease, and it was widely believed that his life had been shortened by his having undertaken the strenuous role of Tristan. His wife, Malvina Schnorr von Carolsfeld, a Danish soprano, sang Isolde opposite him at the premiere.

Schoeffler, Paul (b. Dresden, 15 Sept. 1897; d. Amersham, Berks., 21 Nov. 1977) German baritone. He studied in Dresden and made his début there in 1925 as the Herald in *Lohengrin*. He remained a member of the Dresden company until 1938 when he joined the Vienna State Opera. He took Austrian nationality and remained with the Vienna Opera until his retirement in 1965. Schoeffler sang a wide repertory of Italian and French as well as German roles, but in the post-war period came to be regarded as the outstanding interpreter of the role of Hans Sachs. He sang at Covent Garden both before and after World War II and at the Metropolitan Opera, New York, in the post-war years.

Schorr, Friedrich (b. Nagyvárad, 2 Sept. 1888; d. Farmington, Conn., 14 Aug. 1953) Hungarian bass-baritone. He studied in Vienna, and made his début in Graz in 1912 as Wotan. In the 'twenties and 'thirties he was generally considered the most outstanding Wotan. He specialized in Wagner, and was a notable Hans Sachs and Dutchman. He did not sing in Berlin or Bayreuth after 1933, but continued to appear at Covent Garden and the Metropolitan Opera, where he made his last opera appearances in 1943.

Schramm, Friedrich (b. Frankfurt, 26 Jan. 1900; d. Basle, 29 Mar. 1981) German producer. He was active in a number of German theatres in the 'twenties and 'thirties, and after the war became Generalintendant at Wiesbaden from 1951 to 1962. He helped to build up Covent Garden's Wagner repertory with new productions between 1947 and 1951. His father, Hermann Schramm, was a well-known character tenor who had sung David in *Die Meistersinger* at Bayreuth in 1899.

Schröder-Devrient, Wilhelmine (b. Hamburg, 6 Dec. 1804; d. Coburg, 26 Jan. 1860) German soprano. She made a great impression on Weber when he conducted a performance of his *Freischütz*, in which she sang Agathe, and on Beethoven who rehearsed her as Leonore in his *Fidelio*. When the young Wagner heard her as Leonore, he wrote to her to declare that she had inspired him to become a composer of opera. In due course, she created the roles of Adriano in Wagner's *Rienzi*, Senta in *Der fliegende Holländer* and Venus in *Tannhäuser*. By all accounts, she was a great singing actress.

SCHRÖDER-FEINEN, URSULA (b. Gelsenkirchen, 21 July 1936) German soprano. After singing a variety of roles in Gelsenkirchen, she began to specialize in the Strauss and Wagner dramatic soprano roles, and since 1970 has been greatly in demand in Europe and America as Senta, Ortrud, Brünnhilde and Kundry, all of which roles she has sung at Bayreuth. She has a warm voice of great power, and a sympathetic stage personality.

SCHUMANN-HEINK, ERNESTINE (b. Lieben, 15 June 1861; d. Hollywood, 17 Nov. 1936) Czech contralto. At the turn of the century she was a leading exponent of the roles of Fricka, Erda and Waltraute, which she sang at Bayreuth, Covent Garden, and the Metropolitan Opera. She became an American citizen and remained with the Met until 1932, after which she made a new career in Hollywood films.

Astrid Varnay as Brünnhilde.

SEIDL, ANTON (b. Pest, 7 May 1850; d. New York, 28 Mar. 1898) Hungarian conductor. He helped Wagner prepare the score of the *Ring* for its first complete performance in 1876, and on the composer's recommendation was appointed chief conductor at Leipzig. He took a Wagner company on tour throughout Europe in 1883, with great success. He conducted the first American performances of *Meistersinger, Tristan, Rheingold, Siegfried* and *Götterdämmerung*, and *Parsifal* in Bayreuth in 1897.

SILJA, ANJA (b. Berlin, 17 Apr. 1940) German soprano. Greatly influenced by Wieland Wagner, with whom she had a close relationship, she sang in a number of productions at Bayreuth between 1960 and 1966. Her forceful acting as Senta, Elsa, Eva, Elisabeth, Venus and Freia was more generally admired than her singing, for her technique was imperfect and her emission of tone uneven. After Wieland Wagner's death she concentrated less intensely upon the Wagner roles.

SLEZAK, LEO (b. Krásná Hora, 18 Aug. 1873; d. Tegernsee, 1 June 1946) Austrian tenor. He made his début in Brno in 1896 as Lohengrin, and was one of the most popular members of the company in Vienna from 1901 to 1927. He had a large voice of unusual sweetness and a huge physique to match. Lohengrin was his major Wagner role, in which he was greatly admired. After his retirement from the stage, he wrote a number of books and also appeared in films.

SOLTI, SIR GEORG (b. Budapest, 21 Oct. 1912) Hungarian conductor. His international career began in Munich where he was music director from 1947 to 1952. He became music director of the Royal Opera House, Covent Garden, in 1961, and remained for ten years during which time he improved standards there. Although he does not specialize, he is generally thought to be one of the finest Wagner and Strauss conductors of the day, and perhaps less impressive in Italian opera and the classical symphonic repertoire. He conducted the first commercial gramophone recording of the complete *Ring* with the Vienna Philharmonic Orchestra, and is the conductor of the 1983 Bayreuth *Ring*, staged in commemoration of the one-hundredth anniversary of the death of the composer.

STOLZE, GERHARD (b. Dessau, 1 Oct. 1926) German tenor. He made his début in Dresden in 1949 in the small role of Moser in *Die Meistersinger*, and went on to specialize in character roles. He sang Mime and David frequently at Bayreuth in the 'fifties and 'sixties, and also appeared frequently in Vienna.

Sucher, Rosa (b. Velburg, 23 Feb. 1847; d. Eschweiler, 16 Apr. 1927) German soprano. She was London's first Isolde and Eva, and also sang Elsa, Senta and Elisabeth in London. She was active at Bayreuth between 1886 and 1894, and gave her farewell performance as Sieglinde in Berlin in 1903. Later, she taught singing in Vienna.

Suthaus, Ludwig (b. Cologne, 12 Dec. 1906; d. Berlin, 7 Sept. 1971) German tenor. He made his début as Walther in Aachen in 1928, sang mainly in Stuttgart throughout the 'thirties, and in Berlin from 1941 until 1965. His first Bayreuth appearances were in 1943, and he was heard in Vienna, London and New York after the war. An impressive Tristan and Siegmund, he was greatly admired by Furtwängler, who chose Suthaus for his recording of *Tristan und Isolde* with Flagstad in 1958.

Svanholm, Set (b. Västeras, 2 Sept. 1904; d. Stockholm, 4 Oct. 1964) Swedish tenor. Like Lauritz Melchior, he sang as a baritone for several years before retraining as a tenor. His first Wagner roles were Lohengrin and Siegmund in 1937. He sang in Salzburg, Vienna and Bayreuth during the war, and then appeared abroad with great success at Covent Garden and the Metropolitan Opera until the mid-'fifties, during which time he was recognized as the leading Tristan and Siegfried. In 1956 he became the Intendant of the Stockholm Opera.

Talvela, Martti (b. Hiitola, 4 Feb. 1935) Finnish bass. In the 'sixties he appeared at Bayreuth in most of the Wagner bass roles, among them Fasolt, Hunding, Hagen, Daland and Mark. He has also sung in Karajan Wagner productions at Salzburg, and was admired at Covent Garden as Gurnemanz. A tall and powerfully built man, he has a dark bass voice of unusual power.

Ternina, Milka (b. Vezisče, 19 Dec. 1863; d. Zagreb, 18 May 1941) Croatian soprano. At the turn of the century she was one of the leading dramatic sopranos. She sang Kundry at Bayreuth in 1899, but when she appeared in the same role in the 'unauthorized' New York *Parsifal* of 1903, Cosima Wagner banished her from Bayreuth. Possessor of a beautiful voice and a fine dramatic intelligence, she was considered the finest Isolde of her day. She was forced by paralysis to retire in 1916.

Thomas, Jess (b. Hot Springs, S. Dakota, 4 Aug. 1927) American tenor. He began his international career in the late 'fifties, and sang frequently in Bayreuth, Munich and Vienna in the 'sixties and early 'seventies. His fine physique and intelligent artistry as much as his natural vocal resources led to his success in several of the Wagner roles, especially Walther and Tristan. He first appeared at the Metropolitan Opera in 1963, and was Tristan in Peter Hall's 1971 production of *Tristan und Isolde* at Covent Garden.

Thorborg, Kerstin (b. Venjan, 19 May 1896; d. Dalarna, 12 Apr. 1970) Swedish mezzo-soprano. She sang throughout Europe in the 'thirties (and at the Metropolitan Opera until 1950) and was much admired as Ortrud, Fricka, Brangaene and Kundry. Ernest Newman considered her the greatest Wagner mezzo he had heard.

Tichatschek, Joseph (b. Teplice, 11 July 1807; d. Dresden, 18 Jan. 1886) Czech tenor. He was greatly admired by Wagner, and created the title-roles of *Rienzi* (1842) and *Tannhäuser* (1845).

Tietjen, Heinz (b. Tangier, 24 June 1881; d. Baden-Baden, 30 Nov. 1967) German conductor and producer. In charge of all German theatres from 1927 to 1945, and artistic director at Bayreuth from 1931 to 1944, Tietjen was responsible for most Bayreuth productions during that period, and also conducted *Der Ring*, *Die Meistersinger* and *Lohengrin*. His productions were lavish and traditional. He worked as a producer at Covent Garden after the war, staging *Der fliegende Holländer* in 1950 and *Parsifal* and *Die Meistersinger* the following year. In 1958, he combined with Wieland Wagner in a production of *Lohengrin* at Hamburg, which he conducted and Wagner staged.

Toscanini, Arturo (b. Parma, 25 Mar. 1867; d. New York, 16 Jan. 1957) Italian conductor. Renowned principally for his conducting of the Italian operatic repertoire, especially Verdi and Puccini, and to a lesser extent for his performances of the classical symphonies, Toscanini was an admirer of Wagner, and introduced *Götterdämmerung* to Italy in 1896. He conducted *Tristan und Isolde* and *Tannhäuser* at Bayreuth in 1930 and '31, and was also responsible for Adolphe Appia's only Wagner staging, when he engaged the designer for *Tristan und Isolde* at La Scala in 1923.

Traubel, Helen (b. St Louis, 20 June 1899; d. Santa Monica, 28 July 1972) American soprano. She studied in St Louis and began her career as a concert singer. It was not until she was in her mid-thirties that she turned to opera. Her success as Sieglinde at the Metropolitan Opera in 1939, and the departure of Kirsten Flagstad in 1941, led to her becoming that company's leading Wagner soprano. She remained with the Met until 1953. She sang in Central and South America, but never in European opera houses. She was considered a fine Brünnhilde and Isolde. After leaving the Met, she continued to sing in concerts, and in night-clubs. She was also the author of two novels, both murder mysteries.

Treptow, Günther (b. Berlin, 22 Oct. 1907; d. 28 Mar. 1981) German tenor. He made his début in Berlin in 1936 as the Steersman in *Der fliegende Holländer*, and went on to become a leading Wagner heroic tenor of the war years and the following decade, appearing with great success in Vienna and at Bayreuth, the Metropolitan

Wieland Wagner.

Opera and Covent Garden. His finest roles were Siegmund and Siegfried in *Der Ring*, and Tristan.

Varnay, Astrid (b. Stockholm, 25 Apr. 1918) American soprano. Of Austro-Hungarian parentage, she studied with her mother, a coloratura soprano, and with Herman Weigert, whom she married. She made her début at the Metropolitan Opera in 1941 as Sieglinde, and remained with the company until 1956 as a leading dramatic soprano, specializing in the Wagner and Strauss repertory. She appeared frequently at Bayreuth between 1951 and 1968. With a fine voice and great acting ability, she was a strong rival to Flagstad. After the mid-'sixties, she began to concentrate on mezzo-soprano roles in operas by composers other than Wagner, though she remained a superb Ortrud for many years.

Veasey, Josephine (b. London, 10 July 1930) British mezzo-soprano. In the 'fifties, 'sixties and 'seventies she sang a number of Wagner roles at Covent Garden, among them Fricka, Waltraute and Venus. She was chosen by Herbert von Karajan to sing Fricka in his production of *Der Ring* which he conducted in Salzburg, Milan and New York.

Vinay, Ramón (b. Chillan, 31 Aug. 1912) Chilean tenor. He studied in Mexico and sang for five years as a baritone before making his tenor début in New York in 1943. He sang Wagner dramatic tenor roles at Covent Garden and Bayreuth in the 'fifties, and was also a superb Otello in Verdi's opera, in which he was coached by Toscanini. After 1962, he turned again to baritone roles, and sang Telramund at Bayreuth. After his retirement in 1969, he worked occasionally as a producer of opera. He had a voice of affecting quality, and was a most expressive actor.

Völker, Franz (b. Neu-Isenburg, 31 Mar. 1899; d. Darmstadt, 5 Dec. 1965) German tenor. He made his début in Frankfurt in 1926, without having had any formal vocal training, and in Vienna, Berlin and Munich in the 'thirties was highly regarded as a dramatic tenor with a voice of lyric beauty. He was Bayreuth's leading tenor between 1933 and 1942, appearing there as Siegmund, Lohengrin, Parsifal, and Erik in *Der fliegende Holländer*. After the war, he continued to sing in Munich until 1952, and then taught in Stuttgart.

Waechter, Eberhard (b. Vienna, 8 July 1929) Austrian baritone. He studied in Vienna, made his début there in 1953, and has been a member of the Vienna State Opera ever since. A fine lyric baritone in Mozart and Verdi, he scored a great success at Bayreuth with both of his Wagner roles, Amfortas and Wolfram, which he sang there between 1957 and 1963. Covent Garden audiences found him a moving Amfortas in 1959.

Wagner, Cosima (b. Bellagio, 24 Dec. 1837; d. Bayreuth, 1 Apr. 1930) The illegitimate daughter of Franz Liszt, she married Wagner in 1870, after her divorce from the conductor Hans von Bülow, and helped the composer to establish his Festival Theatre at Bayreuth. After Wagner's death, she continued to manage the Bayreuth Festival performances for several years, even after she had theoretically handed over control to her son, Siegfried (q.v.), in 1908.

Wagner, Johanna (b. Seelze, 13 Oct. 1826; d. Würzburg, 16 Oct. 1894) German soprano. Niece (by adoption) of Richard Wagner. She created the role of Elisabeth in *Tannhäuser* at the Dresden premiere in 1845. In 1861, her singing voice having deteriorated, she turned to the dramatic stage, but took up a singing career again when her voice returned. She sang a Norn and a Valkyrie in the first Bayreuth *Ring* in 1876.

Wagner, Siegfried (b. Triebschen, 6 June 1869; d. Bayreuth, 4 Aug. 1930) German composer and conductor. Son of Richard and Cosima Wagner, he conducted at Bayreuth from 1896, began to produce opera there in 1901 and was Artistic Director from 1908 until his death. He composed fifteen operas, twelve of which reached the stage but none of which aroused more than respectful attention.

Wagner, Wieland (b. Bayreuth, 5 Jan. 1917; d. Munich, 17 Oct. 1966) German producer and designer. Son of Siegfried Wagner, he studied stage design briefly with Alfred Roller in 1934, and designed *Parsifal* at Bayreuth in 1937. During the war years, he designed *Die Meistersinger* at Bayreuth, and produced operas, including a complete *Ring*, elsewhere in Germany. He and his younger brother Wolfgang were joint directors and administrators of the Bayreuth Festival when it was allowed to re-open in 1951. His own productions of his grandfather's operas at Bayreuth revolutionized the staging of those works in the post-war period. His son Wolf Siegfried is now active as a producer in Germany.

Wagner, Winifred (b. Hastings, Kent, 23 June 1897; d. Überlingen, 5 Mar. 1980) English opera administrator. Born Winifred Williams, she married Wagner's son Siegfried in 1915, and helped him to manage the Bayreuth Festival. On the death of both Siegfried (q.v.) and his mother, Cosima Wagner (q.v.), in 1930, Winifred assumed sole control of the Festival. An enthusiastic Nazi and a personal friend of Hitler, she cultivated the Führer as a friend of Bayreuth, and gained several advantages for the Festival during the 1933–44 period. After the war, her sons were allowed to re-open the Festival Theatre only on the understanding that their mother would not be involved in the enterprise.

Wagner, Wolfgang (b. Bayreuth, 30 Aug. 1919) German producer and designer. Though primarily active at Bayreuth as an administrator, Wolfgang also produced and designed some productions and, since his brother Wieland's death, has become more actively involved in production. He has produced and designed all of the Wagner operas from *Der fliegende Holländer* onwards.

Hermann Winkelmann as Walther.

Walker, Edyth (b. Hopewell, NY, 27 Mar. 1867; d. New York, 19 Feb. 1950) American mezzo-soprano. She studied in Dresden and Berlin, and made her début in Berlin in 1894. From then until the end of World War I, she pursued a distinguished career in Europe and at the Metropolitan Opera, New York. She sang Kundry and Ortrud at Bayreuth in 1908. Although most of her roles were those which a mezzo-soprano might be expected to undertake, she was also a greatly admired Isolde. She retired in 1918 and taught first at the American Conservatory at Fontainebleau and then, after 1936, in New York.

Walter, Bruno (b. Berlin, 15 Sept. 1876; d. Los Angeles, 17 Feb. 1962) German conductor. After conducting in a number of German cities he was taken up by Gustav Mahler, whose assistant he became in Vienna. He remained in Vienna from 1901 to 1912, and then became the artistic and administrative director of the Munich Opera, a post he held until 1922. He continued to be active, in Vienna and elsewhere, until the Anschluss, when he made his way to the USA, and conducted opera at the Metropolitan for many years. One of the great conductors of the century, noted for the warmth and humanity of his interpretations of the Viennese classics from Mozart to Mahler, Walter was also renowned for his Wagner performances. Covent Garden heard him in Wagner in the 'twenties, and he conducted a famous recording of the first act of *Die Walküre* (and parts of the second act: the political situation in Europe prevented his completion of the work) with Lotte Lehmann, Lauritz Melchior, and the Vienna Philharmonic Orchestra.

Ward, David (b. Dumbarton, 3 July 1922) Scottish bass. He studied in London, and later in Munich with the distinguished Wagner baritone Hans Hotter, and made his début at Sadler's Wells Theatre, London, in 1953. He soon established himself as a Wagner specialist, first with the Sadler's Wells company and later with the Royal Opera at Covent Garden, and was an impressive Dutchman and Wotan. At Bayreuth, 1960–62, he sang Titurel, Fasolt, and the Nightwatchman in *Die Meistersinger*. He was a sensitive artist, with a bass voice of fine quality.

Weber, Ludwig (b. Vienna, 29 July 1899; d. Vienna, 9 Dec. 1974) Austrian bass. He studied in Vienna, sang with various German companies until 1945, and then became a member of the Vienna Opera until his retirement in 1960. He was also heard at Bayreuth from 1951 to 1960. One of the finest basses of the century, particularly in such Wagner roles as Hagen and Gurnemanz, he was also an impressive Daland. After his retirement, he taught at the Mozarteum in Salzburg.

Windgassen, Wolfgang (b. Annemasse, 26 June 1914; d. Stuttgart, 8 Sept. 1974) German tenor. He studied with his father, the tenor Fritz Windgassen, and made his début in Pforzheim in 1941. His first important Wagner role was Siegmund in 1950. At Bayreuth, where he sang from 1951 to 1971, and elsewhere, he quickly established himself as the leading Wagner tenor of the time. Though his voice was somewhat light for the heroic tenor roles, he succeeded in them by virtue of his musicianship and technique. Windgassen's repertory included Parsifal, Siegmund, Siegfried, Loge, Lohengrin, Tannhäuser, Erik, Walther and Tristan.

Winkelmann, Hermann (b. Brunswick, 8 Mar. 1849; d. Vienna, 18 Jan. 1912) German tenor. His performances as Lohengrin and Tannhäuser in Vienna were so successful that they were brought to the attention of Wagner, at whose invitation he created the role of Parsifal in the Bayreuth premiere of that opera in 1882. He also sang Walther and Tannhäuser in Bayreuth, and appeared as London's first Walther and Tristan.

Wolff, Fritz (b. Munich, 28 Oct. 1894; d. Munich, 18 Jan. 1957) German tenor. He made his début at Bayreuth in 1925 as Loge, and continued to appear at Bayreuth and other German theatres until the mid-'forties. He was a distinguished Lohengrin, Parsifal and Walther.

Zimmermann, Erich (b. Meissen, 29 Nov. 1892; d. Cologne, 10 Aug. 1970) German tenor. He studied in Dresden and made his début there in 1918. An experienced character-tenor and actor, he was active in German and Austrian opera houses and at Covent Garden until after World War II. He was considered one of the finest Mimes and Davids of the 'thirties and 'forties.

INDEX

Numbers in italics refer to captions

Adam, Theo, 194
Alvary, Max, 194
Appia, Adolphe, *80*, 89, 105, 156, 179–80, 188, 194
Arhus, Frl. von, *115*
Arnold, Heinz, *24*, 26
Atherton, James, *105*
Auber, Daniel, 16
Austral, Florence, 194

Bahr-Mildenburg, Anna, 194
Bailey, Norman, *35*, *36*, *98*, *101*, 109, *183*, *187*, 194, *194*
Bakman, Patrick, *105*
Un ballo in maschera (Verdi), 188
Balslev, Lisbeth, *36*
Bayreuther Blätter, 175
Becher, Gianrico, 26
Bechstein, Ludwig, 44
Beecham, Thomas, 194
Bellini, Vincenzo, 14, 18
Benois, Nicola, *23*, 26, *97*, *180*
Benthaak, Bernd, *53*
Berglund, Joel, 194
Bergman, Ingmar, 168
The Big Broadcast of 1938 (film), *129*
Bismarck, Otto von, 101
Bispham, David, 194–5
Bisseger, Peter, *50*
Bjoner, Ingrid, *97*, 195, *200*
Blackwood's Magazine, 29
Blankenburg, Heinz, *85*
Blatchley, John, 109, 161
Bockelmann, Rudolf, 195
Bodanzky, Artur, 195
Böhm, Karl, 195
Böhme, Kurt, 195–6
Boulez, Pierre, 168
Brandt, Marianne, 196
Brant, Karl, 141
Branzell, Karin, 196
Brazda, Jan, *159*
Brenneis, Gerd, *101*, *188*
Brilioth, Helge, 196
Brioschi, Anton, *12*
Brivkalne, Paula, *20*
Brömme, Ursula, *24*
Brook, Peter, 67
Brouwenstijn, Gré, *53*, 196
Brückner, Gotthold, 141
Brückner, Max, *30*, *46*, *61*, *78*, *93*, *119*, *121*, 141, 150
Buesst, Aylmer, 196
Bülow, Cosima von, see Wagner
Bülow, Daniela von, 52
Bülow, Hans von, 52, 92, 101, 196
Bulwer-Lytton, Edward, 18, 20
Bumbry, Grace, *52*, 53, 196
Burghart, Hermann, *12*
Burian, Karel, 196–7
Bury, John, *87*, 89
Büsching, J. G., 12

Callio, Timo, *72*
Cannan, Phyllis, *9*
I Capuleti ed i Montecchi (Bellini), 14
Cardenio und Celinde (Immermann), 12
Cassilly, Richard, *50*, 197
Cathcart, Allen, *101*
Chéreau, Patrice, *162*, *164*, *165*, *166*, 168–9, *169*, 197
Christoff, Boris, *180*
Coates, Albert, 197
Coates, Edith, *64*
Coates, John, 197
Connell, Elizabeth, *53*, *144*
Corrodi, Annelies, 70
Cox, Jean, *196*, 197
Craig, Edward Gordon, 88
Crespin, Régine, *68*, 197
Crook, Paul, *143*
Curry, Diane, *159*

Dalmorès, Charles, 197
Damrosch, Walter, 197
Davis, Colin, *6*, 7, 8, *9*, 57, 197
Demougeot, Marcelle, 197–8, *197*
Dempsey, Gregory, *139*
Demuth, Leopold, 198
De Reszke, Édouard, 198
De Reszke, Jean, 198, *198*
Dernesch, Helga, 198
De Sabata, Victor, 198
Destinn, Emmy, 198
Doepler, Carl Emil, *110*, *113*, *115*, *119*, 141
Dönch, Karl, *97*
Donington, Robert, 156
Donizetti, Gaetano, 14
Dowd, Ronald, *49*, 198
Downes, Edward, 198
Dreher, Johannes, 26
'Dresden Amen', 14
Dvořákova, Ludmila, 198
Dyck, Ernest van, 198, *199*

Eames, Emma, 198–9
Easton, Florence, 199
Ebert, Peter, 161
Edelmann, Otto, 199
Ekwall, Knut, *116*
Elmendorff, Karl, 199
Erede, Alberto, 199
Erhardt, Otto, *64*, 67–8, 70, *97*
Ernster, Deszö, 199
Ershov, Ivan, 199
Eschenbach, Wolfram von, 172
Estes, Simon, *36*
Evans, Geraint, *101*, *106*, 199–200
Everding, August, 90, *188*, 200

Farrah, *170*, *187*
Farrell, Eileen, *85*
Fassbaender, Brigitte, 200
Fassbender, Zdenka, 200
Die Feen (The Fairies), *10*, *12*, 12–14, 26, 64
Felsenstein, Walter, 57, 73
Ferrario, Carlo, 88
Fischer, Emil, 200
Fischer, Herta, *183*
Fischer-Dieskau, Dietrich, *101*, 200
Fisher, Sylvia, *64*, 200
Flagstad, Kirsten, *195*, 200–1
Die Fledermaus (J. Strauss), 188
Fleischer-Endel, Katherina, 201
Der fliegende Holländer (The Flying Dutchman), 14, 18, 23, *26*, 27–42, 50, 57, 64, 65, 97
'The Flying Dutchman Galop' (Williams), *26*
Formichi, Cesare, 201
Fra Diavolo (Auber), 16
Frantz, Ferdinand, 201
Franz, Paul, 201
Die Frau ohne Schatten (R. Strauss), 13
Fremstad, Olive, *115*, 201, *201*
Fretwell, Elizabeth, *36*, 201
Frick, Gottlob, 201–2
Friedrich, Götz, *53*, 57, *57*, *146*, *150*, *152*, *156*, 161–8, *161*, 188, 202
Fuchs, Ernst, *188*
Fuchs, Marta, 202
Furtwängler, Wilhelm, 109, 202

Gadski, Johanna, 202
Gano, Dave, *32*
Garrard, Don, *36*, *143*
'Der getreue Eckart und der Tannenhäuser' (Tieck), 44
Gielen, Josef, *68*, 70
Goldberg, Reiner, *9*
Goodall, Reginald, 109, 202
Gorr, Rita, *180*, 202
Götterdämmerung (The Twilight of the Gods), 10, 113, *121*, 125–32, *125*, *132*, *133*, *139*, 141, *144*, 146, *146*, 152, *152*, *156*, *165*, *169*, 172
see also *Der Ring des Nibelungen*
Gozzi, Carlo, 12, 13
Graf, Herbert, *23*, 26, *180*, 185, 202
Grant, Clifford, *141*
Greindl, Josef, 202–3, *202*
Grob-Prandl, Gertrud, 203
Grümmer, Elisabeth, 203
Gudehus, Heinrich, 203
Gura, Eugen, 203
Gutman, Robert, 175

Hafgren, Lily, 203
Hager, Ghita, *159*
Hager, Paul, *105*
Hall, Peter, 90, 168, 185, 203
Hammond-Stroud, Derek, *139*, *141*
Hands, Terry, *170*, *187*
Hans Heiling (Marschner), 14
Hanslick, Eduard, 87, 146–50, 152, 177
Harper, Heather, 203
Harshaw, Margaret, 203
Hartleb, Hans, *106*
Hartmann, Rudolf, 70, *72*, *94*, *101*, 105, 109, 158, 203
Heine, Heinrich, 28, 29, 30, 32, 36, 44
'Heldentum und Christentum' (Wagner), 175
Helm, Anny, 203
Herincx, Raimund, *144*
Hérold, Louis, 16
Hertz, Alfred, 203
Herz, Joachim, 67, 203–4
Hill, Hainer, *68*
Hirzel, Max, *64*
Hitler, Adolf, 70, 100, 101
Die Hochzeit (The Wedding), 12
Hoengen, Elisabeth, 204
Hoffman, Grace, 204
Hoffmann, E. T. A., 44
Hoffmann, Joseph, 105, *116*, 141, 150
Hofmann, Ludwig, 204
Hofmann, Peter, *169*, *187*

Hofmannsthal, Hugo von, 13
Holm, Richard, 204
Homer, Luise, 204
Hopf, Hans, 204
Hotter, Hans, *80*, *136*, 158, *203*, 204
Howard, Ann, *141*
Howell, Gwynne, *141*
Humperdinck, Wolfram, 97
Hunter, Rita, *36*, *144*, 204–5
Hurry, Leslie, 158
Hüsch, Gerhard, 205
Hyde, Walter, *204*, 205

Idylls of the King (Tennyson), 172
Illustrated London News, *123*
Illustrirte Zeitung, *16*, *29*
Immerman, Karl, 12
Interrupted Melody (film), *85*

Jadlowker, Hermann, 205
Jager, *192*
Janowitz, Gundula, 205
Janssen, Herbert, 205
Jeritza, Maria, 205
Jerusalem, Siegfried, *71*, 205–6, *205*
Johns, William, *105*
Jones, Gwyneth, *36*, *57*, *85*, *152*, 206
Joukowsky, Paul von, *172*, *174*, 177, 179
Jung, Carl Gustav, 156
Jung, Manfred, *169*
Der junge Siegfried, 113

'Der Kampf der Sänger' (Hoffmann), 44
Kantsky, Johann, *18*
Kappel, Gertrud, 206
Kapplmüller, Herbert, *89*, 90
Karajan, Herbert von, 57, 71, *71*, 73, *80*, 90, *101*, 109, *133*, *146*, 159, 161, 185, *188*, 192, 206
Kaslik, Vaclav, *50*, 57
Kaulbach, Wilhelm von, *74*, *76*
Kay, Barry, *101*, *106*, 109
Kempe, Rudolf, 206
Kesling, Diane, *105*
King, James, *146*
Kipnis, Alexander, *64*, 206
Kirschen, Martin, 161
Klein, Herman, 52
Klein, Peter, 206
Klemperer, Otto, 70, 206
Klose, Margarete, 206
Knappertsbusch, Hans, 180, 206
Knight, Michael, *146*
Kollo, René, 71, *72*, *74*, 206–7, *207*
Koltai, Ralph, *53*, *139*, 161
Konetzni, Hilde, 208
Konya, Sandor, *68*, *97*, *180*, 208
Kozub, Ernst, *136*, *182*
Kranich, Friedrich, *46*, *80*
Kraus, Ernst, *206*, 208
Krauss, Clemens, 208
Krauss, Felix von, 208–9
Kriemhilde's Revenge (film), *125*
Krips, Josef, 209
Kunz, Erich, 209
Kupfer, Harry, *36*, 41, *56*

Lang, Fritz, *125*
Langdon, Michael, *136*
Large, Brian, 41
Larsén-Todsen, Nanny, 209
Lawrence, Marjorie, *85*, 209
Lehmann, Lilli, *208*, 209
Lehmann, Lotte, *64*, 67, 109, 209
Leider, Frida, 209
Leinsdorf, Erich, 64
Lemnitz, Tiana, 109
Das Liebesverbot (The Ban on Love), 14, *15*, 16, 26
Liebl, Karl, *180*
List, Emanuel, 209
Liszt, Franz, 60, 64, 77, 92
Ljungberg, Göta, 209–10
Lloyd, Robert, *141*
Lohengrin, 10, 50, 57, 59–74, 85
London, George, 161, 210
Lorenz, Max, *195*, *209*, 210
Love of Three Oranges (Prokofiev), 12
Lubin, Germaine, 210
Ludwig II, King of Bavaria, 92, 116, 172

McIntyre, Donald, *36*, *74*, *146*, *152*
McManus, Christopher, *9*
Magee, Brian, 168–9
Mahagonny (Brecht/Weill), 8
Mahler, Gustav, *79*, 88, 210–11
Mallinger, Mathilde, *93*
Malory, Sir Thomas, 172
Marryat, Captain, 29
Marschner, Heinrich August, 14, 18
Martin, Janis, *146*, *188*
Matacic, Lovro von, *182*
Materna, Amalie, *174*, *210*, 211
Maurel, Victor, 211
Mayr, Richard, 211
Mazura, Franz, *187*
Measure for Measure (Shakespeare), 14
Mehta, Zubin, 90
Mein Leben, 12, 28
Die Meistersinger von Nürnberg (The Mastersingers of Nuremberg), *9*, 10, 64, 91–110, 113, 172, 175, 177
Melchinger, Ulrich, *160*, 185, *185*
Melchior, Lauritz, *64*, 67, 109, 211
'Memoirs of Herr von Schnabelewopski' (Heine), 29
Mendelssohn, Felix, 14
Merrill, Nathaniel, *97*, 109, *183*
Meyerbeer, Giacomo, 18, 20, 23
Minton, Yvonne, *187*
Mitford, Mary Russell, 18
Mödl, Martha, 211
Moll, Kurt, *187*
Mori, Toshitaka, *185*
Morte Darthur (Malory), 172
Moshinsky, Elijah, 70
Motley, design team, *98*, 109
Mottl, Felix, 211
Mozart, Wolfgang Amadeus, 10, 13
Muck, Karl, 211
The Music of the Future (Wagner), 84
Die Musik und die Inszenierung (Appia), 88

Naccarato, John T., *159*, 161
Nagano, Yonako, *185*
Napier, John, 70
Neidlinger, Gustav, 211
Nentwig, Franz Ferdinand, *159*
Newman, Ernest, 67, 180, 211
Nietzsche, Friedrich, 176
Nilsson, Birgit, *67*, *85*, 211, *211*
Noerr, J., *76*
Nordica, Lilian, 211–12
Norman, Jessye, *50*

Oftendingen, Heinrich von, 44
O'Hearn, Robert, *97*, 109, *183*
Ohms, Elisabeth, 213
Onegin, Sigrid, 213
Osten, Eva von der, 213
Oswald, Roberto, *105*

Pach brothers, *176*
Paglialunga, Augusto, *159*
Palli, Tina Sestini, *182*
Panofsky, Walter, 159
Papp, Gustav, *24*
Parker, Eleanor, *85*
Parsifal, 10, 14, 30, 40, 88, *170*, 170–92
Parzival (Eschenbach), 172
Peduzzi, Richard, *164*
The Perfect Wagnerite (Shaw), 156
Perron, Karl, 213
The Phantom Ship (Marryat), 29
Pixis, Theodor, *29*, *90*, *113*
Pollent, Karoline, 16
Ponnelle, Jean-Pierre, *36*, *40*, 41, 90, *90*
Popp, Lucia, *9*
Porter, Andrew, 53
Preetorius, Emil, *30*, 40, *67*, *94*, 159, 213
Prey, Hermann, 213
Prohaska, Jaro, *212*, 213
Prokofiev, Serge, 12
Puccini, Giacomo, 12

Quadro, Angelo, *78*
Quaglio, Angelo, *61*
Quell, Frank de, *50*, *180*

Ralf, Torsten, 213
Redon, Georges, *123*
Reinmar, Hans, 213
Reiss, Albert, 213, *213*
Reissiger, Karl, 21
'Religion and Art', 176
Remedios, Alberto, *98*
Rennert, Günther, *159*
Rethberg, Elisabeth, 213
Das Rheingold (The Rhinegold), 8, *110*, *113*, 113, *115*, 120, *125*, *132*, *136*, *141*, 141, *143*, 146, *146*, *150*, *159*, *161*, *162*, *164*, *165*
see also *Der Ring des Nibelungen*
Richardson, Marilyn, *101*
Richter, Hans, 109, 141, 213–14
Richter-Forgách, Thomas, *161*, 185, *185*
Ricketts, Charles, *178*
Ridderbusch, Karl, 214
Rienzi, 12, *16*, 17–26
Der Ring des Nibelungen (The Ring of the Nibelungs), 7–9, 10, 40, 77, 87, 97, 111–69, 172, 175
see also *Das Rheingold, Die Walküre, Siegfried* and *Götterdämmerung*
Ritterzeit und Ritterwesen (Büsching), 12
Robinson, Forbes, *136*
Röckel, August, 133
Rode, Wilhelm, 214

Roller, Alfred, *79*, 88–9, 179, 214
Rooy, Anton van, 214
Rose, Elisabeth, *24*
Rose, Jürgen, *53*, *161*
Rosenthal, Harold, 89
Rosing, Katharina, *115*
Rossini, Gioacchino, 14, 150
Roswaenge, Helge, 214
Rysanek, Leonie, *68*, 214–15, *214*

Salome (R. Strauss), 67
Saltzmann-Stevens, Minnie, 215
Sanjust, Filippo, 188
Sawallisch, Wolfgang, 215
Scaria, Emil, 215
Scheidemantel, Karl, 215
Schenk, Otto, 57, *58*
Schikaneder, Emanuel Johann, 13
Schipper, Emil, *215*
Schlusnus, Heinrich, 215
Schmedes, Erik, 215
Schmidt, Jaques, *164*
Schneider-Siemssen, Günther, 57, *58*, 71, *71*, *80*, 90, *101*, 109, *133*, *136*, *146*, 158, 159, 161, *188*, 192, 215
Schnorr von Carolsfeld, Ludwig, 215
Schoeffler, Paul, 215
Schopenhauer, Arthur, 65, 84
Schorr, Friedrich, 109, 215
Schott, publisher, 92
Schramm, Friedrich, 215
Schröder-Devrient, Wilhelmine, 20–1, *29*, *45*, 50, 215–16
Schröder-Feinen, Ursula, 216
Schumann, Robert, 60
Schumann-Heink, Ernestine, 216
Seidl, Anton, 216
Serapionsbrüder (Hoffmann), 44
Shakespeare, William, 14
Shanks, Donald, *146*
Shaw, George Bernard, 68–9, 150–2, 156
Shaw, Glen Byam, 109, 161, 179
Shirley, George, *146*
Siegfried, 113, *119*, *123*, 123–5, *130*, 132, 133, *139*, 141, *141*, *143*, *150*, *164*, *166*, 172
see also *Der Ring des Nibelungen*
Siegfried (film), *125*
Siegfrieds Tod, 113
Sievert, Ludwig, *21*, 26, *94*, *177*
Silja, Anja, 216
Skelton, Geoffrey, 179
Slezak, Leo, 109, 216
Smith, Patrick J., 57
Söhnlein, Kurt, *46*, 53, *80*, *93*, *178*
Solti, Georg, *87*, 216
Sotin, Hans, *9*
Stassen, Franz, *15*
Steber, Eleanor, *67*
Stein, Peter, 168
Stewart, Thomas, *105*
Stolze, Gerhard, 216–17
Strassburg, Gottfried von, 77, 84
Strauss, Richard, 13, 52, 53, 67, 70
Sucher, Rosa, 217
Sutcliffe, Jeremy, *9*
Suthaus, Ludwig, 217
Svanholm, Set, 217
Svoboda, Josef, 57, 90, *146*, *150*, 161

Talvela, Martti, *188*, 217
Tannhäuser, 9, 14, *42*, 43–58, 64, 65, 85, 92, 172
Tchaikovsky, Modeste, 146
Tchaikovsky, Peter Ilich, 141–4, 146
Tear, Robert, *9*
Der Templer und die Judin (Marschner), 14
Tennyson, Alfred Lord, 172
Ternina, Milka, 217
Thierry, Joseph, 88
Thoma, Hans, 150
Thomas, Jess, 217
Thorborg, Kerstin, 217
Tichatschek, Joseph, *18*, 20, *45*, 50, 217
Tieck, Johann Ludwig, 44
Tietjen, Heinz, 40–1, *67*, 69, 70, *94*, 105, 152, 217
Tomova-Sintov, Anna, 71, *72*
Toms, Carl, *105*
Toscanini, Arturo, 52, 89, 217
Traubel, Helen, 217
Traxel, Josef, *21*
Treptow, Günther, 217–18
Tristan und Isolde, 40, *74*, 75–90, 97, 105, 113, 175
Troyanos, Tatiana, *85*
Turandot (Puccini), 12

Uecker, Gunther, 188

Der Vampyr (Marschner), 14
Varnay, Astrid, *30*, *216*, 218
Veasey, Josephine, 218
Verdi, Giuseppe, 88, 188
Vinay, Ramón, *80*, 218
Vogl, Heinrich, *113*
Vogl, Therese, *113*
Voigt, Heinrich, *24*
Völker, Franz, 218

Wächter, Michael, *29*
Waechter, Eberhard, 218
Wagner, Cosima (Cosima von Bülow), 40, 52, 53, 69, 92, 105, 150, 152, 176, 177, 179, 218
Wagner, Friedelind, 152
Wagner, Johanna, 50, 218
Wagner, Minna, 18, 32, 44, 77, 92
Wagner, Rosalie, 12
Wagner, Siegfried, 52–3, 69, *80*, 152, *178*, 218–19
Wagner, Wieland, *21*, 26, *32*, 41, *49*, *52*, 53, 57, *68*, 70–3, *80*, *85*, 88, 89, *94*, *97*, *98*, 105, *130*, *132*, 156, 159, *178*, 179–85, 188, *218*, 219
Wagner, Winifred, 53, 69, 219
Wagner, Wolfgang, *30*, 41, 53, *67*, 70, 105, *108*, *132*, 159, 161, *182*, 185, 219
Wakhevitch, Georges, 71, 161
Walker, David, *98*, 109
Walker, Edyth, 219
Die Walküre (The Valkyrie), 8–9, 113, *113*, *116*, 120–3, 132, *132*, 133, *136*, 141, *144*, *146*, *166*, *169*
see also *Der Ring des Nibelungen*
Walter, Bruno, 109, 219
Walter, Paul, *180*, 185
Ward, David, 219
Warwick, John, 161
Watson, Claire, *72*, *136*

Weaving, John, *143*
Weber, Carl Maria von, 14
Weber, Ludwig, 219
Wells, Patricia, *105*
Die Welt als Wille und Vorstellung (Schopenhauer), 84
Wenkoff, Spas, *57*, *89*
Wesendonk, Mathilde, 77, 84, 85, 172
Wedendonk, Otto, 77
Wiener, Otto, *97*
Williams, W., *26*
Windgassen, Wolfgang, *21*, *85*, 219–20
Winkelmann, Hermann, *170*, *174*, *219*, 220
Wolff, Fritz, 220
Wollitz, Eduard, *183*
Wood, Sir Henry, 179

Zampa (Hérold), 16
Die Zauberflöte (Mozart), 13
Zimmermann, Erich, 220
Zylis-Gara, Teresa, *71*

ACKNOWLEDGEMENTS

All quotations from the writings of Richard Wagner are in the translations by William Ashton Ellis (*Richard Wagner's Prose Works*, London, 1895–9).

The quotations from Cosima Wagner (in the *Tannhäuser* chapter) and Friedelind Wagner (in the *Ring* chapter) are quoted from *Wagner at Bayreuth* by Geoffrey Skelton (Barrie & Rockcliff, London, 1965).

The quotations from George Bernard Shaw are from the 1 and 8 August 1896 issues of *The World* (*Lohengrin* chapter), and the 22 July 1896 issue of *The Star* (*Ring* chapter).

The quotations from Eduard Hanslick are from his *Music Criticisms*, trans. Henry Pleasants (USA, 1950).

The quotations from reviews in *Opera* magazine are reproduced with the kind permission of the editor, Harold Rosenthal.

The author and publishers wish to thank the following for permission to reproduce photographs:

Adolphe Appia Foundation, page 80;
Associated Press, page 89 *above*;
Australian Opera, pages 41, 53 *right* and 100 *below*;
Clive Barda, pages 6, 7, 8, 9 *above* and *below*, 10, 42 *above* and *below*, 74, 84 *right*, 106 *above* and *below*, 107, 110, 154–5, 186 and 187 *below*;
Bayerische Staatsoper, Munich, pages 24 *below*, 25, 72, 159 *left*, 196 and 200;
BBC Copyright Photographs, pages 34 and 194;
BBC Hulton Picture Library, pages 192, 193, 204, 206, 208, 210 and 219;
Bildarchiv Bayreuther Festspiele, pages 30, 33 *below*, 38, 48 *above* and *below*, 52, 54, 55, 66 *above* and *below*, 67, 68 *below*, 81 *above* and *below*, 85 *right*, 90, 93 *above* and *below*, 95 *above* and *below right*, 97 *right*, 98 *above*, 108, 109, 121, 129, 130, 131, 132 *above* and *below*, 133 *above* and *below*, 164 *above* and *below*, 165 *above* and *below*, 173 *below right*, 174 *above*, 179 *above* and *below*, 180 *left*, 182, 203, 214 and 218;
Bildarchiv Hamburgische Staatsoper, pages 160 *below* and 189;
Bildarchiv Preussischer Kulturbesitz, Berlin, pages 18, 19 *below*, 28, 29 *left*, *centre* and *right*, 44, 45 *above*, 60, 75, 76, 77, 78 *below*, 91, 92, 95 *below left*, 112, 117, 123, 175, 198, 199, 202, 209, 212, 213 and 216;
Cassel Staatsoper, pages 160 *above* and 184 *above* and *below*;
Zoe Dominic, pages 36 *above*, 69 *above*, 73, 86, 101 and 207;
English National Opera, pages 36 *below*, 37, 49, 99 *left* and *right*, 140, 141 *above* and *below*, 142, 143 *above* and *below*, 144 and 145;
Houston Grand Opera, page 104 *above* and *below*;
Illustrated London News, pages 122 and 178;
Kobal Collection, pages 57, 84 and 128;
Siegfried Lauterwasser, pages 70, 71, 82–3, 102 *above* and *below*, 103 *above* and *below*, 134–5 and 190–1;
Mander and Mitchenson Theatre Collection, pages 11, 12, 13, 15, 17, 19 *above*, 22, 27, 43, 59, 61 *below left*, 113 *below*, 115 *above*, 116, 126, 127, 172 *below* and 201;
Metropolitan Opera, photos by James Heffernan, pages 40, 58 *above* and *below*, 71 *below*, 85 *left*, 96 *above*, 124, 147 *above* and *below* and 183 *below*;
Metropolitan Opera Archives, pages 124 *above* and *below* and 125;
Motley Books Ltd, pages 79, 94, 111, 113 *above*, 114, 118, 119 *right* and 177;
New Orleans Opera Association, page 32;
Oper Berlin, pages 100 *above* and 188;
Opera Magazine, pages 20, 21 *above* and *below*, 56, 89 *below*, 96 *below right*, 181 and 185;
Phonogram International, pages 168 and 169;
Roger-Viollet, pages 61 *above*, 195 and 197;
Royal Opera House Covent Garden Archives, pages 45 *below*, 64 *left* and *right*, 65, 136–7, 172 *above*, 173 *below left*, 174 *below* and 176;
San Francisco Opera Association, pages 39 *above* and *below* and 159 *right*;
Scottish Opera, page 146;
Seattle Opera, page 158 *above* and *below*;
Donald Southern, pages 68 *above*, 69 *below*, 136 *left*, 148 *above* and *below*, 149 *above left* and *above right*, 152 and 156;
Stadttheater, Leipzig, page 24 *above*;
Teatro Colón, Buenos Aires, pages 33 *above* and 105;
Teatro Communale, Florence, page 183 *above*;
Teatro alla Scala, pages 23, 35, 50, 96 *below left* and 180 *right*;
Unitel, Munich, pages 162 *left*, 163, 166 and 167;
Vienna Staatsoper, pages 53 *left* and 205;
Richard Wagner Museum, pages 31 *above* and *below*, 46 *above*, 47, 61 *below right*, 62–3, 78 *above* and 115 *below*;
Reg Wilson, pages 51, 87 *left*, 98 *below*, 138, 139, 150 *left*, 151, 153, 155 *below*, 157, 171 and 187 *above*.